REBOUNDERS

REBOUNDERS

HOW WINNERS PIVOT FROM
SETBACK TO SUCCESS

RICK NEWMAN

BALLANTINE BOOKS
NEW YORK

Published in the United States by Ballantine Books, an imprint of The Random
House Publishing Group, a division of Random House, Inc., New York.

BALLANTINE and colophon are registered trademarks of Random House, Inc.

Library of Congress Cataloging-in-Publication Data
Newman, Rick.
Rebounders : how winners pivot from setback to success / Rick Newman.
p. cm.
Includes bibliographical references and index.
ISBN 978-0-345-52783-7 (hardcover : alk. paper)—
ISBN 978-0-345-52785-1 (eBook)
1. Success in business.   2. self-realization. 3.   Career changes.   I. Title.
HF5386.N395 2012
650.1—dc23   2012004143

Printed in the United States of America on acid-free paper

www.ballantinebooks.com

2   4   6   8   9   7   5   3   1

First Edition

Book design by Christopher M. Zucker

CONTENTS

FOUR SURPRISES ABOUT FAILURE

What am I doing wrong?

This is a lousy question to have to ask yourself. Most people, when faced with a major disappointment, come up with a lot of other explanations before they begin to examine their own culpability. There's usually an incompetent boss, a backstabbing colleague, a vengeful ex-spouse, or some other handy villain to pin the blame on. If not, then the corporation, the government, the system, or some other monolithic abstraction is an easy culprit. As a last resort, we can always fault plain-old bad luck.

I avoided asking myself that uncomfortable question for years—but finally ran out of convincing alternative explanations. I had been divorced for a while. A custody battle had gone against me, forcing me to move two hundred miles, to another city, in order to be near my two kids. That meant giving up a prominent job with a lot of valuable connections—the lifeblood of success for a journalist like me—and taking a more obscure one where I started with an empty Rolodex. It was a scary decision. The new town was more expensive. I already feared insolvency due to legal bills and child-support payments. The many friends and family members I had been leaning on would suddenly become a long-distance crutch. No matter. I might find myself lonely and broke, but somehow it would all work out, I gamely told myself while trying to recall what, exactly, had been so ennobling about Job's famous misery. Anyway, it wouldn't last long, I figured. I'd find a way to recover and come roaring back, better than before. It would probably even toughen me up.

After a few years, the thrill of character building had completely worn off. I lived in a cluttered rental apartment that could scarcely accommodate my growing kids during the weekends and other times they were with me. It felt shabby, and there was no extra money to do much about it. Many other people I knew—including my ex-wife—seemed to be in an upgrade phase of life, moving to a bigger house, buying a nicer car, and taking enviable vacations. For me, it was like trudging up a long stairway, gasping for air, while other people were cruising upward on an escalator. Then my industry started to struggle, as news began to appear free on the Internet, and newspapers and magazines began to lose money, then go out of business altogether. Layoffs became routine, and raises a rarity. I networked like a fanatic, worked freelance jobs, and explored other career possibilities, but nothing made much of a difference. As I crested the age of forty, I was falling behind instead of getting ahead, with a set of options that seemed to be narrowing and a deepening disillusionment that wasn't supposed to afflict people like me.

I told myself all the things I was supposed to: I was healthy and so were my kids, a blessing that's impossible to overstate. I was better off than other people in my orbit, especially some colleagues who had been laid off and didn't even have a paycheck anymore. Despite the loneliness of the new city, I had made some terrific new friends. My long-distance family was still supportive. I did some mental math and estimated that 98 percent of the world's population—AIDS sufferers in Africa, flood victims in Bangladesh, parents with screaming kids standing in endless lines at Disney World—were worse off than I was. What was I so unhappy about?

Deflated ambition, that's what. Things weren't going the way I expected. My plan to become a world-renowned journalist wasn't developing, and instead I was growing roots as a rank-and-file toiler considered clever, and maybe even talented, but nothing special. There were legions of me, and in a business that was suddenly shrinking and discarding a lot of able professionals, I felt headed for oblivion if I didn't do something to distinguish myself.

I had plenty of rationalizations that explained my predicament. The divorce was a huge distraction. The judge who decided the custody dispute obviously disliked me. The move was a major career disruption. The Internet was way beyond my control. But the setbacks were stacking up, and it began to dawn on me that maybe some of my decisions hadn't been as shrewd as I'd thought. I felt that I had been a good dad who deserved better treatment in divorce court, but maybe I had, in fact, been too concerned about my own needs or career. Moving to be near my kids was the right thing to do, and I fortified myself for the rigors of it by convincing myself that I was on some kind of preordained quest, like King Arthur or Harry Potter. But maybe I was fooling myself with false grandiosity. To overcome the career setback, I applied the doctrine of hard work: Keep applying effort until you get what you want. But it wasn't paying off. So after I pondered the awful possibility that maybe I was doing something wrong, and causing my own frustration, I asked myself an even worse question: *Was I failing?*

It was hard to tell. To some people, failure means you can't feed your kids or get sober long enough to show up for their soccer games, or even hold a job. I was able to do all that. But failure can also mean that you don't fulfill your own expectations, or those of others. That you accomplish less than you should. That you violate the Parable of the Talents, which had stuck with me since Catholic school. I had always been terrified of burying my talents, whatever that meant, because the sad sack who did that in the Bible got banished to the outer darkness, where there was ghastly weeping and gnashing of teeth. Had I somehow buried my talents, by getting into the wrong business or failing to see better opportunities or not trying hard enough? How could I even answer such questions, anyway?

I applied my journalistic instincts to the question, and started to research failure. What I found was more enlightening than I expected.

A lot of renowned and successful people had failed at something, occasionally at something big. The lucky ones failed early and learned quickly, while others failed later or took longer to get over it. But the important thing always seemed to be that they learned from failure, and used that knowledge to become better and more successful. I interviewed former Coca-Cola president Don Keough one day and asked him about failure. "Built into success is failure," he told me. "Ask one hundred people, 'What have you learned from success?' and most of them will just look at you. But ask, 'What have you learned from failure?' and you'll get lots of answers." One of his most instructive failures, Keough told me, had been listening to researchers and consultants who insisted the company should launch New Coke in 1985, a move now considered one of the biggest gaffes in corporate history. "The whole process made me a professional skeptic," Keough said twenty-four years later. "I learned to look beyond data and apply common sense, ask questions beyond the first question."

I also interviewed broadcaster Tavis Smiley, who had always wanted to be a politician and got started in broadcasting only after failing to get elected to the Los Angeles City Council. "I ran, I lost, I was devastated," Smiley told me. To keep his name and his ideas on voters' minds, he started doing short radio commentaries, which eventually caught on and led to a rewarding career in broadcasting that he never expected. He even wrote a book, *Fail Up,* about the surprising ways that mistakes and setbacks had ended up propelling him forward. "I drew three lessons from all that," he told me, in the preacherlike cadence that has drawn millions of fans to his TV and radio shows. "Sometimes rejection is redirection. Sometimes a dead end is really a finish line. And third, sometimes the universe has more in store for us than we imagine."

I came across the famous commencement speech that late Apple CEO Steve Jobs gave at Stanford University in 2005, describing the despair he felt after getting fired, in 1985, from the company he had helped create. "What had been the focus of my entire adult life was gone, and it was devastating," he told rapt listeners. The hiatus, however, forced him to rediscover what he was passionate about and rededicate himself to that. "I didn't see it then, but it turned out that getting fired from Apple was the best thing that could have ever happened to me," Jobs said. "The heaviness of being successful was replaced by the lightness of being a beginner again, less sure about everything. It freed me to enter one of the most creative periods of my life." Apple, of course, hired Jobs back in 1996, reversing a long slide for the iconic company and launching the era of the iPod, iPhone, and iPad, which made Apple the most valuable technology company in the world.

In a moving commencement speech at Harvard in 2008, the British author of the Harry Potter novels, J. K. Rowling, described the tension she felt early in her career when she chose the whimsical path of writing novels over the steadier trade work that her once impoverished parents urged. She described her own years of failure and doubt as she ended up divorced with a child, jobless, and "as poor as it is possible to be in modern Britain, without being homeless." But that misery forced her to strip away all of the inessential things in her life and direct all of her energy into the only work that mattered to her, which was her writing. "Failure gave me an inner security," she said. "Failure taught me things about myself that I could have learned no other way. I discovered that I had a strong will, and more discipline than I had suspected; I also found out that I had friends whose value was truly above the price of rubies."

During a commencement speech at Dartmouth in 2011 (you may be wondering, like me, *Where were these great speakers during* my *graduation ceremony?*), late-night TV host Conan O'Brien talked about the misery he felt after losing his dream job as host of *The Tonight Show*—and the surprising breakthroughs that came after that. "It was the most satisfying and fascinating year of my professional life," he said of the uncertain time following his departure. "I have never had more fun, been more challenged—and this is important—had more conviction about what I was doing. Whether you fear it or not, disappointment will come. The beauty is that through disappointment you can gain clarity, and with clarity comes conviction and true originality."

As I continued my inquiry, one revelation followed another, and I made these four important discoveries:

1. **SETBACKS CAN BE A SECRET WEAPON.** We're naturally drawn to tales of success. Nobody celebrates failure, and many people try to disguise their flops. Yet setbacks can be the most powerful and formative events we ever experience—as long as we regard them as learning opportunities, not as defeat. When I began to study successful people and ask them to tell me their stories, it became clear that the pivotal events in their lives weren't the breakthrough moments when everything finally fell into place, but the quit points that usually came much earlier, when success was in doubt, support was scarce, and it wasn't at all clear what to do. Many people give up when they hit such quit points—and you never hear their stories because they don't accomplish much. For those who persist, however, those low moments of fear and failure often constitute a crucible that makes them more capable once they've endured it. Over the last fifty years or so, a whole body of scientific research has shown that overcoming setbacks can make people stronger, smarter, and more durable. Psychologists call this quality resilience. The message, however, hasn't quite penetrated mainstream thinking. It's time it did.

2. **SMALL ADVERSITIES MATTER, JUST LIKE BIG ONES.** Like a lot of people, I downplayed my own struggles because they didn't seem Oprah-worthy. When whole families are debilitated by poverty and parents are losing their children to disease or violence, it feels petty to gripe about an undersized apartment or a flatlining career. But many non-traumatic events count as legitimate adversities: job or relationship stress, money woes, a nagging illness, midlife frustration, loneliness, betrayal by a friend, getting robbed, even crabby kids, or getting stuck in traffic. Small setbacks aren't an excuse for shirking responsibility or blaming somebody else, which is the way people with a sense of entitlement often react to them. What they are is an opportunity. Small challenges are the building blocks of resilience, helping us develop a kind of "stress inoculation" if we react to them effectively. That's how we develop the vital skills that will help us cope with bigger setbacks in the future.

As a parent, I felt a lightbulb blink on as I discovered how important it is for kids to face small (and safe) hardships that help them learn they can solve problems on their own and get better at doing difficult things. Like many parents, it makes me uncomfortable if my kids are uncomfortable. But it would be worse if I solved every problem for them, which unfortunately is what many parents do, in the name of protecting their kids. The most capable people are those who believe their own actions can lead to a better future. You get that way through practice—by using your own resources to solve problems or make a bad situation better. Like learning math or getting the hang of a bicycle, it's less intimidating if you start small and work your way up to bigger challenges.

3. **WE'RE ADDICTED TO ALLURING SHORTCUTS AND INCOMPLETE SLOGANS.** Everybody wants to believe that success is easy, and there's no shortage of people telling us it's so. But it's not really true that you can do anything you set your mind to, or cut your workweek to a mere four hours just by reading a book, or get great abs with a few painless exercises. Here's the slogan that misled me: Do something you love and success will follow. I did, in fact, love my work as a journalist, yet I was stuck in a mid-career rut with declining opportunities and a growing sense of gloom. I finally figured out that there were a few corollaries to that slogan that must not have fit on the bumper sticker. Doing something you love often requires sacrifices, for one thing, since the odds are that other people love it, too, and there's a lot of competition for work. Just loving what you do probably isn't enough, either; you also have to be good at it, often really good. And if you love to do something that nobody's willing to pay for, then don't expect to make a living at it. Consider it a hobby instead.

4. **OPTIMISM IS OVERRATED.** Sure, it's important to keep a positive attitude when things don't go your way, but for some people optimism is the same as denial. If you believe that things will work out automatically, simply because they should, you might be ignoring problems that will undermine what you're trying to accomplish. You might even take foolish risks because you overestimate your own abilities. Optimism overlaps with overconfidence, and in modern times this has brought about the

dot-com debacle, which caused a stock market crash; the second Iraq war, which was nowhere near the "cakewalk" some experts thought it would be; and a devastating housing bust built on the false premise that home values would never, ever decline.

Successful people who have weathered a few storms rarely believe things will simply work out. They're more apt to practice "defensive pessimism," imagining worst-case scenarios so they're prepared when things go wrong. They do, however, tend to have a powerful faith in their own problem-solving abilities and the knowledge—gained through experience—that hard work and adaptation bring success. In my own case, I had assumed that my career would flourish and my standard of living would recover after I got divorced and moved—without a specific plan for how to make that happen. That left me feeling pretty disappointed when it didn't happen. As a reflex, I learned to be defensively pessimistic, anticipating what could go wrong. A few friends felt I became too dour, always planning for the worst possible outcome. But it made me feel better, because the worst outcome almost never happened, and that in itself felt like success.

Some people, I began to realize, react to failure much better than others. I began to call them Rebounders, because they have an enviable set of skills that enables them to bounce back from adversity, whether it's big or small. Rebounders know how to solve problems and overcome setbacks, often because they've done it before. So they tend to react with calm determination, and even a sense of humor, when something goes wrong. They'd rather solve problems than complain about them or blame somebody else. They treat small challenges just as they would big ones, sweating the details and applying care to get it right. They analyze their mistakes and learn from them, and change their mind from time to time, when new information turns out to be better than old information. Wallowers, by contrast, often do the opposite. They get rattled when something goes wrong, even something small, because they're not accustomed to solving their own problems. They complain or get indignant instead of simply trying to fix things. They spend a lot of time figuring out who to blame for a problem, usually absolving themselves. They rarely question their own judgment and tend to overestimate their own abilities. Since Wallowers find it difficult to analyze their own mistakes, they often repeat them instead of improving upon them. They tend to be the people who get stuck in their careers and don't understand why and who remain convinced that their tribulations are somebody else's fault.

There are some very rich, well-known Wallowers. Richard Fuld, for instance, built Lehman Brothers from a rump Wall Street firm into an industry powerhouse, earning himself a tidy $250 million in the process. But as the firm's CEO, he became blind to poor and massive risks his firm was taking, convinced that Lehman's problems were coming from outside the firm, not from within. At the moment of crisis, when he could have saved his firm, he misread facts that others saw clearly, ascribed far more value to his firm than anybody else did, and vastly overestimated his own ability to orchestrate a solution. When Lehman failed in 2008, triggering the worst financial panic since the Great Depression, Fuld erupted in a spasm of denial and blame. During hours of testimony over the ensuing months, he blamed the government, the media, Lehman's lenders, and Lehman's competitors for the meltdown—but largely absolved himself.

In the same month that Lehman Brothers collapsed, a little-known, $100-million Pennsylvania company called Erie Plastics also failed, a victim of canceled contracts, too much debt, and a deep recession that blindsided the owners. I was surprised when the CEO agreed to talk to me about his doomed firm, since people rarely like to tell the press about their failures. But the CEO, P. C. "Hoop" Roche, was comfortable talking. As the owner of Erie Plastics, he had lost much of his own fortune when his firm declared bankruptcy, finding himself out of a job—and needing one—at the age of sixty-five. Three of his five adult kids had worked at Erie Plastics, and they were also among the 375 people who lost their jobs when the company closed. But Roche didn't blame other people for what happened. He faulted himself, and even put together a presentation he gave to business groups on the lessons to be learned from his painful ordeal. Among them: Never allow one customer to dominate revenues. Plan for the unexpected. React to a crisis swiftly and aggressively. And when the going gets tough, drink less and exercise more. I wasn't surprised to hear from Roche about a year later, when he told me that he got a new job as CEO of a business-networking group, transforming the "iceberg" on his résumé—a Chapter 11 filing—into wisdom he'd be able to share with other business leaders. His deepest regret was that his big failure hadn't happened sooner, giving him more time to apply what he learned. "You hear stories about successful people that make it sound like they wake up one day, have a great idea, and all of a sudden they're a millionaire," he told me. "Anybody who knows a millionaire knows there's blood, sweat, and tears on the floor. It's a fight. Sometimes a decades-long fight."

Hoop Roche: Rebounder. Richard Fuld: Wallower. The difference is that Roche had the self-awareness and humility to recognize his own mistakes and convert them to valuable knowledge he and others could benefit from. Fuld seemed to scoff at the idea that he could make a mistake, which forced him to look for other explanations, evade the truth, and wallow in denial.

We all know people who fit these descriptions, and probably a few who have qualities from both. There was a time when it didn't matter all that much, because you could still get ahead despite flaws that might have otherwise held you back. After World War II, the middle class boomed. A comfortable life and a fulfilling retirement were within easy reach, even for people who lacked a college degree or particular talent. Entrepreneurs with a good idea and a strong work ethic could find banks willing to lend them money and plenty of customers, and often become quite wealthy. Business titan Warren Buffett has quipped that anybody lucky enough to have been born in the United States in the twentieth century won the "ovarian lottery": They inherited enormous advantage simply by being born in the right country at the right time.

Opportunity is still plentiful, but a lot of the rules that governed success over the last seventy years are changing. We're in the middle of a long period of revolutionary upheaval—due mostly to digital technology and globalization—that will transform society, as the Industrial Revolution did beginning in the late 1700s and electrification did a century after that. Old businesses and professions will continue to become obsolete remarkably fast, while new ones rapidly spring up in their place. There will be more surprises, speed bumps, and disappointments than we're used to. We'll need to compete for our livelihood like athletes, because nobody's going to give out raises and promotions anymore just for showing up. The way we react to those challenges will become the differentiator between success and mediocrity. Wallowers who struggle to adapt or get bitter because things don't go the way they expect will quickly run out of chances. The people who get ahead will be Rebounders. They'll spot the opportunities first and enjoy more of them, because they'll spend less time on regret and recrimination and more time analyzing their setbacks, or just trying again. Talent, education, hard work, and luck still matter, but Rebounders have an edge that separates them from the pack.

Many people throughout the world have already seen the evidence of these wrenching changes in their own lives. In my own case, I've been stunned to see hardworking people I know get evicted or ask for help paying off debts more onerous than I ever would have guessed. One acquaintance who had lived a six-figure lifestyle just a few years earlier ended up living in a shelter. And those were the people whose lives I was able to follow. Others simply drifted away, a For Sale sign or a disconnected phone number the last telltale sign of something gone wrong.

The Rebounders in this book are people who encountered obstacles that are both familiar and extraordinary, from frustrated ambition to jarring career setbacks to near-death experiences. My list is admittedly eclectic. It includes people whose work I enjoy or admire, and whose experiences reflect the kinds of challenges many people face. I chose to zoom in not on the triumphant, breakthrough moments when all of their struggles finally paid off, but on the lonelier moments when they were humbled by failure and it was far from obvious what to do. I wanted to know what kept them going, where their confidence came from, how they found their way in the dark, and what they learned along the way. I wanted to identify the connective tissue between setback and success. In essence, I wanted to map the anatomy of resilience.

There were also several types of people whom I decided don't qualify for my list. Some comebacks are legitimate, for instance, but many are hype events orchestrated to boost some celebrity's sagging career or enliven a TV feature that doesn't contain much of an actual story. People promoting their own revival—such as Donald Trump with his 1997 book *Trump: The Art of the Comeback,* or aging rock musicians who mount comeback tours—are usually phony Rebounders more focused on self-promotion than self-improvement. It's hard to be a Rebounder if you're a raging narcissist, which is why Charlie Sheen, Mel Gibson, LeBron James, and most reality TV stars will never make my list, no matter how impressed they become with their own second, third, or fourth acts. I've also chosen to exclude people who bounce back from adversities of their own making. Some people become addicts or hellcats or sociopaths because of pain inflicted on them by others, but we too readily forgive the antics of people who simply don't control themselves. Besides, there's already a glut of addiction memoirs and celebrity-rehab stories.

As I analyzed the distinctions between Rebounders and Wallowers, I learned that there are good ways and bad ways to fail. The better you fail or react to a setback, the faster you'll recover, and the more you'll benefit from what you learn. I'm a journalist, not a psychologist, so I'm not prescribing a course of action for people struggling with hardship. Instead, I'm reporting back on my observations after an intensive study of Rebounders, so that readers can select the insights that might be useful in their own lives. The Rebounders in this book reacted to stressful events in many different ways, but there were some qualities that seemed to overlap or recur. In general, these attributes align with the characteristics that psychologists consider the key elements of resilience. Rebounders accept failure, for instance, instead of pretending that this basic human experience will never happen to them. They take purposeful action when confronted with a challenge, and don't let anger, indignation, guilt, or other bad feelings dominate them. They're open to new ideas and not bound by rigid, dogmatic thinking that never changes. They prepare for things to go wrong and don't squeal with outrage if they have to make sacrifices in order to accomplish something important to them. Rebounders are impatient to succeed, like everybody else, but they learn to wait for their moment to arrive. They tend to have heroes and role models, who help inspire them. And while passion helps drive them, they learn sooner or later that passion isn't enough— Rebounders usually have an additional boost that lifts them through tough times. These attributes will become apparent as I describe how a dozen prominent Rebounders worked through their own difficulties, and I'll explain each of these nine attributes in more detail in Chapter 14.

It's also important to keep in mind that anxiety, depression, discouragement, fear, worry, and many other challenges we face today are nothing new. They've been part of every generation in modern history, and all along, there have been people with the grit needed to surmount challenges and keep pressing forward. The most resilient people are usually the winners, and the tougher the times are, the further ahead they get. Since that's true in any era, I've included a brief historical sweep in the chapters ahead to demonstrate the timelessness and universality of resilience. But most of the Rebounders in this book are contemporary figures whose names or accomplishments are familiar to many.

Studying genuine Rebounders helped me answer some of the uncomfortable questions I put to myself during my own low moments. I had, in fact, been doing a few things wrong. For one thing, I was too fixated on goals I had set in the past, which I failed to adjust even though circumstances changed. My tunnel vision led to a mismatch between what I wanted to accomplish and what it would actually take to accomplish it, which was part of the reason I was coming up short. I had enough confidence to make risky decisions, but I also made airy, overoptimistic assumptions about how everything would work out, setting myself up for disappointment. And I thought too rigidly about failure, equating it with defeat and telling myself that I couldn't let it happen.

I'm still not sure if I've been failing, but the question has stopped bothering me because whatever happens, I've been learning something important that I didn't know before. If this has been happening through failure, fine with me. I also realize that the more I know about Rebounders and how they do it, the better I get at it myself. Problems seem less intimidating. It gets easier to drop something that hasn't been working, stop banging my head against the proverbial wall, and try something new. I've begun to take a kind of pride in the hardships I face, because I get the sense that life will be more meaningful when I overcome them. If I don't overcome them, it'll be easier to live with than before. I've learned that it's cool to be a Rebounder. And also essential.

REBOUNDERS

CHAPTER 1

WHAT MAKES A REBOUNDER

Millions of people have quoted Friedrich Nietzsche, the starchy German philosopher, without knowing what kind of philosophy he espoused or even who he was. In 1895, Nietzsche provided a motto for generations of strugglers when he published his famous aphorism number 8, from the book *Twilight of the Idols:* "What doesn't kill me makes me stronger." Nietzsche was paraphrasing poets and philosophers who had observed a connection between adversity and triumph since the days of Job and Odysseus. Yet the bumper sticker pithiness of his aphorism gave this ancient meme a modern interpretation that ordinary folks have used ever since to ascribe meaning to their travails. That's not exactly what the German provocateur intended. Nietzsche suffered from a variety of severe illnesses, including blinding migraines and debilitating gastrointestinal problems, yet he came to view his suffering as a gift. He felt that his medical maladies had given him an intense appreciation for life and helped him achieve the kinds of extraordinary insights he needed for his philosophical work, in which he frequently questioned and sometimes skewered accepted values. "Being sick can even become an energetic stimulus for life, for living more," he wrote in his autobiography, *Ecco Homo*. To him, the resilience that came from enduring difficult challenges was a kind of exceptional strength, available only to a few. It was a privileged status, not a common condition.

In 2010, researchers Mark Seery of the University at Buffalo and Alison Holman and Roxane Cohen Silver of the University of California, Irvine, published a study that tested Nietzsche's aphorism. Could painful struggle really make people stronger and healthier? By that time, decades of research had shown that resilience—the capacity to cope with adversity, overcome it, learn from it, and even be transformed by it—was a vital human quality. It was clear that hardships decimate some people, as expected, while others seemed to recover with little or no damage. But most of that research focused on a single event, like death or divorce, without measuring the effects of cumulative adversity—the whole range of things that can happen to people over time. And there was no real evidence that disruptive events could make people more resilient. In a way, that was consistent with Nietzsche's thinking, because he felt the kind of extraordinary strength that emerged from his own suffering was rare.

Seery and his colleagues wondered if the phenomenon might be more common. So they surveyed nearly 2,400 adults ranging in age from 18 to 101, asking whether they had ever experienced any of thirty-seven negative events, ranging from the loss of a loved one to financial stress to natural disaster. They asked the same questions several times over three years, to account for new problems as they developed. Along the way, they also asked whether the participants suffered from depression, anxiety, or other factors that impaired their ability to function normally, to gauge their mental health.

What they discovered is that there's good adversity and bad adversity. The typical person in the study had a median age of forty-nine and had experienced seven adverse events, with the death of a loved one being most common, followed by a family member's illness, relationship stress, and violent episodes. One unfortunate soul had endured seventy-one discrete adversities. About 8 percent of the participants, on the other hand, had experienced no adverse events. But they weren't as lucky as you might think. As the researchers expected, people with a high history of adversity experienced a relatively high level of mental health problems. But so did people with no adversity. People who had experienced moderate amounts of adversity turned out to be the healthiest, with the lowest levels of emotional distress and the highest levels of satisfaction. Nietzsche, it turned out, was more right than he knew: Enduring a few slings and arrows can make people happier than living a charmed life and experiencing none at all. This phenomenon was actually common. The researchers even noticed a particular number of adversities that seemed to correlate with the most resilient people: three.

Resilience is the core strength of a Rebounder. And while Rebounders have been around forever, the science that helps us understand their special qualities is relatively new, and still evolving. In Nietzsche's day, resilience, as it was understood, was largely considered innate: Either you came preloaded with it, or you were out of luck. Sigmund Freud, the founder of modern psychology, felt that an individual's personality was largely fixed by the age of five. Years of intensive therapy might help to uproot psychosis or other disorders, but if you weren't born a winner, there probably wasn't much you could do about it. That view began to change as psychologists explored the characteristics that allowed people to survive, and even thrive, after adversities and setbacks. In the 1960s, psychiatrist Aaron Beck developed something called cognitive therapy, which allowed people to overcome depression or anxiety simply by thinking more objectively about what troubled them, with less self-pitying emotion. Beck's innovations made it clear that people could improve their response to challenges and learn to live better, without the need for years of Freudian therapy. In the 1990s, psychologist Martin E. P. Seligman developed a new discipline known as positive psychology, meant to categorize and explain not what goes wrong but what goes right with people—and use that knowledge to help them become healthier and more durable. Legions of other researchers have probed the myriad attributes and phenomena that generate the protective factors once called invulnerability, and now known as resilience. The U.S. military has even funded some of the research, hoping it might help inoculate soldiers against the psychological brutality of combat and reduce the incidence of post-traumatic stress disorder (PTSD).

The insights and tools provided by all this research create a road map for how to become a Rebounder. Researchers have, in fact, proven that some resilience is innate. A variety of studies have shown that about one-third of people are born with a natural reservoir of resilience that allows them to cope effectively with challenges or setbacks, overcome them, and end up better off. That seems to be true whether you're born wealthy or poor, in affluent places like America or Europe, or less-developed areas where life is harder. And it plays out in many ordinary events. Back in 1975, a team of researchers led by psychologist Salvatore Maddi began a twelve-year study of 450 executives at Illinois Bell Telephone, which was part of Ma Bell—AT&T—when it had monopoly status and was the nation's dominant phone service provider. The court-ordered deregulation of AT&T in 1981 led to severe cutbacks at IBT, which is a familiar corporate scenario these days but was unusual at the time. By the end of 1982, IBT had downsized from 26,000 employees to 14,000. Nearly half of the workers in the study group got laid off, while many of the others had to adapt to new responsibilities or other stressful changes.

Within a few years of the disruption, Maddi and his team found that the one-third rule applied. The resilient people who stayed at IBT rose quickly and became company leaders, while those who left landed good jobs or started their own companies. The other two-thirds became corporate America's walking wounded, struggling in their new jobs or wallowing in unemployment. They sought relief in drugs or alcohol, battled with spouses, and even turned violent on occasion. It would be nice to report that corporate tactics have become gentler since then, but unfortunately those downsized IBTers were more pioneering than they knew.

Maddi and his team found that the one-third of workers who fell into the resilient group had three qualities in common: They remained committed to their work even when conditions got tough, avoiding the kind of gossip, recrimination, and political infighting that's tempting to engage in but usually accomplishes little. They believed they could do something to control what happened to them, which helped prevent them from feeling powerless. And they viewed unexpected change as a chance to grow or find opportunity, which made them optimistic even as they knew they faced stressful challenges. The vulnerable two-thirds, by contrast, did things familiar to anybody who has ever been involved with a team of any kind, or encountered a mere sliver of humanity: They complained, blamed others for their problems, exaggerated their distress, and busied themselves with trivial tasks, while pretending bad things weren't happening. When the layoffs came, these Wallowers got axed in out-sized proportion.

So hooray for the lucky one-third of us who are born with natural antibodies against stress. But what about the other two-thirds? And what if you're not sure which fraction you belong to? Or you want to supplement your natural resilience, just in case? One of the most important insights about resilience is that it's as learnable as any other skill, and it doesn't take years of psychoanalysis or other rigorous effort to accomplish. In fact, the natural vicissitudes of life often help us build durability. All we have to do is let them happen, and learn from them.

The opportunities to learn resilience and add to our natural supply of it begin when we're kids. Most parents instinctively recoil at the thought of their children enduring stress, discomfort, or failure, since it's a parent's job to protect their kids against danger, not expose them to it. Yet decades of research now makes it clear that "controlled" exposure to adversity helps kids become confident and adaptable. That doesn't mean setting them loose in some kind of *Lord of the Flies* experiment. But it does mean letting kids experience failure that's appropriate for their age, and letting them figure out how to overcome it on their own. Several of the Rebounders I interviewed and studied endured some kind of unusual stress as children, such as an alcoholic or abusive parent, divorce, financial strain, or neighborhood violence. Others who grew up more comfortably had an inclination, and the freedom, to seek adventure and fend for themselves in ways that would make many parents uncomfortable today. I've been careful not to draw oversimplified conclusions from my own concentrated sample of research, but it seems safe to say that some people feel comfortable taking measured risks as adults because they learned as kids that they can survive scary challenges.

Parents don't need to hire adversity consultants or send their kids to failure camp if they want them to benefit from a taste of hardship, because the right kinds of challenges happen naturally enough. Young kids who play hide-and-seek experience a kind of controlled tension, since they're temporarily cut off from the group that supports them. Early sleepovers and other events where kids feel separation anxiety are a kind of adversity, forcing kids to make themselves comfortable without the reassuring presence of their parents. Being treated unfairly by a coach or teacher or other kids can be a rough experience that makes kids feel unprotected. And losing at something—a game, a tryout, an academic challenge—generates disappointment. But when it's all over and kids realize that the world hasn't ended, they become a bit more durable.

There's plenty of convincing research showing that when kids cope with manageable challenges like these, they end up feeling more competent and stronger. They develop "stress protection" and learn that they can handle setbacks, which makes the next challenge seem less intimidating. Most important, they learn that they have some power to control what happens after a setback, instead of being captive to the vicissitudes of fate. About one-third of kids show strong resilience on their own—there's the one-third rule again. Between the ages of five and nine, most kids begin to learn resilience through everyday experiences—a phenomenon that child psychologist Ann Masten dubbed "ordinary magic" because it happens naturally, without the effort or even awareness of parents. Starting around nine, kids can be taught how to develop deeper Rebounding skills, much as they're taught math or manners. Over time, a well-taught Rebounder will develop layers of emotional durability that will help him or her master everyday challenges, grow through setbacks, and survive trauma without becoming damaged.

Parents can aid this development—but they can interfere with it, too. "Helicopter parents" who hover over their toddlers to prevent anything unpleasant from happening to them foster dependence, not resilience. Praising a child's innate talent or intelligence—instead of encouraging hard work or practice—doesn't build confidence, as many parents believe. Instead, it makes kids think that success should come easily, without effort. Then, when something goes wrong or turns out to be hard, they're left without the resources to rise to the occasion, which generates self-doubt, not confidence. Self-esteem slogans like "You're special!" or "You can do anything you set your mind to!" create unrealistic expectations of a seamless path through life. So do sports games with no score—meant to prevent one team from "losing" and therefore feeling ruinous disappointment—and "participation awards" given simply for showing up. Parents who routinely intervene with coaches or teachers, to plead for better grades or a more favorable spot in the lineup, are teaching their kids that success comes from somebody else's actions, rather than their own. Some researchers even think that super-safe playgrounds with soft surfaces, short slides, and injury-proof play areas—in lieu of banging seesaws, dizzying tire swings, and monkey bars you have to work up to with age—may stunt children's emotional development. Instead of allowing kids to progressively confront fears and anxieties, as happens when a child climbs higher and higher on a jungle gym, for example, they provide an antiseptic environment where there are barely any challenges to master.

The same principles apply to adults, whether they learned resilience earlier in life or not. The stakes are obviously higher, though. Nobody's going to shower the typical thirty- or forty-year-old with vapid praise, or intervene to prevent discomfort. Adults need to solve problems on their own, and they'll either learn to do it, like a Rebounder, or suffer repeat setbacks, like a Wallower. The good news is that resilience is learnable at any age, and it pays dividends no matter when it starts to work in your favor. We tend to think that success comes from natural gifts like intelligence or talent, but the connection isn't nearly as strong as it might seem. Renowned psychologist Howard Gardner has shown that the most widely understood form of intelligence—the kind measured on an IQ test—accounts for only about 20 percent of what makes people successful. Raw talent can provide a head start, but as basketball wizard Michael Jordan learned when he was cut from his high-school basketball team, it better be amplified by effort and determination. All around us, in fact, are underachieving prodigies who fall short of their promise: Golfer John Daly, actress Lindsay Lohan, off-the-charts genius Chris Langan, who has a sky-high IQ but could never attain his dream job as a professor because he couldn't finish college. There are many other naturally talented people whom none of us will ever hear of, because they lack the fortitude to rise above mediocrity. "Nothing is more common than unsuccessful people with talent," President Calvin Coolidge said long ago. "The world is full of educated derelicts."

Gardner and others developed the idea that there are many other types of intelligence—besides the kind that measures brainpower—that account for the larger portion of what makes people successful. One of the most important traits Gardner identified was a "special talent" some people have for identifying their own strengths and weaknesses—a key component of resilience. That kind of self-awareness allows people to have a realistic understanding of why things go right, and why they don't. It's also the foundation for self-improvement, since you need an accurate and timely diagnosis in order to troubleshoot a problem. Dick Fuld might have been able to save Lehman Brothers if he had realized that the fundamental cause of its woes was a culture of risk-taking and greed—a culture he encouraged—not the animosity of short-sellers, competitors, the press, and other outsiders.

Resilience is the great equalizer, because if you don't have enough, you can get more. It's possible to boost your IQ slightly, but your intelligence quotient is much more fixed than your resilience quotient. Practically everybody has some "resilience factors" they can build upon, to become as durable in the face of setbacks as the most natural-born Rebounder. Basic resilience factors include trust, loyalty, a desire to improve your life, and the ability to form friendships, and they're so common that even underprivileged kids growing up in broken families possess some of them. Left undeveloped, these traits wither into uselessness. But once tapped and nurtured, those nuggets of resilience can be so powerful that they outgun intelligence or talent. If you had to choose between a high IQ and high resilience, you'd be better off choosing resilience.

As your mother told you (or should have): All things are best consumed in moderation. That includes adversity. Traumatic experiences like rape, incest, abuse, or destructive violence are unlikely to produce happy outcomes under any circumstances, and usually require medical attention, the way any serious injury would. Adversity is never something to take lightly. In their study of Nietzsche's aphorism, Seery and his colleagues cautioned that it's dangerous to assume that painful experiences will promptly trigger happiness. Even if that were possible, it's not as if people whose lives had gone too smoothly would start driving around looking for potholes, to notch a few flat tires and get into the optimal adversity zone. In his 2011 address at Dartmouth, comedian Conan O'Brien added a corollary to the popular saying. "Nietzsche famously said 'Whatever doesn't kill you makes you stronger,' " he quipped. "What he failed to stress is that it *almost* kills you. Disappointment stings and, for driven, successful people like yourselves it is disorienting."

The point is to understand that there can be an upside to stressful events, which can transform and improve the way we react to them. The narrative that unfolds over the following chapters will reveal how a dozen prominent Rebounders discovered and built their own resilience, with takeaways that will be relevant to the everyday struggles many people face. Some of the Rebounders I studied seem to be part of the one-third minority who are born with the natural gift of resilience. But even so, they had to figure out how to use that gift when faced with unexpected challenges they had never deliberately prepared for. Usually it takes a while. It's trial and error. Rebounders often root around in the toolbox that contains the unique components of their personal resilience, until they find the right tools for the job. Other Rebounders have more to learn, like scrappy athletes who lack natural talent but still manage to compete with the best, thanks to heart, determination, and intense practice. They learn resilience along the way, sometimes through intentional effort. But most of the time they're accidental Rebounders. Their examples are powerful, because they reveal that even when learned haphazardly, resilience can be a springboard to success. How much more effective it must be, then, when cultivated with conscious effort.

CHAPTER 2

THE ELEMENTS OF PERSISTENCE

Americans find it gratifying to think of their nation as a land of natural geniuses or trailblazers destined for greatness. But that's highly romanticized. Since its founding, America has been a nation of failers. What makes it a remarkable place is that America is also a nation of Rebounders.

Benjamin Franklin, America's first self-help guru, ran away from his parents in Boston at the age of seventeen, finding work as an apprentice for a dim-witted Philadelphia printer. Franklin thought he saw a way out, but his first business venture left him out of money and stranded in London for eighteen months, unable to pay the return fare. After finally making it home, Franklin foundered again when a wealthy man he thought would be his business patron died. It took clever scheming and a bit of deception for Franklin to finally open his own printing shop, funded by the affluent father of a colleague. That gave him the means to publish his own newspaper and *Poor Richard's Almanack,* the folksy bestseller that would pave the way for an illustrious career as a politician, diplomat, and sage of the American Revolution. Many of Franklin's popular insights and aphorisms came from his early struggles to establish himself. "To be thrown upon one's own resources," he said, "is to be cast into the very lap of fortune, for our faculties then undergo a development and display an energy of which they were previously unsusceptible."

George Washington lost his father at the age of eleven, which forced him to forego a college education, a gap in his upbringing that nagged at him his entire life. He bumbled through a variety of frontier skirmishes early in his military career, suffered financial duress even when ensconced at the stately Mount Vernon, and lost more battles than he won during the Revolutionary War. Yet Washington developed a talent for politics and a commanding presence, plus another key attribute: "the deeply rooted toughness of children forced to function as adults at an early age," as his biographer Ron Chernow writes. Somehow those frequent struggles and hard lessons produced a military titan who overcame continual crisis during the Revolutionary War and turned the ragtag Continental Army—undermanned, underequipped, underpaid, and undertrained—into a force able to defeat the British redcoats.

America itself essentially failed under the Articles of Constitution, the first governing document adopted after the Revolutionary War. The Articles bound the states into a "firm league of friendship" that was so weak, the central government had no power to levy taxes, defend the country, or pay its debts. That left the upstart nation unraveling before it was even sewn together. The founders, fortunately, were enlightened enough to recognize the flaws in their first draft of a constitution, and they got it right on the next try.

The importance of a second chance—or even a third or fourth one—became a singular hallmark of American society in the mid-1800s, when the United States established the world's most forgiving bankruptcy code. Back in the Old World, where most Americans or their ancestors came from, debtors unable to pay what they owed were routinely tossed into barbaric prisons. But financial panics and depressions were common back then, and it seemed counterproductive—feudal, even—to ruin responsible men merely trying to provide for their families and generate some wealth. So by mid-century, most bankrupts in the United States could get some relief from the courts and resume their lives. Providing a way out of bankruptcy fueled entrepreneurship and the kind of risk taking that helped make the United States a global industrial power by the 1900s—and generated some mighty fortunes in the process.

So many industrial titans from that era failed before they succeeded that the fail-first model could almost be taught in business school. Some of the notable Rebounders who got second chances include Henry Flagler, John D. Rockefeller's partner in Standard Oil; Cyrus McCormick, who developed the mechanical reaper that later led to the formation of International Harvester Company; Henry J. Heinz; Milton Hershey; and Henry Ford. Their fail-first model was followed in later years by Walt Disney, Sam Walton, and Chester Carlson, who invented the photocopier in 1938 and waited twenty-one years before finding a business partner willing to commercially produce it. In politics, Andrew Jackson, Abraham Lincoln, Theodore Roosevelt, and Harry Truman were Rebounders who muddled through business misadventures or major personal setbacks on their way to becoming triumphant leaders. It took abject failure for a busted, inebriated stock analyst named Bill Wilson to form Alcoholics Anonymous in the 1930s. Even Norman Vincent Peale, who published *The Power of Positive Thinking* in 1952, endured repeated rejections by New York publishers before his wife rescued the manuscript from the trash and helped find a publisher that sent the book on its way to becoming one of the all-time bestsellers. Anybody who has failed in America, in other words, belongs to a rich tradition.

On December 9, 1914, there was a tremendous fire in West Orange, New Jersey, on the campus housing Thomas Edison's manufacturing operations. An explosion in one building had ignited chemicals throughout the plant, fueling the furious blaze, which destroyed thirteen buildings altogether. Hundreds of townspeople pressing against police lines watched Edison's phonograph works, his movie-processing plant, and other facilities vital to his far-flung franchise burn to the ground. Edison, who was sixty-seven at the time, might have been devastated. But no one thrived on setbacks the way Edison did, and he relished the challenge of rebuilding. "He seems to be the least perturbed of anyone . . . over the loss of his immense factories," *The New York Times* reported two days after the fire.

Edison vowed that he'd be producing phonographs again in less than two weeks—a target he missed, but only by a few days—and he took advantage of the disaster to dramatically improve his factories. He borrowed an "efficiency engineer" from his pal Henry Ford—who by then was changing the world with his mass-production assembly lines—in order to arrange his workers and machinery in the most productive way. The assembly-line makeover allowed Edison to upgrade all the fireproofing in his buildings, making the new plant one of the most modern anywhere. Within two months, his buildings were rebuilt, better than ever. "Where others might see disaster and failure," Edison biographer Paul Israel writes, "he was always optimistically looking for opportunities and seeing the possibility of new directions for improvements."

Most people today get their fill of Thomas Edison in grade school, with few insights into the man beyond his electric lighting scheme, the phonograph, the motion picture camera, and a few other groundbreaking inventions. Yet Edison was perhaps the ultimate Rebounder, and there are deep parallels between the challenges he faced then and those we encounter today. Edison came of age in an era when new technology was transforming the way people lived and worked, much as the Internet, computing power, and digital communication are doing today. Edison cultivated failure in his hundreds of laboratory experiments, because he knew that rich learning—and sometimes, major commercial breakthroughs—came from studying mistakes and capitalizing on them. He endured three economic depressions in his career and ran short of money many times. Yet he rarely got discouraged, and by the end of his prodigious career, he had made an enormous contribution to human progress. Edison also drew a timeless line between determined achievers and dreamy poseurs when he said that "Genius is one percent inspiration and ninety-nine percent perspiration," a truism that draws knowing nods of agreement from entrepreneurs everywhere. Had he lived one hundred years later, Edison probably would have helped lead the digital revolution, on par with Bill Gates and Steve Jobs—if not a step ahead of them.

Edison grew up a rambunctious boy in northern Ohio and eastern Michigan, in a family whose fortunes rose and fell—like many families' at the time—with the patriarch's entrepreneurial prospects. The young Edison left school early, with one popular version of the story claiming that a disapproving teacher found him to be "addled." (Today, the diagnosis would probably be attention deficit disorder.) It's also possible the family simply couldn't afford school, which wasn't compulsory or publicly financed at the time. Whatever the case, Edison's mother, Nancy, taught him at home for several years, which was fairly common.

Mrs. Edison was gentle but overprotective, and young Tom gave her plenty to worry about as he courted danger and tested the bounds of home. Edison loved to conduct experiments; even as a kid, and managed to get his hands on chemicals and other materials that occasionally produced explosions, scorched clothes, and, more than once, a fire. Edison started working in earnest when he was thirteen, heading out in the morning for long days at the railroad, where he was thrilled to do odd jobs and get to know the older workers. He ran his own stands selling fruit and periodicals, while in his spare time he read everything he could get his hands on and learned how to operate the telegraph, which was on the verge of becoming a transformative technology, similar to the Internet in the 1990s. Throughout his life, Edison was known for supreme confidence that rarely left him questioning himself, which many acquaintances probably figured he was born with. Maybe. But Edison's boyhood seems to have been a model experiment in itself, a series of small challenges that gradually grew bigger as the boy became adept at handling them. Even when something went wrong—as it did one day when some of Edison's chemicals spilled on a train, producing an explosion and getting him temporarily banned from the rails—Edison learned that he had the ability to land on his feet. He was becoming resilient, which would end up being one of his greatest strengths.

Edison left home for good when he was about seventeen, "tramping" around the Midwest in a manner that would drive today's parents mad with worry. He had become a skilled telegraph operator, which enabled him to get good work almost anywhere he turned up. So Edison and a few adventurous friends began hopping rides on trains, which brought them to Fort Wayne, Indianapolis, Cincinnati, Louisville, New Orleans, Memphis, and many other places. At one point they hatched a scheme to go to Brazil, but changed their minds when they heard an insurrection was under way. Edison experimented and tinkered the whole time, occasionally getting fired because he was often more interested in his books and homemade contraptions than in the work he was getting paid for. That, plus his constant purchases of books and equipment, left him constantly short of money. But his parents were in worse shape. When Edison returned home around the age of twenty-one, he discovered that the military had commandeered the family home. His leisurely, adolescent education had concluded.

To start earning real money he moved to Boston, which was the Silicon Valley of the 1860s, a hotbed of telegraph operators and financiers eager to earn their fortune exploiting the telegraph and other new technology. Edison had some qualities that were rare, if not unique: He was a technical and creative genius, with nearly superhuman stamina that allowed him to work eighteen-hour days routinely. But Edison's legendary persistence—the "perspiration" part of his formula—wasn't simply the result of hard work. Edison succeeded, over and over, for three reasons that are as valid for innovators today as they were then. First, instead of making all-or-nothing gambles on one or two consuming ideas, Edison developed many ideas at once and prioritized those that seemed to be most promising. He was an inveterate multitasker. Second, he learned to let pragmatism be his guide, prioritizing inventions that had some obvious use over those that were merely interesting or that he grew emotionally attached to. Finally, Edison found remarkable value in failed experiments and other setbacks, which often produced insights and nuggets of knowledge that contributed to other breakthroughs later on. Edison rarely felt discouraged when he hit a quit point, because to him every setback was a signpost that might point to a more productive outcome in a different direction.

Edison didn't need to fail repeatedly before he recognized a mistake. Once would do. Like other ambitious young men in Boston, Edison worked long days as a telegraph operator, while spending much of his remaining time experimenting, studying scientific matters he hadn't yet learned, and building his own inventions. It must have been thrilling to Edison in 1868 when he constructed a device that seemed like it could be his first big success, even attracting investors willing to help cover his costs. The gizmo was an electric vote-counting machine, which he figured would help speed the work of state legislatures, or even the U.S. Congress, when it came time to tally votes on various measures. Once it caught on, Edison would market it to deliberative bodies all over the world. The machine, based on technology used in telegraphs, would allow lawmakers to vote by simply moving a switch at their desks, instead of the more laborious process of rounding up votes manually—and it earned Edison his first patent. But when he tried to market the device, legislators weren't interested. It turned out that walking around to tally up votes was the essence of politicking, a key opportunity to strike last-minute deals. What seemed like an inefficiency to Edison was a valued part of the process to those involved in it. Edison's first patented invention was a flop.

Edison made a rookie mistake that many first-time entrepreneurs have repeated since: He came up with a clever innovation before bothering to find out if anybody would be willing to pay for it. Unlike many others, however, Edison saw the problem right away, vowing to "never waste time inventing things that people would not want to buy." In fact, the quick recognition of his own mistake— rather than a more comfortable explanation faulting the legislature, his investors, or anybody besides himself—showed that Edison could accurately assess his own abilities, a trait many Rebounders have. That kind of "cognitive ability" helps people get better results the next time they try something hard, which in turn breeds confidence and the deep learning needed for extraordinary accomplishments. Instead of evading accountability by blaming others—or blaming themselves, which generates guilt and self-doubt—Rebounders like Edison tend to put blame aside completely and approach setbacks clinically, like a problem that needs to be deconstructed into smaller and smaller parts until it's well understood and solvable. For the most part, Edison stuck to his own simple lesson for the next fifty years, which helped him make some of the toughest decisions of his career. Late in his career, when Edison made a few costly mistakes, it was largely because he forgot to heed his own advice.

Edison's most significant invention—the modern lightbulb—is often characterized as an overnight breakthrough that popped into the inventor's head like a new sandwich recipe or a fresh use for duct tape. The very idea of a Eureka moment is often illustrated with an image of Edison's lightbulb, signifying a sudden flash of insight. Yet the development of electric light was a painstaking process that offered Edison many quit points and involved dozens of setbacks. Edison beat many competitors to the prize because he was more pragmatic than they were, more thorough, and more open-minded about learning from failed experiments than others who would have seen them as dead ends.

When Edison began tinkering with electric light in 1877, he was hardly the first. Scores of hobbyists and well-financed inventors had been trying to develop a commercially viable lighting system for years, with plenty of demonstrations and exhibitions but nothing that worked for general use. Creating light in a laboratory was the easy part. To work in the real world, the lamps would have to be durable, long lived, relatively simple, and cost effective. There were endless complexities involving the power source, electrical properties, materials for the bulb, and the method of constructing it. By then, Edison had built his famous laboratory in Menlo Park, New Jersey, with a team of researchers working under him. One of the biggest problems he and everybody else working on the electric light encountered was the metal in the lamp, which tended to melt as current ran through it. Edison thought platinum had the right properties to serve as the filament without melting, but the metal was as scarce then as it is now, and he knew he'd need an abundant supply. So he consulted numerous experts and sent queries throughout the world, hoping to discover a vast new cache of the valuable mineral. He struck out, one of the many setbacks on his quest.

Edison's investors, and others familiar with his progress, began to whisper that the whole effort might flop. But Edison simply had to find another way, and by figuring out what didn't work, he gathered insights that led him to experiment with vacuum technology, which solved the problem of the melting metal. There was still a long way to go, however. All along, Edison knew that a lighting system had to be affordable, so that municipalities and other big customers would buy it. So he designed his system to be financially competitive with gaslight, which lit most cities at the time, and even considered ways to wire his bulbs into gas fixtures that were already in place. Another prominent inventor, William Sawyer, had made some breakthroughs of his own on the electric lamp, and gotten generous funding, too. But most people have never heard of William Sawyer, and here's why: He moved too quickly from building a lamp that worked under controlled laboratory conditions to manufacturing his system, and it turned out to be unreliable. Edison, by contrast, spent months testing and refining his lamps before he started to sell them in large quantities, working out many bugs to ensure his system would be durable. He also focused on building an entire electrical system that would provide not just light but also heat and the energy to power industrial machines that were still driven by steam. He didn't turn the quick profit that some of his rivals were after, but his electrical systems ultimately transformed towns and cities throughout the world. By the time he founded the Edison General Electric Company (now known as GE) in 1889, the lesson he learned in Boston had guided him quite well.

Another early lesson for Edison was the value of backup plans, and if one project didn't pan out, he usually had another to turn to. Edison was virtually broke when his vote-counting machine failed, for instance, and he might have grown forlorn had he been banking on that alone to jumpstart his career as an inventor. But at the same time, he was working on other inventions, like an improved telegraph (which he always seemed to be working on) and various devices that would report stock and commodity prices in financial exchanges. Those became modest successes, providing some income, garnering the attention of leading businessmen and proving the merits of multitasking. Edison also worked on improvements to Alexander Graham Bell's telephone that made it practical for general use, which Bell hadn't yet done. Bell had beaten several other inventors, including Edison, in the race to develop a "talking telegraph." But his phone had a major weakness: The transmitter generated a weak current that limited the distance sound could travel, making the phone impractical over longer distances. A couple of years earlier, Edison had experimented with carbon in his efforts to improve the undersea cables that carried telegraph transmissions. It hadn't worked out—another failed experiment. But as Edison studied Bell's phone, he realized that the properties of carbon he had seen earlier might make it ideal for the telephone transmitter. Several months of experiments validated the idea, and Edison's carbon transmitter became a standard component of Bell's telephone—all the way until the 1980s, when digital technology displaced it.

Edison didn't fret over much, but like many self-made innovators, a shortage of funding vexed him on and off for much of his career. That financial pressure, however, turned out to be an unwitting contribution to his pragmatism, and ultimately to his success. As Edison established himself as an inventor, he earned enough to send some money back to his parents in Michigan, and to comfortably support his own family once he was married. But staffing and equipping his lab cost a fortune, and his elaborate experiments required a constant flow of funds from deep-pocketed investors. "I cannot stand this worrying much longer about bills," he complained to one business partner. "You cannot expect a man to invent and work night and day, and then be worried to a point of exasperation about how to obtain money for bills." As many entrepreneurs know: Oh yes you can.

A desperate need for money during the Panic of 1873—a full-blown depression that was worse than any downturn in our day—left Edison unable to pay his bills, forcing him to make partial payments or beg the forbearance of those he owed. His own customers did the same thing. To get out of debt, Edison sold the rights to several of his lucrative inventions to notorious financier Jay Gould, who had become a kind of vulture investor profiting from others' misfortune. Some entrepreneurs become despondent when forced to surrender the rewards from their most prized innovations, but Edison took it in stride; after all, there would be more inventions. He faced similar problems during financial panics in 1890 and 1893, managed them, and stayed focused on new creations.

Like many businesspeople, Edison complained at times about pressure from impatient investors who sometimes wanted results faster than he could deliver. Yet the scrutiny he received from people whose money he was spending made him a more efficient and prolific inventor. He had a habit of spending freely on staff, books, and equipment for his lab, leaving little cushion in case something went wrong, which happened frequently. Edison usually found his way out of a jam, but the discipline forced on him by business partners became hallmarks of his success. He learned, for example, to test ideas with small, inexpensive experiments before scaling up to larger, costlier ones. That helped disprove flawed hypotheses early on, providing a big advantage over rivals who went broke conducting big tests that didn't pan out, or who simply skipped key tests because they couldn't afford them. Edison also learned to give up on "dead experiments," as he called them—projects that seemed interesting or worthwhile but couldn't be linked to an obvious payoff. That's one way Edison learned to perspire over the right projects. As he grew wiser, he told colleagues that more money is lost over not knowing when to stop than in almost any other way.

Edison proved the value of his own pragmatism when he abandoned it, mostly in the latter part of his career, paying a steep price. In 1892, General Electric merged with another company, a deal Edison opposed and that, among other things, led to his name being dropped from the company. Miffed, he reduced his role with the power company and devoted himself to something completely different: a vast mining project that came to be viewed as his most spectacular flop. Edison had dabbled in mineralogy, mostly when he needed to learn about the properties of various metals, for this or that invention. Iron ore mines in the eastern United States had been falling far behind newer mines in the Midwest, where the quality of the ore was better and the equipment was more modern. Edison believed he could invent technology that would make eastern mining less expensive, and profitable once again. He spent a decade—and much of his personal fortune—proving himself wrong.

The huge operation he set up at an old mine in Ogden, New Jersey, did, in fact, produce some breakthrough technology. But even that wasn't enough to make it profitable, and the mine became known as "Edison's folly." Maybe Edison was due for a flop, after so many successes, but had he followed his own established practices it might not have happened. Instead, Edison financed nearly the whole thing himself, which gave him total control but meant there were no outsiders demanding tangible signs of progress. Edison was often overoptimistic about how long it would take for his inventions to pan out, and the investors and other experts he usually worked with served as a useful counterbalance. Going it alone, however, Edison pressed on well past the point at which he should have pulled the plug—a rare instance when persistence worked against him. He seemed to love the camaraderie and rigorous routines of life at the mine, where he worked around the time that Theodore Roosevelt was preaching about the virtues of the "strenuous life" as an antidote to the soft living of the emerging leisure class. So Edison may have let his enthusiasm for the work cloud his judgment as a businessman. Some Edison biographers also suspect that the inventor was so hurt by his falling out with friends and partners at General Electric that he overcompensated by trying too hard to succeed at the mine. If so, it showed that Edison could be susceptible to the false sirens of emotion, and was human after all. It cost him more than $2 million of his own money—well over $50 today.

In characteristic fashion, Edison was so wired to glean knowledge from failure that the debacle at Ogden led to some profitable new lines of business. He had invented the world's most advanced crushing and grinding machines, able to reduce huge slabs of rock nearly to powder. That didn't save his mine, but it did produce a kind of sand that Edison thought would be ideal for an improved form of Portland cement, which was becoming a common building material. So he began to study the cement industry and decided he could build a giant kiln, twice the standard size, that would turn out more cement, cheaper. This time, he was right. Several of Edison's cement innovations became standard throughout the industry, and ultimately he earned decent money from them.

Still, Edison succumbed to hubris later in his career, particularly when it came to one of his most-loved inventions, the phonograph. By the early 1900s, Edison's machine was competing with another line sold by the Victor Talking Machine Company, which included the famous Victrola. The financial crisis of 1907 drove down sales of both makes. As the crisis subsided, Victor's sales recovered and quickly eclipsed their earlier peak. But sales of the Edison machine continued to fall. The problem, it turned out, was that the Victor machines played a type of disk that was cheaper to make and easier to use, and held more music than the Edison recordings. As a result, Victor drew more performers and was able to offer a much broader selection of music than Edison.

Edison's managers implored him to greatly expand the selection of recordings and offer the kind of music people wanted to buy, but Edison didn't listen. He believed consumers would patronize the technology that offered the best sound quality—even though there was no evidence of that—so he focused his efforts on distinguishing the Edison phonograph and its recordings through their high-fidelity sound. Meanwhile, he continued to select all the artists in the Edison catalogue himself. That produced a selection of music chosen by one man in his sixties—who happened to be nearly deaf. Edison seemed to have completely forgotten what he learned in 1868, disregarding ample evidence that consumers wanted more recordings and believing he could dictate a nation's musical tastes.

Hubris is rarely justified, but Edison's overconfidence came from a remarkable record of Rebounding so many times before. One aspect of his life may best encapsulate his ability to confront and harness adversity: his deafness. No one is certain of the causes, but it's clear that Edison's hearing was impaired by the time he was a teenager, and as an adult he was completely deaf in one ear and about 80 percent deaf in the other. The hardship caused Edison some distress. He once said that the worst thing about it was his inability to hear birds chirp. And since he was a gregarious chap who loved to banter, acquaintances could tell he felt pained when somebody told a funny story and he couldn't join in the laughter. But Edison never felt sorry for himself or used his disability as an excuse. In fact, he considered it an asset, insisting throughout his life that being unable to hear blocked out distractions and made it easier to concentrate. When learning, later in life, that a new medical procedure might help restore his hearing, he didn't even pursue it, fearing it might disrupt the precise way he learned.

Students of Edison have long speculated that his deafness forced him to learn in an individualistic way that transcended conventional instruction and allowed him to see possibilities that most others didn't. But more broadly, the way Edison handled his deafness goes a long way toward explaining why he was so successful. Edison focused on what he could control—his learning, his experiments, his business dealings—and spent almost no time lamenting the disability he couldn't control. Like other early adversities, he learned to cope with his loss of hearing gradually, when it was modest, then in bigger ways, when he was nearly totally deaf. We'll never know if Edison's deafness actually made him better off, but his belief that it did may have made it so. In the years since Edison multitasked in his lab, researchers have found that some successful people create "positive illusions" that lead them to believe they've got more working in their favor than they really do. That can cause trouble for people who are far less capable than they think. But it can also make talented people more comfortable taking risks, and many people more resilient. In any event, it's hard to imagine that Edison could have been nearly as productive had he bemoaned his disability to colleagues and investors or spent much time seeking miracle cures. Complainers tend not to get much done.

A lot has changed since Edison's time. But a lot hasn't. Dreamers still chase beloved ideas that they hope will spare them the rigors and tedium of ordinary work, regardless of whether there's a market for those ideas or not. Entrepreneurs still commit all their efforts to a single cause, mistakenly believing that making a Plan B, C, or D would betray their dedication to Plan A. People in every field and phase of life still sweep their failures under the rug, hoping that nobody else will notice and they themselves will forget—meanwhile discarding nuggets that might yield rare value, if only they were examined more closely. Edison himself never claimed a magical Eureka moment, or used his own lightbulb to represent a flash of insight that led to easy success. His breakthroughs were laborious, and many occurred only because he had the confidence to challenge his own assumptions. We've learned a lot since Edison's day. But we've forgotten some important things, too.

CHAPTER 3

WHEN HARDSHIP IS A PRIVILEGE

Thomas Edison died on October 18, 1931, at a time when America faced its worst crisis since the Civil War. For reasons that still aren't entirely clear, the United States and much of the rest of the world had become mired in the Great Depression, a miserable and maddening spectacle during which banks routinely failed, family savings disappeared, stock markets collapsed, and barbaric poverty ravaged millions. The man who led America through the first phase of the Depression turned out to be one of history's most notorious Wallowers, proving that natural ability and professional attainment don't equate to resilience or Rebounding skills. Herbert Hoover had been a precocious engineer whose life and career, until he became president, had been "nearly all sunshine and had seemed to move only forward," according to Amity Shlaes in *The Forgotten Man,* her 2007 chronicle of the Depression. Hoover was one of the first graduates of Stanford University, becoming one of the world's foremost mining experts while still in his twenties. As a relief official during World War I, Hoover helped provide food to millions of starving Europeans, earning a reputation for logistical genius. He was an energetic and effective commerce secretary after that, and when Hoover ran for president in 1928, he was considered one of the most capable and successful men in America. But Hoover had a fatal flaw: He was a man who "had never known failure," as the writer Sherwood Anderson put it. Virtually everything Hoover touched before the Depression went according to his carefully constructed plans, and he had never learned how to abandon failed ideas or recalibrate after a humiliating setback. As one effort after another failed to halt, or even slow, America's grinding descent in the early 1930s, Hoover's overconfidence crumbled and he began to seem paralyzed. "Hoover could not stand to think about the troubles mounting across the country," wrote Shlaes. Instead of Rebounding, he retreated to a cloistered world of fly-fishing and denial, becoming the face of imperious neglect. He got trounced when he ran for reelection in 1932.

In Ocean County, New Jersey, a placid seaside community about fifty miles south of New York City, a young boy named John Clifton Bogle tried to puzzle out the changes happening to his own family as the Depression took its corrosive toll. Bogle, known as Jack, had been one of two twin brothers born on May 8, 1929, just a few months before the Wall Street crash that marked the start of the Depression. In the crash, Bogle's parents lost a sizeable inheritance that had come from a lucrative family business, which forced them out of their spacious home close to New York City and into a much smaller one farther away. Bogle's father became a heavy drinker. While ignorant of the details, young Jack did know that there never seemed to be money for anything. Spending on trifles was unimaginable, and the boy worried about where the money would come from to fix a flat tire or handle other routine problems that arose. Bogle started to earn his own money by the time he turned ten, by delivering newspapers, scooping ice cream, and handling mail at a nearby post office. One of the proudest moments of his childhood came when he bought a bicycle with his own cash.

Bogle's father eventually lost his job, then moved out as his parents separated. Bogle's mother, who prized education, persuaded a wealthy relative to help Jack, his twin, and their brother get work scholarships to Blair Academy, a boarding school one hundred miles away. After high school, however, the family had no money left to pay for any of them to go to college. Jack, who had performed best at Blair, got into Princeton, where a scholarship covered part of the cost, and he took jobs as a ticket manager for the athletic department and a waiter in the student dining hall to pay for the rest. Bogle was one of the have-nots at Princeton, serving food to the wealthier kids who didn't have to work their way through school. But he felt lucky to be there, and he was also learning that hardship breeds advantages that privilege doesn't. Years later, with his career in shambles and his plans wrecked, the fortitude he had learned at a young age would help Bogle mount a crusade that transformed an entire industry and helped enhance the personal wealth of millions of middle-class families—not to mention his own.

After some early struggles with calculus and other subjects, Bogle hit his stride at Princeton, gravitating toward writing and economics. Years of privation made him determined to build a successful career, and he chose a topic for his senior thesis that he thought would get him there: "The Economic Role of the Investment Company." It earned Bogle high honors and did, in fact, help him start his career. After graduating, he interviewed for a job with Wellington Management Company, an investing firm founded by Walter L. Morgan a year before the 1929 stock market crash. Morgan, an accountant, had been lucky enough to learn his first hard financial lesson in the early '20s, when he used borrowed money to buy stock in an oil company that went bust. The robust economy gave him time to recover and pay back what he borrowed, and the sting of that setback made him a conservative investor by the time he founded Wellington. Morgan's caution helped his firm weather the Depression better than most. By the time Bogle came calling in 1951, Wellington was one of the leading firms in its field, and Morgan was regarded as a wise man of investing.

Bogle and his thesis impressed Morgan, who hired the smart young Princetonian and became his mentor. As the protégé grew and learned, Morgan tapped Bogle to be his successor, the man who would run Wellington when Morgan retired. Bogle was fairly young when that happened—a mere thirty-seven when he became executive vice president in charge of day-to-day operations. The firm needed his youth and energy. Its conservative approach to investing began to seem staid and outdated in a new razzle-dazzle world where slick marketing campaigns drew more customers than consistent but dull performance. By 1966, Wellington had lost 10 percentage points of market share in a decade and become the doddering old grandfather of its industry. Morgan gave Bogle a mandate: Fix all that.

The whiz kid running Wellington decided the answer was to merge with an investing firm in Boston that ran a high-flying mutual fund called Ivest, which had generated returns four times higher than the overall stock market. There were flattering magazine profiles of the four partners who ran Ivest, all under thirty-five years of age. They were even featured in a book, called *The New Breed on Wall Street.* A merger would invigorate Wellington and expand its offerings, while aligning the Boston upstarts with one of the industry's marquee names. The deal was finalized on June 6, 1966, with toasts, gifts, and congratulations all around, capped by applause in the financial press. Bogle became president and CEO of the merged firm, which would be headquartered at the old Wellington offices outside of Philadelphia, with an expanded office in Boston. Bogle would own 28 percent of the voting power, while the four Boston partners each got an ownership stake that would grow to 10 percent in five years' time, or 40 percent in total. For a couple of years, it looked like a brilliant deal. The Ivest Fund continued to soar and lure investors. Wellington regained some luster and developed other funds meant to mimic Ivest. And the markets mostly rose in the months following the merger, providing a natural lift.

But one seam at a time, the deal began to unravel once the champagne stopped flowing. Bogle, thrifty and traditional at heart, had deep doubts about the trendy, aggressive strategies of the Boston hotshots. Disagreements about strategy began to surface among the five partners—with Bogle usually outnumbered four to one. Bogle was autocratic, even by his own admission, and the more he got to know his new partners, the less he liked them. His disdain began to flare in meetings and phone calls. One of the partners complained that Bogle "gives directions by order rather than by discussion." Another Bostonian groused that Bogle was "out of touch with the ugly realities of the company."

Bogle had other vulnerabilities. In 1960, when he was thirty-one, he suffered his first heart attack. Doctors discovered that he had a chronically weak heart, and told him they didn't think it would hold out another ten years. Bogle neither scoffed nor capitulated; he simply went back to work. Problems flared again in 1967, when Bogle spent six weeks at the Cleveland Clinic having a hole sawed into his chest and a pacemaker implanted. Doctors there predicted that he'd never return to work. But his personal physician began to understand that Jack Bogle didn't abide by the usual rules of medicine, that he possessed a "mystical quality," poorly understood by doctors, which amounted to extraordinary perseverance. Bogle's heart problems unnerved a few of the executives at Wellington, and a company director even phoned Bogle's doctor to ask about his longevity. The doc gave a reassuring answer.

Dissension at Wellington intensified, however, as the stock market began to drift down in 1969. It bounced back for a while, but began to plunge in 1973, the start of a bear market that would last five years. The downdraft exposed deep weaknesses in the Ivest Fund, which became a dog, falling in value by far more than the overall market. After a short time in the sun, Wellington Management Company turned ice cold. Customers bailed out, leaving the firm managing less money in 1973 than it had at the time of the merger, seven years earlier. The whole industry was suffering, but Wellington was doing worse. Its own stock, which had traded at forty dollars in 1967, fell to a paltry eight dollars.

Rivalries among the top executives became all-out warfare. The Boston four now controlled 40 percent of the firm's votes compared to Bogle's 28 percent. By the end of the year, the Boston group formally asked Bogle to resign, offering him a payout to leave. Bogle refused. He'd rather fight a winner-take-all battle. But the new breed of Wall Street outflanked the old guard, with the Boston partners finally locking up enough votes on the Wellington board to vote Bogle out. Bogle knew it, and he told his wife, Eve, what was going to happen. When Bogle arrived at a board meeting on January 23, 1974, he knew he was going to be fired that day. While accepting his fate, he fought to the end. It was a painful meeting, with several directors—long-time friends of Bogle—reluctant to get to the pressing matter at hand. Finally, one of the directors asked if Bogle would resign, sparing the board the burden of firing him. No, he said, the board would have to do the dirty work itself. Out of principle, Bogle then read a 28-page memorandum in his defense, suggesting reforms that would tilt the company back toward the direction he felt it needed to go. But it only delayed the inevitable, and finally there was a vote. With Bogle abstaining, it was ten to one in favor of firing Bogle. Boston won, and Bogle lost. The prodigy from Princeton was out of a job.

Bogle was far from destitute. His peak salary had been $100,000 per year, equivalent to roughly $500,000 today. His six kids ate up a chunk of that, and Bogle had also gotten into the habit of giving a sizeable portion of his pay to charity every year. But he had long followed his own investing advice, living below his means and saving as much as possible. A lavish lifestyle didn't interest him anyway, and Bogle had never measured his success in dollars. He was a builder, rather, whose identity had become rooted in the company that had hired him out of college, nurtured his career, and ordained him as its leader. Losing Wellington felt nearly as bad as losing his fortune might have felt. "Bogle was heartbroken," his biographer Robert Slater wrote. On a train ride the next day, the stress overwhelmed him, and Bogle broke down in tears, heaving. "I was totally wiped out," he recalled years later. "I don't recall another time like that, when I was wiped out by it all."

Bogle knew his wings had been clipped as he sorted out his future. It would take a while to recover. He looked for another job, but found limited offerings because he wanted to keep his family in Philadelphia, where there were few big financial firms. He considered buying a small investing firm in Delaware, but that would have required him to spend more time away from home, which he resisted. Then another option materialized. Bogle had a second role at Wellington, as chairman of the various mutual funds the firm administered. The funds were organized as separate companies that were linked to Wellington Management but technically independent of it. The same person had traditionally been chairman of both, but Bogle urged the fund directors to break with tradition and retain him as chairman and chief executive. Some were Bogle backers who felt that Wellington had just fired its most talented executive, and they persuaded the whole group to keep Bogle on as chairman of the fund company. It would be an awkward arrangement, requiring humility and patience. As chairman of the fund company, Bogle would have a lofty title but limited responsibility. One critic derided the job as "chief clerk," responsible for record keeping and other back-end duties. The Boston partners would still control the profitable parts of the arrangement: investment management and marketing. Pride wasn't an obstacle for Bogle, and he welcomed the opportunity, much as he had felt lucky to be at Princeton, even if it meant waiting on fellow students who were wealthier. "All of a sudden," he said later, "it gave me an opportunity to start something new. And better." The prospect of more conflict with the Boston four didn't faze him. "I really like a good fight," he acknowledged. "It gets your blood pumping. It's exhilarating."

Back in school, one of Bogle's strongest subjects had been math, but he also enjoyed writing and had a flair for historical allusions. Getting fired and knocked down a few rungs on the ladder of achievement reminded him of the Greek myth of Antaeus, the son of Poseidon, who had gained fame as an unbeatable wrestler. Antaeus's secret—and his vulnerability—was that he gained indomitable strength when he was in contact with the ground, which meant that he got stronger when he was knocked down. The only way to defeat Antaeus was to lift him in the air. Bogle saw parallels to his own experience, one of many instances in which he would cast his own odyssey in epic or mythical terms, with himself as the earnest protagonist buffeted by powerful forces occasionally stronger than himself. Bogle's heady rise during his first fifteen years at Wellington had left him ungrounded, and vulnerable to the bad judgment that led to the merger with the Boston firm, which he now considered a "disgraceful mistake." Getting fired, by contrast, reconnected him with the ground and helped renew his strength. "When I got fired," he said later, grinning, "nobody ever would have imagined that that wouldn't be the end of me."

Bogle also knew that personalizing the fight with his adversaries from Boston could interfere with his judgment and sap his energy. And he felt a troubling sensation familiar to anybody who feels wronged. "I did struggle a lot with the idea of some kind of revenge," he recalled. "I talked to a friend of mine and asked him, How do you deal with that?" His friend suggested he visit Ezra Zilkha, a businessman who was heir to a Middle Eastern banking fortune and had a reputation as a kind of philosophical guru. So instead of dwelling on vindictive schemes, Bogle went to see Zilkha one day, explaining his problem. In an Arabic accent that conveyed ancient wisdom, Zilkha told Bogle: "What you must do is light a little candle of hatred and then put it way in the back of your mind. And then every once in a while open it up and give it a little air. You don't want the candle to go out. But you don't want it to burn you up, either." The advice made Bogle feel better, and gave him a chuckle he badly needed.

Bogle began to foment a plan that went all the way back to his senior thesis at Princeton. The Wellington funds were still struggling badly, and Bogle, not content to be chief clerk for long, outlined seven options that would allow the fund directors to escape the control of the management company, slash costs, pass the savings on to investors, and distinguish their funds from others that charged higher fees. It all made sense, but it was heresy. The management company run by the Boston crew earned much of its income from services provided to the funds. The fees it charged did, in fact, lower the returns earned by people who invested in the funds, but that was how the whole industry operated. Bogle was basically proposing that investors would be better off without the middleman, which would be the first time anybody ran mutual funds that way. "In a lot of ways it was outlined in my senior thesis at Princeton," Bogle recalled. "Mutual funds should be managed for the shareholder, not for the manager. They should be run in the most economical, efficient, and honest way possible." The fund directors saw the logic, but they weren't quite ready for a war with the management company. So in June 1974, they decided to adopt the least controversial of Bogle's seven options, taking over administrative duties from the management company, a small part of the services Wellington provided.

Bogle had a toehold, but the Boston partners, now on high alert, weren't about to hand him any easy second chances. The first riposte came quickly. The new arrangement created more distance between Wellington Management Company, controlled by the Boston four, and the fund company headed by Bogle, called the Wellington Group of Investment Companies. This meant that only one of them could use the storied Wellington name, and the management company won that battle easily. At first, Bogle saw it as a disastrous setback, since he was no longer associated with the Wellington name, which was still a strong brand that also happened to form part of his personal identity. But a couple of allies convinced him to see it differently: He could now choose his own name for the firm he ran, signaling a fresh start and a new direction. That swayed him.

While picking out some new wall hangings for his office, Bogle was browsing a book with prints of British naval battles, including several depicting the victories of Admiral Lord Nelson, who hounded the French and Spanish navies during the Napoleonic Wars. In 1798, after an audacious rout of the French Navy near the mouth of the Nile River, Nelson had written, "Nothing could withstand the squadron under my command. The judgment of the captains, together with the valor and high state of discipline of the officers and men of every description, was absolutely irresistible." Bogle found the words stirring, and envisioned a company driven by the same fighting spirit. So he named the fund company after Nelson's flagship, HMS *Vanguard*. The official name was The Vanguard Group, owned by the eleven mutual funds and their 380,000 shareholders operating on an at-cost basis.

Though the fund managers had passed on most of his initial ideas for lowering costs, Bogle knew there were many other ways to lower fees, and therefore raise returns to investors. For one thing, Bogle knew a dirty little secret: Money managers provided far less value than they claimed. He had done the research himself and shown that funds managed by "experts" who were constantly trading stocks performed worse over time than overall market averages, when all the fees were accounted for. The unusual success of funds like Ivest, which the managers typically attributed to their own brilliance, was almost always due to pure randomness, with a few outliers outperforming (and underperforming) the pack every year. It was inevitable that sooner or later those funds would come careening back toward the middle—or toward the other side of the bell curve. Bogle laid it all out in a series of memos for his fund directors.

Immediately after the new firm got started in May 1975, Bogle proposed that it start an "index" fund that wouldn't be managed by so-called experts trading stocks every day. Instead, it would be "passively managed," simply holding shares in all the firms comprising the S&P 500 stock index, so its performance would mirror the overall stock market. The advantage would come from extremely low costs, compared with the pound of flesh exacted by most fund managers. The board members pointed out that Vanguard's charter didn't allow it to do its own investment management. That was Wellington's job. Bogle argued that the fund wouldn't be "managed"—it would simply follow a set formula dictating what stocks it should hold. He knew that was disingenuous. But as Bogle's confidence grew, so did his audacity.

This time, the directors agreed with Bogle's idea, making Vanguard the first firm ever to create a stock index fund. But like many innovative new ideas, it barely survived its debut. The initial public offering for the fund, in 1976, was expected to bring in $150 million worth of investors' money. It raised just $11 million, which wasn't even enough to buy shares in all five hundred firms. Critics dubbed the fund Bogle's Folly, and some of his own colleagues suggested scrapping the idea. But Bogle trusted his math. No, he said, it will just take some patience. Vanguard stuck with it.

Bogle then focused on other ways to cut costs. Wellington marketed Vanguard's funds through a network of brokers and retail outlets that charged hefty fees for their services. That was another standard practice that racked up costs and robbed investors. Bogle wanted to cut out the brokers, eliminate Wellington's whole distribution role, and pass the savings along to investors. That turned into an epic battle, with both sides aware that the outcome could be ruinous for Wellington or Vanguard, or both. If the Vanguard board approved Bogle's plan, then Wellington would lose a huge chunk of business. But Bogle's plan to bypass the retail network and rely on telephone marketing and word-of-mouth sales was risky too, since customers might balk at the new approach. Brokers cut out of the deal might even bad-mouth Vanguard or spread false rumors.

Bogle was sure that his logic was correct, but he harbored his own doubts about how customers would react. For two months the Vanguard board debated, dithered, and argued with Wellington. Finally, in February 1977, the Vanguard board voted to end its distribution arrangement with Wellington. To the relief of Bogle and everybody else at Vanguard, it worked. The feared liquidation of accounts didn't happen. With this radical step, Vanguard would be the first major mutual fund firm to eliminate sales fees, dramatically shifting its focus from marketing shares to serving shareholders.

Vanguard was becoming a rebellious upstart, but there was little euphoria, because it all happened at an awful time for the financial industry. The bear market had ended in 1975, but battered investors were still spooked. Inflation was creeping toward double digits, gobbling up most of the return that investors were able to eke out in mutual funds or most other investments. The turmoil between Vanguard and Wellington generated awful publicity that didn't help. There was a net cash outflow from Vanguard funds for eighty straight months as customers pulled their money out. Some worried that the new Vanguard wouldn't survive the 1970s.

Other roadblocks kept popping up. In 1978, the Securities and Exchange Commission ruled that Vanguard was not allowed to make key changes that were essential to its new structure. It was a major setback that threatened the whole company, and Bogle was furious. The SEC left the door open, however, to a revamped plan that would still allow the cost savings Bogle wanted, in a way that regulators deemed acceptable. Bogle and his team got to work on the changes and the reams of paperwork required. After three tense years, the SEC finally completed its review of Vanguard's business model—and reversed its earlier decision, endorsing the firm's structure as a new standard for the industry. Seven years after getting fired, Jack Bogle had been vindicated.

Vanguard had become more familiar to investors by then, with Bogle seizing every chance he got to pontificate against high fees that dunned investors. He was becoming a celebrated rebel, champion of the little guy and darling of the press, and the spoils began to pour down on Vanguard. After a long period of declines, the assets managed by Vanguard exploded. By 1990, they were nineteen times what they had been in 1980, making Vanguard the second-largest mutual fund company in America, after Fidelity. The stock index fund derided as "Bogle's Folly" in the 1970s caught fire in the 1980s, and by 2000 had become one of the largest mutual funds in the world, copied by many others. As Bogle envisioned, Vanguard's costs were the lowest in the industry by far, which boosted returns and frequently landed Vanguard funds among the top performers in their class. Magazines like *Forbes* and *Institutional Investor* published glowing profiles of Bogle, dubbing him a maverick and "the conscience of the industry."

Bogle's heart troubles persisted the whole time. He had at least six heart attacks in total, followed by a heart transplant in 1996. That was an ongoing challenge, but it also gave Bogle a larger-than-life luster, bordering on legend. A group of fans, calling themselves the Bogleheads, began to form in 1998, when Bogle was sixty-nine. The fan club grew into a cottage industry with its own website (www .bogleheads.org), trade shows, and several Boglehead books advocating their hero's philosophy of shrewd investing that avoids flash and focuses on the basics.

In retrospect, triumphant tales like the Jack Bogle story seem preordained, as if no force on earth could stop the protagonist from fulfilling his mission. But a closer look reveals many momentous pivot points that could have produced an ordinary outcome instead of an extraordinary one. Bogle's rise through the ranks at Wellington Management Company in the 1950s and '60s was impressive but not extraordinary. He worked hard and applied his talents, and the firm rewarded him with frequent promotions. But Bogle was simply climbing a ladder set before him, not taking unusual risks or creating anything new.

Beginning in 1974, however, he faced a series of quit points where it would have been understandable, and probably even rational, for him to stop fighting, give up, and try something else. After getting fired as CEO, he could have been satisfied with the role he salvaged for himself at the fund company and quietly fulfilled his duties, instead of launching a disruptive reform plan and trying to remake the business. He could have given up when Vanguard's first index fund flopped or when the SEC invalidated the firm's business model. All along, Bogle's heart problems provided ample excuse to take extended leave or to retire, to look after his health. Each time Bogle hit one of those quit points, he refused to capitulate, even if his ultimate goal remained distant.

Jack Bogle was obviously born with intelligence and other gifts that gave him advantages. But so are a lot of determined people who end up succumbing to bad luck, self-doubt, faulty judgment, or forces that are simply more powerful than they are. Bogle became a breakthrough Rebounder because he continually created advantages for himself and shunned the unproductive behavior that leads to stagnation. He spent his energy on purposeful action when he could easily have been dominated by indignation, worry, or rumination. Like many Rebounders, Bogle also viewed his life and career as an epic narrative, with himself in the central role. Accurate or not, aligning himself with the overachieving underdogs of history gave Bogle a far deeper sense of purpose than somebody who simply goes to work every day.

As Vanguard became successful, Bogle got in the habit of giving long speeches to the "crew," as he called his employees, whom he likened to Lord Nelson's loyal shipmates. He talked frequently about the firm's early struggles and often described Vanguard as "a company that might never have existed." Its competitive battles—particularly against rival Fidelity—were similar to Nelson's continual quest "for an enemy ship that wants to fight." He even compared his comrades from the early days at Vanguard to the warriors who fought with Henry V at the famed Battle of Agincourt in 1415: "We few, we happy few, we band of brothers."

It's easy to imagine some eye-rolling among the Vanguard "crew members" as the old man launched into yet another grandiose recounting of the glory days. But Bogle's sense of mission paid off for Vanguard, partly because his various trials gave him a sense of fragility that seemed to go hand in hand with his confidence. Bogle had an ironclad belief that hard work could help him overcome misfortune. But he was no blind optimist, simply waiting for things to go his way. He was much more of a defensive pessimist, constantly asking his colleagues during Vanguard's formation, "What can go wrong?" Even as Vanguard enjoyed breakout success in the 1980s and '90s, Bogle's speeches to the crew would often follow a familiar pattern: First, a bit of boasting about milestones reached, then, a set of stern warnings about unseen threats and the dangers of complacency. The exhortations must have become tiresome, yet Bogle turned out to be right. In the spring of 1987, for example, a bond market shock produced a deluge of phone calls from worried customers, and Vanguard, overwhelmed, had to turn some callers away. Finally! The kind of trouble Bogle was always looking for! After a task force looked into it, Vanguard instituted a new system requiring every employee to get customer service training, so this Swiss Army, as Bogle called it, could man the phones in a crisis. Later that year, on October 19, the stock market fell by 23 percent, the biggest one-day crash ever. At Vanguard, all hands came on deck to answer calls—including Bogle—which produced rave reviews of its handling of the crisis. At Fidelity, meanwhile, many callers turned irate and panicky as they got recorded messages or busy signals. A year later, Vanguard's assets had soared by 22 percent, three times the industry average. By 2011, with $1.6 trillion in assets under management, it had become the world's largest mutual fund company.

Long after Bogle had retired as Vanguard's CEO, I met him at the Vanguard offices in suburban Philadelphia, where he continued to do research and write books. I asked Bogle if he could account for the extraordinary persistence that led to the creation of Vanguard. He didn't have a stock answer, but he did insist that having to work for everything he got, beginning in his childhood, endowed him with values that propelled him his entire life. "If you grow up the hard way," he mused, "maybe the odds are 70 percent you can make something out of your life. If you grow up the easy way, maybe the odds are 40 percent."

Bogle, always striving to be mathematically correct, noted that his offhand computation was highly imprecise. But he saw in his own life the connection between childhood hardships and adult achievement that researchers had been studying for years. He was a real-life example of "survivor's pride," a phenomenon discovered by psychologist Emmy Werner of the University of California, Davis, and others, who found that overcoming challenges early in life helps some children develop a sense of mastery and confidence that allows them to take risks as adults, without debilitating worry over what will happen if they fail. Pampered children never given a chance to fail, by contrast, tend to lack a sense of mastery, since tough problems are usually handled by someone else. So perhaps Bogle wasn't being completely coy when he expressed a sense of superiority over the silver-spooners he waited on at Princeton: "Deep down, I think I felt sorry for them," he told me. "They weren't born with all the advantages I had."

Bogle also developed an abiding appreciation for the deep lessons learned through failure, which starts with recognizing your own failures in the first place. "I have come to regard failure as another essential of leadership," Bogle wrote in his 1999 bestseller, *Common Sense on Mutual Funds*. "It is often best if things do not come too easily in this life." On a list of lessons for entrepreneurs that Bogle generated, number two was, "Turn disaster into triumph." Number four was, "Get fired."

In 1997, a Yale University student named Thatcher Lane Gearhart wrote about John Bogle in his senior thesis on entrepreneurship. Gearhart had studied the history of Vanguard and realized that Bogle might have been just another corporate executive, never driven to found Vanguard, if his career at Wellington had gone smoothly. "Were Bogle not forced to act out of the ordinary," Gearhart concluded, "he would not have acted out of the ordinary." Bogle endorsed his conclusion, including it in *Common Sense* a couple of years later. If the Yale student was right, Vanguard owes its existence to a disgraceful mistake made by a headstrong Jack Bogle in 1966, with the penance paid in 1974 and redemption deferred until 1981. Millions of Vanguard investors are no doubt grateful that Bogle screwed up.

CHAPTER 4

THE DANGERS OF OPTIMISM

Jack Bogle learned that getting fired can be an enlightening and empowering experience. But that's not usually how it feels in real time. Bogle's insight came years later, and at the time it happened, he felt miserable—and he was lucky enough to have some money in the bank. Many others get a rougher deal from the employment gods, who don't seem to consider financial preparedness when deciding who shall benefit from the perverse opportunities they bestow. If they did, they might get better results, because for a lot of people, losing a job is a disaster that's bloody hard to recover from.

I was at a conference of business leaders in New York one day, scribbling a few uninspired notes about branding and marketing and other stuff I had heard many times before, when the keynote speaker stepped to the podium in a conventional gray suit. It had been an unproductive morning, and sitting through a self-congratulatory speech filled with corporate clichés wouldn't make it any better. So I packed up my things and got ready to make a quiet exit the moment the speech got boring. It didn't get boring though, and at one point the speaker mentioned how he had been unemployed, middle-aged,

and nearly broke when he started a long career comeback that ultimately made him worthy of featured-speaker status. A Rebounder!
When he finished his talk, I followed him off the stage, introduced
myself, and asked to learn more.

If you've ever eaten in an airport, noshed on fried chicken, or
snuck away for a cup of coffee and a donut, chances are Jon Luther
had a role in your meal. In the 1990s, Luther helped run a concession
company that converted the dilapidated food dispensaries at airports
in Los Angeles, Newark, Fort Lauderdale, and many other cities into
pleasant, name-brand eateries with food that was actually fresh—
perhaps the only thing that's gotten better about air travel over the
last two decades. After that he became president of Popeye's, the
fried chicken chain, and then in 2003, Dunkin' Brands hired Luther
as its CEO, making him responsible for nearly ten thousand Dunkin'
Donuts and Baskin-Robbins stores. At each of the chains, Luther
earned credit for turning around ailing brands, improving quality,
creating a sense of purpose and excitement, and, along with all of
that, boosting profitability.

But all of that was after the comeback, and for a while, when in his
forties, Luther worried that he might never reverse a sharp career
downturn that left him struggling to pay his bills and pushed his
boldest ambitions far out of reach.

Luther started out in Buffalo, where he grew up in a tough,
working-class neighborhood. He left the local liberal arts college
after two years because of too much partying and too little studying.
He flipped burgers and tended bar, and his interest in hospitality led
to a two-year degree from a small hotel school in upstate New York.
He married his wife, Sharon, while still in school, figuring at the
time that he'd always work and live in Buffalo. His first real job was
managing the cafeteria at a Wurlitzer plant in North Tonawanda,
New York, where four hundred hungry Polish women came for lunch
every day.

Luther left the Polish women behind and started working for Aramark, the big concessionaire that provides food at sports arenas, hos-
pitals, universities, and other institutional settings. After four years
in Buffalo, there was no way to get ahead at the company unless he

moved someplace else, so he and Sharon decided to say good-bye to a big circle of family and friends and move to Connecticut, where Luther got the chance to run a division. Eventually he ended up at Aramark headquarters in Philadelphia, running the company's luxury restaurant division, which was prestigious but had one shortcoming: It wasn't profitable. When Aramark decided to shut it down, they offered Luther other jobs at the company, but he felt it was time to break free of the corporate mothership and do something on his own. He knew of a small restaurant company in Maine that was for sale, and he hoped to organize some investors, move to New England, and start running his own operation.

A back injury deferred that dream. While training for a marathon, Luther suffered a herniated disc that required surgery and rehabilitation and sidelined him for nine months. The opportunity in Maine got away. By this time, Luther had a son just starting college and a daughter heading there soon, which meant that poking around for another deal, without a steady income, wasn't an option. He got a job offer from the Marriott hospitality chain, which provided the income he needed and brought the family to the suburbs of Washington, D.C. But the desire to run his own company stuck with him, and after a couple of years at Marriott, Luther started talking again with some of the same investors who had been considering the deal in Maine. They offered him the chance to run a food service company called Benchmark, which would have outlets in South Carolina, Cleveland, and Boston. Luther envisioned a prosperous little firm that would grow quickly, then get bought by a big conglomerate like Aramark, earning him a generous payday and springboarding him to even bigger things. So he left Marriott, invested most of his life savings in Benchmark, and started commuting from Washington to the sites of the new business.

His dream popped quickly. The economy began to slow, and the investors he had been working with started to get cold feet. Then the top deal maker, Luther's main backer, left to start his own firm. That left a disorganized group of reluctant investors running a company they no longer wanted. Luther offered to raise enough money himself to buy them out, but they turned him down, preferring to bleed

Benchmark of its cash and sell off the equipment they had purchased piece by piece. As a newcomer to the cutthroat world of deal making and venture capital, Luther hadn't counted on fickle investors willing to take a loss if they suddenly saw a better outlet for their money. He thought the investors were just as committed as he was. But he learned otherwise when they decided to sell the whole operation, and abruptly fired him one day in late 1990—an outcome Luther had barely contemplated. He had been so optimistic about Benchmark's prospects that when he signed a contract with the partners, he insisted on few protections for himself if things didn't work out. As a result, the investors treated Luther like just another piece of equipment they needed to liquidate. He got a mere thirty days' severance pay, lost all his stock in the company, and was out his entire investment. They even reclaimed Luther's company car, sending a repo man to his home to snatch it in the middle of the night.

It was a shocking comedown that left Luther out of a job, and nearly out of money. Both of his kids were in college by then, and a nationwide recession was beginning. "It was just a mess," he told me. "I'm sitting on the street with two kids in college, wondering, What do I do now? I was in huge debt, with a big mortgage, and I had lost everything I had invested in Benchmark."

Luther started to do consulting work when he could get it, but the restaurant business usually stalls during a recession, and gigs were scarce. To stretch money, he cashed in a couple of insurance policies, which brought in a few thousand bucks. He and his wife cut out their own restaurant meals, vacations, luxuries, and other obvious things they could live without, while trying to shield their two kids from any financial stress. But the bank account still got dangerously low, and Luther used to dread the moment he would approach an ATM, wondering if various checks had cleared and money would come out when he requested a withdrawal. A few times, it didn't. "I had to go back home and scratch my head and say, How am I going to do this?" he told me more than twenty years later. "I tapped out all of my resources."

Luther was also fighting the temptation to return to corporate work just to earn a paycheck. He figured he could get a job in sales with little trouble, because he had done that early in his career with Aramark, and been successful. Even during a recession, companies were usually willing to bring in new salespeople who could help boost business. But that wasn't what he wanted to do with the rest of his life. Though Benchmark had crumbled, and the luxury restaurants at Aramark had been unprofitable, Luther felt he had developed a talent for branding and marketing and executing innovative ideas. Even as Aramark was backing away from the luxury restaurants that Luther ran, he instituted changes that led to prestigious wine awards and other acclaim. He didn't yet have the breakthrough success to prove it, but Luther felt sure that he could be a leader, changing things for the better, instead of toiling for somebody else. At the age of forty-eight, he knew he faced a pivotal moment: His next job would probably determine whether he spent the rest of his career building something he could claim as his own or simply pulling down a paycheck. "I never had huge doubts in my ability," he told me. "I had huge doubts about whether the rest of the world would recognize it."

There's nothing unusual about that predicament. For every self-satisfied star who sails through his career thanks to family connections, good mentors, or lucky timing, there are dozens of others who are just as talented but remain stifled or frustrated because they got a bad break instead of a good one, or tripped over one of the extension cords that run all throughout life. Some people break out of a rut by taking a big risk on something they've always dreamed about. FedEx founder Fred Smith, for instance, is famous for flying to the blackjack tables in Las Vegas in 1973, when his fledgling air-express company was desperately short of cash, and winning $27,000 that he promptly wired to company headquarters, to help meet payroll expenses. Sounds cool, but taking all-or-nothing risks with kids in college and a family to support is a gunslinger's strategy, and a trip to just about any casino provides a glimpse of all the Fred Smith–wannabees who mistakenly thought a few lucky cards would be enough to turn a losing streak around.

Rebounders rarely, if ever, rely on luck alone. What's far more common is a kind of diligence meant to inoculate them against bad luck and help turn fortune their way. Luther realized he had been out of his league trying to work a deal with sharks from the venture capital world. He was experienced at sales and the inner operations of food-service companies, but even in school, math and science had bored him. As a businessman, he knew little about finance or buying and selling companies. So while marginally employed as a consultant, he called an old friend from Aramark, who had recently become the chief financial officer of another company, and asked for help. His friend agreed to meet with him occasionally for a few months and tutor him on balance sheets and financial statements and the intricacies of corporate money maneuvering. That convinced Luther to dive in even deeper, so he scrimped the funds to pay his own way through a short executive program on finance at the University of Pennsylvania's Wharton School of Business. And in his consulting work, he deliberately looked for jobs involving mergers and acquisitions, which he considered a weak part of his portfolio, since his primary experience in these had been getting merged out of a failed startup and acquiring nothing but debt.

Waiting for the right opportunity felt like a game of chicken, because the tuition bills and debt payments seemed relentless. If Luther's intuition was wrong, and the opportunity he was waiting for didn't materialize, he'd only have a bigger hole to dig out of when he acknowledged defeat and went back into sales. The road to redemption, ironically enough, ran through the food-industry mecca known as . . . Buffalo. The burger joint where Luther had worked as a teenager was owned by the father of a high-school friend, who ended up being pals with a guy named Jerry Jacobs, who ran a family-owned business called Delaware North. Jacobs's company owned the Boston Bruins and the Boston Garden arena where they played, and also had contracts to provide the food at a variety of stadiums and arenas and even Yosemite National Park. The weakest part of the company serviced airports, which seemed like a dead-end business catering to municipal clients that were short of money on account of the recession, and not all that motivated to delight the flying public with great food anyway. Luther's name came up when Jacobs started looking for somebody to turn around the airport division. After several discussions, Jacobs offered him the job.

There were a lot of reasons to turn it down, including the fact that

Buffalo is rarely a gateway to the big time. Luther saw other warning flags as well. Jacobs was known as one of the toughest bosses in the business. His two sons worked at Delaware North and were being groomed to run it, which meant that some decisions might be governed by family issues rather than sound business practices. Plus, Luther would be running the worst part of the company. But there were some important factors on the positive side of the ledger, too. Most important, taking over a failing operation would give him the chance to rebuild his career and prove to others what he felt he was capable of. "If I don't make it here," he told himself, "this could be the end of my aspiration to do great things." So he accepted the offer.

When Luther moved back to Buffalo with his wife, he became the president of a money-losing subsidiary known as CA One, operating thirty-eight airport restaurants that were far down the food chain from the luxury bistros he once ran. Many were stuck with overpriced leases negotiated years earlier, when air travel was booming. High costs and falling revenues left understaffed restaurants serving stale, unappetizing food. Management was unmotivated. Employees stole. Morale was poor. Resentful customers spent as little as they could, since the food served on board the airplanes was often better. Luther's mission was to reverse the whole cycle of decline, or at least reduce Jacobs's losses.

He started by asking the airports to slash their rents, in exchange for a pledge to remake the restaurants, bring in more customers, and boost revenue by 30 percent. That was an extremely aggressive target for such a stagnant business. Instead of the blind faith that had left him abandoned in the Benchmark deal, Luther now practiced a kind of defensive optimism: While he believed in his ability to improve the business, he also knew it might not work, and he prepared himself and everybody else for disappointing results. He made sure never to sugarcoat the pitch to his bosses or assure them everything would work out. Instead, he'd make the strongest case he could to convince Jacobs that the new investments were worthwhile, but make sure everybody understood all the risks, too. It worked. Jacobs and his lieutenants seemed to trust Luther, putting aside major doubts and providing most of the money he asked for.

The first level of reforms was to make some airport dining areas more like the food court at a mall, with familiar brands and food that, while not spectacular, was at least tasty and affordable. So at several airports he brought in chains like Au Bon Pain and Burger King. But national franchises tend to charge hefty licensing fees, so in other airports, CA One simply created its own brands, such as Lefty's Tavern and Jake's Coffee. Some colleagues argued that new brands invented by corporate fiat would never gain traction with the public, but Luther's passion for marketing persuaded them. "If it walks and talks like a brand, it's a brand to people," he told the doubters. "People use the same airport over and over again. As long as you're consistent, nobody will know it's not a street brand." That seemed to work, and Luther tweaked the scheme to add some local flair, with innovations like the Red Rocks Cafe at Denver International, which served barbecue sandwiches and Colorado craft beers. In Tucson, he pushed the concept a step further by recruiting well-known local establishments like the El Charro Mexican Restaurant and the Last Chance Saloon to open outlets at the airport, giving travelers a chance to experience genuine local favorites. It wasn't exactly the Stork Club, but for harried travelers, friendly service in a joint that felt like a neighborhood pub was a huge improvement over the utilitarian beverage stands they were used to.

Los Angeles became a turning point. The airport was taking bids for the contracts on six dining locations, and Luther's old employer, Marriott, seemed like the favorite to win, since it had run those locations for years. But instead of renewing the contract with the established service, airport officials jumped at CA One's offer to highlight local cuisine and gave Luther's firm the contract. Luther's first move was to approach renowned California chef Wolfgang Puck, famous for the celebrity-filled Spago and Ma Maison restaurants. Earlier in his career, Puck had worked at the same Aramark division as Luther, a connection that helped Luther get on the chef's busy calendar. But Puck was incredulous when Luther asked if he'd be willing to open a restaurant at LAX. "Why would I want to do that?" he gasped. "Why would I put my reputation on the line in an airport that has such lousy food?"

Luther shared his vision: "Wolf, you'll get a chance to change it," he said. "If you come into the airports with your cuisine, we can change the entire slope of the airport business." Luther finally converted the business-savvy chef, and the first Wolfgang Puck Express opened in LAX's Terminal 7 in 1995.

Puck's imprimatur helped draw other upscale eateries, including a Daily Grill restaurant in another terminal and the Disney-designed Encounter restaurant suspended by parabolic arches in the center of the airport. The buzz over the new openings made LAX a destination in itself, and celebrities like John Travolta even rented the Encounter for private parties. A year after taking the plunge, Puck told Luther that he had received more compliments on the express outlet at the airport than he had about Spago during its first year—especially since people could stop in on short notice while waiting for a flight, and didn't need to wait weeks for a reservation.

The rest of the world finally started to recognize Luther's capabilities. His new concepts drew strong reviews in the press. Competitors began to copy Luther's ideas, with airports all over America starting to upgrade their restaurants. Luther himself, unknown until then outside of the companies where he had worked, was suddenly described in trade publications as a turnaround artist. Most important, CA One turned a steep loss into a healthy profit, saving the owner a sizeable chunk of his personal fortune. At a companywide meeting one day, executives who ran other Delaware North divisions and were under pressure to deliver better results began to ask how Luther's division managed to turn in such impressive numbers. The president of the company, Richard Stephens, who was Luther's direct boss, stood up to answer. "One word," he said. "Courage." He explained that Luther had come up with creative ideas, taken risks to get them approved, and challenged the owner to spend money he would have preferred to keep in his pocket. Luther didn't let it show, but he got choked up, as the endorsement validated his own belief in himself. "I'll never forget that moment," he told me later. "That's when I got recognized for doing tough things no one else was able to do. I said, Yeah, I guess I do have courage. It was a pivotal moment in my comeback."

At the age of fifty-three, Jon Luther was finally a rising star. Other companies began to call, asking if he'd be interested in helping revive their business, as he had done at CA One. By the end of 1996, Luther felt that in five years at Delaware North he had accomplished what he set out to. "I passed the test," he told himself. "I'm back." He had proven to himself and to many others that he had the talent to lead an organization and inject life into it. The Popeye's fried chicken chain was one of Luther's suitors, and it was an appealing challenge. Popeye's, founded in 1971, had expanded rapidly in the 1980s, but taken on too much debt and been forced to reorganize itself in bankruptcy in the early 1990s. By the time they called Luther, Popeye's was a second-place chain with about one thousand outlets that seemed like nothing more than a Kentucky Fried Chicken copycat, with stagnant sales and a hazy focus. The company's owners asked if he'd come onboard to turn that around, and in 1997, Luther became president of Popeye's. This time he had the leverage to do what he had failed to do at Benchmark in the 1980s: anticipate what might go wrong and negotiate a contract that would protect him if it did.

Popeye's had started in New Orleans and succeeded thanks to a spicy chicken recipe that stood out from other fast-food fare. But as the chain got bigger, its singularity had faded. Luther thought Popeye's could distinguish itself once again by returning to its culinary roots, so he and the chain's executive chef revised the menu to focus on the Cajun and Creole cuisine of the Bayou. He cleared out undergrowth in the company that blocked innovation, much as he had managed to persuade the tight-fisted owner at Delaware North to invest in new ideas. That freed the company's menu experts to come up with new offerings that gave Popeye's a fresh marketing angle, lured new customers, and earned a few industry awards, bringing some badly needed buzz to the brand. Sales soared, and before long, Popeye's was earning more sales per store than any other chain in its category.

Dunkin' Brands was looking for a similar jolt when it lured Luther away from Popeye's in 2003. The offer included some challenges that Luther didn't anticipate. Dunkin', too, wanted to reenergize its brands, but Dunkin' was owned by a British conglomerate, which was then bought by a big French firm. Compared to the autonomy he had at CA One and at Popeye's, Luther had to tug on a long leash to get the attention of his bosses in Europe when he wanted to do something out of the ordinary. So when the French firm decided the American donut chain no longer fit in its portfolio, Luther saw the corporate kiss-off as a chance to recapture the opportunity he had missed twenty years earlier, with Benchmark. He helped organize a group of private-equity firms that bought the company, kicking in some of his own money for a small ownership stake. When that deal went through, in 2006, Luther once again had a free hand to revitalize a tired brand. He sold a sandwich chain that was a drag on the business and raised growth targets for the donut franchise. To get the attention of customers whose money he needed to meet those targets, Luther reprised some of his moves at Popeye's, adding new menu items like sandwiches and coffee drinks, raising quality standards, and running a catchy new marketing campaign: "America runs on Dunkin'." By the time he retired as CEO in 2009, Luther had boosted Dunkin's sales by 50 percent, added six thousand stores, and fulfilled the goal he had started to pursue twenty-five years earlier: He ran the show and put all his talents to use. When Dunkin' went public in 2011, Luther's ownership stake was worth more than $40 million.

As a wealthy man, Luther sounded a bit like a survivor of the Great Depression when he talked about one of his most searing memories: walking up to an ATM and wondering if any money would come out. "I never, ever forgot the ATM," he said. "I never want to worry about that again. It was emotionally traumatic for me. Now, generations to come will never have to worry about an ATM." He's far from the first human being to be motivated by poverty—or the fear of it—but that alone isn't what got Luther through a crucible moment. He also summoned Rebounder skills that helped him identify his weaknesses, strengthen his own capabilities, and sustain the confidence it took to keep taking risks.

Luther describes himself as an "eternal optimist," but his optimism evolved from naïve hopefulness to something more akin to defensive optimism after he stumbled. In the fifteen years that he spent at Aramark, virtually all the risks he took paid off. He rose quickly and got generous raises. Everything did, in fact, work out. But with the Benchmark fiasco, he finally took a risk that backfired, and the penalty was severe because he hadn't prepared for it. Psychologists recognize that mistake as "naïve optimism," a belief that problems will get solved and change will happen smoothly without any extra effort or energy. When things don't turn out that way, naïve optimists often find themselves without resources, because they never learned the deeper skills it takes to surmount adversity. That's when they tacitly admit defeat, giving up on their ambition or retreating to more comfortable ground.

Luther may have started out as a naïve optimist, but he became a "realistic optimist" who relied on himself—not on luck, or on others—to turn things around. Mastering adversity starts with an accurate assessment of your own abilities. That may seem obvious, but most people trying to figure out what went wrong tend to find causes that validate a preexisting belief in their own competence, and let themselves off the hook. When the problem is our own short-sightedness, we often wear natural blinders that prevent us from seeing it and lead us to look for other causes. But Luther realized that in the Benchmark deal, he was an amateur jousting with professionals. He went further by identifying specific things like finance and acquisitions that he needed to learn more about. And instead of blaming the investors for dumping him, he faulted himself for failing to foresee pitfalls and prepare for them. That tempered his optimism but bolstered his confidence, and helped convince him to keep his quest alive.

Clear thinking also allowed Luther to understand what he did well—connect with customers, nurture change, execute creative ideas, and build business. So when he hit the skids and ran out of money, he knew what to do: look for an opportunity to exploit what he was good at, while working hard to improve his subpar skills. "That's why I wouldn't settle," he said. "Because I knew from my marketing days what I could do creatively. You have to have an inner confidence in your ability." When Delaware North approached him, he knew it was the right move. "The opportunity matched my skills perfectly," he told me. Maybe it was a lucky break, but if so, it happened because Luther knew what he was good at in the first place, and turned down other jobs that might have provided a quicker paycheck but a rougher fit.

Luther also allowed himself the time to get it right. He would have preferred to succeed sooner—who wouldn't?—but he didn't panic or try something desperate as the clock ran down. When I interviewed him, he told me of friends he grew up with in Buffalo who peaked early in their lives, resting on laurels they had earned as early as high school. Then they plateaued, either content to stay where they were or uncomfortable going any further. Everybody knows people like that—and we all want to believe we're not one of them. But the thing that differentiates strivers from settlers isn't always a fancy degree or a comfortable career or a quick rise to stardom. Sometimes it's the stumbles that reveal what you still need to learn, stumbles that might not happen if you never ventured beyond familiar terrain. "I always felt I had to work harder because I didn't have that four-year degree," Luther told me at the age of sixty-seven, after he had retired as Dunkin's CEO. "I've always been a continuous learner. And I haven't peaked yet." As long as there's something new to learn, there's always another peak.

CHAPTER 5

HOW PASSION MISLEADS

Most people who accomplish something worthwhile aren't indifferent about it. If they were, they wouldn't be motivated to take the risks or bear the tradeoffs that are often the tollbooths on the road to high achievement. They have passion. It helps them work long hours, deflect naysayers, try difficult things, and stretch their talents as far as they'll go.

Passion is in high demand. If you could package or bottle it, you'd have a miracle potion equivalent to Botox or Viagra. In fact, there are many passion merchants professing to do just that, selling books or videos or seminars meant to help you discover what you love and inject meaning into your life. In the 1970s, philosopher-mythologist Joseph Campbell started telling the college students he taught to "follow your bliss," a mantra that caught on nationwide in the 1980s when Campbell starred in a popular documentary called *The Power of Myth.* Campbell's notion of bliss was complex, rooted in Indian spirituality and other ancient traditions, but ebullient baby boomers equated bliss with passion, and some of them took the advice to mean that they should devote themselves to work that made them feel good. It sounds enlightened, but there's a catch: The things people feel passionate about aren't always easy to earn a living at, and there are probably as many people who have charged passionately into dead ends as there are people who have attained soulless, but comfortable, prosperity.

Some people are truly passionate about making money and becoming phenomenally successful—at what, it doesn't matter so much. Lucky them; their bliss happens to lie along the same path as compensation and material extravagance, so they never have to choose between passion and comfort. Others have a tougher challenge, with a passion for something that's hard to market or so competitive, such as basketball or acting, that only a tiny percentage of the most determined climbers will make it to the top. Many try anyway, devoting their careers to pursuits in which they'll never be quite good or lucky enough. Some take a more pragmatic approach, indulging their passion as a part-time hobby while paying the bills by doing more conventional work.

The dangerous myth about passion is that if you love something intensely enough, you'll be successful at it. Just do something you love, the saying goes, and the rest will fall into place. Many of us know people who disprove that adage, and there's now some scientific data that backs up the anecdotal evidence. In his popular book *Outliers,* journalist Malcolm Gladwell wrote about the "10,000-hour rule" discovered by psychologist K. Anders Ericsson and others trying to figure out what makes standout performers and other high achievers so brilliant. The concept is pleasingly simple: Practice makes perfect, and ten thousand hours of it seems to be a threshold at which greatness becomes possible. Gladwell explained how the 10,000-hour rule helps account for the genius of composer Wolfgang Amadeus Mozart, chess legend Bobby Fischer, Microsoft cofounder Bill Gates, and even The Beatles. None of them started out as masters. They only got that way after years of practice and exposure to their craft. While it's always nice to start out with raw talent, the research suggests that practically anybody can become a virtuoso if they make it to ten thousand hours.

That round number is intuitively appealing, because it's big enough to seem uncommon but small enough to seem attainable. It confirms something we already know—experience counts—while at the same time quantifying it. Yet devoting ten thousand hours to any one thing is a huge commitment that requires a lot more than passion and blocks out many other activities people find enjoyable, so it could be a goal reached only by people who are extraordinary to start with. If you spent forty hours a week doing a given activity, it would take five years to hit the target. And remember, coffee breaks and chitchat time don't count, as they usually do in the workplace. Gladwell pointed out that for artists, performers, and innovators who need to earn a living (or go to school) while they're becoming brilliant, ten years, or one thousand hours per year, is more typical. You can still get good at something by devoting five thousand hours to it, or two thousand hours, but don't expect to develop the kind of expertise that makes you a breakthrough success.

Passion could be one thing that motivates somebody to spend that much time getting better at one single activity. But a lot of people have genuine passion for something they'll never spend ten thousand hours on. Basically, they become hobbyists. There are others who dutifully log their ten thousand hours but never develop passion. Tennis great Andre Agassi certainly must have spent ten thousand hours swinging a racket while becoming one of the world's top players, but he admitted in his autobiography that he hated tennis for much of his career and was driven largely by the insistence of his overbearing father. So the 10,000-hour rule rings true, but it's not clear if passion plays a big role in reaching that threshold or is merely an incidental factor.

Passion and devotion are common among Rebounders, almost essential, really. So I wanted to find out what it's like to have the kind of passion for something that leads you to devote your life to it—and take the risk that you might never succeed in any conventional sense of the word. Can passion mislead us? Or is it inviolable? Should we always follow our bliss, or are there times when we should suspect a trap?

Musician Lucinda Williams followed her bliss down a rutted, unmarked road that seemed to lead nowhere for a long time, with much of the turbulence she encountered becoming material for the gritty songs that would earn her a reputation as one of America's most soulful songwriters. Ordinarily, in my line of work, there would be a helpful adjective in front of a word like musician, the first word in that last sentence, to help the reader quickly develop a mental picture of the person I'm trying to describe. So you'd envision Williams as a country musician, a rock musician, a blues musician, or maybe an iconoclastic musician. But that's always been Lucinda Williams's problem: She lacks a ready adjective. She defies categorization and spent much of her career struggling in the professional dead zone between country, folk, rock, and blues. Record companies repeatedly dropped her because they couldn't figure out how to promote and market her music. She refused to conform to more recognizable styles that would have been far easier to commercialize. For years, every career boost seemed to be followed by a stall, with Williams perhaps destined to be the kind of talented cult performer beloved by a few but unknown by most. Twenty-five years after she started performing, Williams finally produced a bestselling record and earned one of the most coveted adjectives in her profession, becoming a Grammy Award–winning musician. Her uncompromising individuality became the very thing that drew thousands of fans. But for a long time it seemed like a liability that could derail her career and leave her stuck without a backup plan.

Williams was born in Lake Charles, Louisiana, a petroleum town halfway between New Orleans and Houston, known for its Cajun cuisine and colorful nightlife. Her parents divorced when she was twelve, and Williams lived with her father, a poet and professor who moved Lucinda and her two younger siblings frequently as he pursued various teaching posts. By the time she left for college, Williams had lived in half a dozen southern cities, including Jackson, Mississippi, and Fayetteville, Arkansas; plus Mexico City and Santiago, Chile. Her father, a prolific writer who authored more than two dozen books of poetry and read one of his poems at President Bill Clinton's second inaugural in 1997, later expressed regrets about the nomadic life his children endured. But his eldest daughter didn't seem to mind. "It wasn't this big traumatic thing," she told *People* magazine in 1998. "I didn't grow up in an Ozzie-and-Harriet type of environment, but who did?"

Williams spent a year at the University of Arkansas, where her dad was teaching at the time, then went to New Orleans to visit her mom in the summer of 1971. Williams was already more interested in music and songwriting than in school, and in the French Quarter she discovered a little folk bar called Andy's that offered to let her play a few gigs. It didn't pay, but she could collect tips, and if the tourists who wandered in off Bourbon Street were in a generous mood, it could be a profitable way to spend the night. She liked it so much that she called her dad to say she didn't think she'd be returning to Arkansas for the fall semester. "I said, 'Dad, I got this gig down here, I'm really excited and I want to stay down here and do this instead of going back to school.' " She expected him to object, because he had always encouraged his daughter to pursue a solid career, and playing music for tips didn't seem like the most reliable kind of work. But he gave a simple one-word answer: Okay.

Williams stayed in New Orleans for a while, then moved to Texas in 1974, spending the next ten years going back and forth between Houston and Austin. It was subsistence living, musician-style. In Austin, she started out by strumming her guitar near the popular farm market off Guadalupe Street, joining lots of other musicians trying to get noticed in one of America's music metropolises. She started to pick up a few paying gigs, but the competition was tough and nobody saw her as an overnight success. One nightclub manager offered to book her for a couple of nights, but she never heard back from him. She was walking past that club one day when she noticed the performance calendar on the window was filled for the coming month. So she asked him why she wasn't on it. "We've already got a couple of chick singers lined up," he explained.

"So he had met his quota already," Williams said years later. "I'll never forget that. That pissed me off. Really bad."

Williams lived with friends when she could, working as a waitress or a clerk at book and record stores when she needed extra money to pay the rent. In her spare time, she wrote songs. Her ambition was modest. "Pay the rent and just make a living playing music. That was my first goal," she said.

It took years to reach it. Williams began to collect a smattering of fans who felt emotionally drawn to her sweet, woeful songs and her gravelly gumbo of a voice—Janis Joplin–like, with a deeper, smokier drawl. She also began to collect a series of charismatic but unreliable boyfriends, who were like an unwelcome but valuable gift to an aspiring, autobiographical songwriter. One of the first to cause her grief was a Byronesque poet who committed suicide after his wife and another girlfriend (not Williams) discovered his duplicity. It turned out that Williams was merely a supporting cast member in a "frenzy of philandering," as *The New Yorker* described it years later in a long profile of Williams. She poured the anguish into songs, evolving from a writer who copied the styles of others into one developing her own unique voice. Her first album, in 1979, was a collection of traditional blues and country songs written by others, but in 1980 she produced a record that included some of her own songs mixed in with covers. It energized her fans and caught the attention of a few music-industry veterans, but barely sold and earned virtually no money.

With help from a couple of friends who had become devoted to her music, Williams spent the next several years making demo tapes, banging on record-company doors, and piling up rejections. Music executives could tell there was a fetching quality to her music, but they weren't keen to take a risk on a country balladeer with a flair for rock and roll, or a blueswoman with a folky twang, or whatever she was. In 1984, after ten years in Texas, Williams decided she needed to move to Los Angeles, where music was regarded as more of a business and less of a hobby. She was in a relationship that she wanted to end (a recurring theme in her life and career), and leaving Austin seemed like one way to do it. She also felt that Austin was too comfortable for musicians, a place where they could do the same thing forever with like-minded friends and never be pushed out of their comfort zone. "When I left to go out to L.A.," she told me, "everybody I knew in Austin was going, Oh, you're going to hate it out there. They'll eat you alive. You'll be coming back with your tail between your legs. Somehow I knew it was time to go. That was a big break, because there was no music business in Austin. Or Houston. Those are good places to cut your teeth, play songs in front of other musicians, get feedback. But some people never grow out of that comfortable niche thing."

Friends helped her pay for a $400-a-month apartment in L.A., and she did the same thing she had done in Houston: play clubs, get to know people, and work day jobs when she needed extra cash to pay the bills. She also took voice lessons, married a drummer in a country band, and, a short while later, started writing songs about the heartache it caused when she divorced him. After a couple of years, Sony Records offered her a "demo deal," paying her $1,200 a month for six months while she recorded some songs in the studio and the label decided whether to make a bigger commitment and produce a record. Nearly fifteen years after she started playing in public, it felt like her first big break. "I was so excited," she said. "I was just in heaven. I said, 'Wow, I don't have to work a day job.'"

The thrill didn't last. Sony ended up taking a pass, just as other record companies had. Williams felt deflated but undeterred. She believed in her own talent, but she had also begun to learn the difference between talent and drive. Talent to her was a kind of inner wisdom, which she felt she had, and other musicians had. But drive was something different, something she had seen routinely in her father. In one sense he had been a stereotypical poet, with a beard and a beret and a leftist bent. But he was also a ferociously hard worker who often wrote a poem a day, preached the Protestant work ethic, and quoted John Calvin to his kids. "I saw him struggling, but he was always writing, and always creating, and that was success to my mind," Williams said. "Not just creating, but being able to make a living at it. That's all I wanted: be creative, be an artist, make a living." She also got to know many others who wanted to be creative, but seemed less determined to work all the clubs, move to where the action was, and treat their passion like a career. "I've seen so many people with talent but without the drive," she said. "You can't get 'em to get out. They say they're happy living in wherever, just doing whatever they do."

Williams had one other reason to stick with her music: She had no Plan B. In fact, she cackled when I asked her if she did. "I should've had a Plan B," she said, "because I had no skills at all. I couldn't type.

I really took a gamble." Had her father insisted that she return to college instead of staying in New Orleans to play music, she probably would have stayed anyway, she told me. "I was a rebel." She was all in.

Her first real break came from a place she never would have guessed: a punk label based in England called Rough Trade Records. Williams's music was a lot of different things, but one thing it wasn't was punk. Rough Trade was branching out, however, and its executives were less worried about boxing their artists into tidy marketing packages than most of the U.S. labels. So they signed Williams to make a self-titled record—as if it was her debut album—that consisted of many of the same songs Sony had rejected. While she yearned for commercial recognition, and a real paycheck, Williams's goals were still so modest (or her hopes so diminished) that her initial excitement was mostly over having free records to hand out: "I was always having to copy tapes because everybody wanted to hear my songs, so I thought, Yeah, that will be great, then I won't have to make tape copies for all my friends."

Bigger perks would follow, including a bit of vital radio play and rave reviews from national critics. *Rolling Stone* discovered Williams and described her as a "veteran singer-songwriter," even though most of its readers hadn't heard of her yet, and rated her album 3.5 stars out of 5, a strong showing for a musician who hadn't made a record in eight years. The magazine described her album as a "low-key, beguiling affair" featuring songs "almost exclusively [about] longing, loss and desire . . . She sings with a down-home twang in her voice, but she also knows her way around Delta-blues songs." Other reviews were even more favorable, and the acclaim led to a tour. She finally generated enough income from her music to reach the goal she had set more than fifteen years earlier: She didn't have to work day jobs anymore. "That was a real pivotal time for me," she said. "I had written all the songs on the album. I didn't even feel like I came into my own as a songwriter until right around that time. I thought, Wow, I can write. I can do this."

This time, the buzz lasted for a couple of years, but Rough Trade ran into a rough patch and went out of business in 1991, leaving

Williams looking for a label once again. A small alternative label agreed to produce her next album, *Sweet Old World,* which contained more of the gutsy, soul-baring songs that had become Williams's trademark, including a couple she wrote all the way back in the late '70s about the poet-paramour who shot himself. Hardcore fans loved it, but the label was struggling—on its way to folding, too—and lacked the marketing muscle the record needed. It ended up less of a commercial success than the prior record, and Williams remained an "elusive talent," as *Rolling Stone* called her, known mostly to "smart folk-and-country inclined listeners who've frequented the right clubs in Houston, Austin, Louisiana, New York, and Los Angeles."

Breakthroughs seemed to intermingle with setbacks. Other artists, like Tom Petty and Emmylou Harris, began to record her songs on their own albums, a high form of recognition from more successful artists eager to help her along. Mary Chapin Carpenter recorded a version of "Passionate Kisses," which Williams had written for her own Rough Trade album, earning a 1994 Grammy nomination for both songwriter and performer. But the money had run out by then—"the money kinda comes and goes, even now," she said years later—and Williams was nearly broke by the time of the Grammy ceremony in New York. She was also intimidated by the klieg lights and the designer vibe, the polar opposite of the shadowy, smoky joints she was comfortable in. So instead of attending, she stayed home in Nashville, where she had moved with her most recent boyfriend. "The whole thing intimidated the hell out of me," she told *People.* "I was just filled with self-doubt."

"Passionate Kisses" won the Grammy for Best Country Vocal Performance by a female, proving, finally, that Williams's music had at least some commercial appeal. But it didn't end her trouble with record labels. For her next album, Williams teamed up with producer Rick Rubin, the brash cofounder of Def Jam Records who had recently formed a new label, American Recordings. Rubin had helped artists like Johnny Cash, Mick Jagger, the Red Hot Chili Peppers, and many others turn important corners in their careers, so he seemed like a good fit for Williams. But Rubin was also migrating from one distributor to another, and American Recordings drifted into a state of turmoil. Williams's project got hung up on legal technicalities. Another producer, at Mercury Records, was also interested in the record, and while they dickered over who would get it, Williams waited.

She may have demonstrated patience in her ordeals with record companies, but Williams was also gaining a reputation as a prickly, mercurial musician. Part of it was artistic integrity. On her first two albums, she had recorded the kind of music she thought producers wanted to hear, and tolerated last-minute dubbing meant to make the music more listenable. Neither album sold or earned her much acclaim. So she learned to resist that kind of interference, even walking out on one record deal, despite desperately needing the money, after a producer remixed some songs to give them a disco lilt. But she could also be a flighty character who was difficult to do business with, showing up hours late for meetings, hitting the stage well past showtime, and showing general disdain for the suits who were trying to turn her into a profitable act. The long gaps between records didn't help. The music press, generally eager to see her succeed, began to write that Williams was a "neurotic perfectionist" who struggled to finish a project. She never denied that, but it stung all the same, and felt unfair. "You don't see that applied to men as much in the music business," she told me later. "It goes back to the old adage. If you're an aggressive woman you're a bitch, but an aggressive man is cool."

Mercury Records finally ponied up the money to buy Williams's fifth album, releasing *Car Wheels on a Gravel Road* in 1998. Williams had scrapped the first and even the second fully mixed versions of many songs, bringing in a new producer who added a deeper, edgier sound. The risk was that endless revisions would generate an overproduced, inconsistent record that felt more assembled than whole. But the result was a raw, emotive collection that earned the kind of bear hug from critics that artists dream about. The songs created a tableaux of the steamy Southern landmarks, populated by impassioned, desperate characters that Williams had spent twenty-five years distilling into powerful music. She sang about roadhouses, prisons, impossible lovers, tattoos, scars, regrets, secrets, and lost innocence, all with a fiery energy suggesting that hope still burned somewhere. *Spin* magazine dubbed *Car Wheels* "album of the year." *Rolling Stone* called it a "country-soul masterpiece." While predicting correctly that no single song on the album would become a hit, *Rolling Stone* raved that Williams demonstrated a "near-absolute mastery of the pop song craft that has been crystallizing at the conjunction of blues and country for half a century. . . . Her lyrics are easeful, trenchant, imaginative, concrete, and waste free, her tunes always right there and often inescapable." The perfectionism paid off.

At the age of forty-five, Williams finally crested the career hump that had been stretching out like a never-ending rise on the prairie. *Car Wheels* earned Williams her second Grammy, not for country or blues or rock, but for Best Contemporary Folk Album. This time, she showed up to collect her award. She began to earn recognition far beyond the music press, as the mainstream media grew attached to the soulful singer with the hardscrabble career. There were profiles in *People* and *The New Yorker,* plus another in *Newsweek,* which called her music "stunning." After her next recording, *Essence,* came out in 2001, *Time* magazine labeled Williams America's best songwriter. Just as important, a new category of music began to form around the very blend of sounds that had become Williams's hallmark. Beginning in the mid-1990s, a few radio deejays began using the word Americana to describe Southern roots music that blended country, blues, rock, and folk. It was partly a semantic distinction, but it also addressed the problem record labels had faced since the very beginning of Williams's career, by giving a name and an identity to music that fell between other established categories. That helped radio stations explain what they were playing, the same way the term rock and roll had helped explain the new sound that musicians like Elvis Presley created when they blended elements of blues, gospel, and jazz. The movement caught on, boosting airplay for artists like Lyle Lovett, Dwight Yoakam, Rosanne Cash, and even Bob Dylan. Eventually, it became a Grammy category of its own.

In the first two decades of her career, Williams released five records, barely earning enough money to live on until *Car Wheels* broke through in 1998. After that record, she released six more in fourteen years, a respectable output for any musician, and especially one who consistently earns praise for originality and depth. Williams never had a Top 40 hit, but that was never what she was aiming for, and from *Car Wheels* on, all of her recordings charted, with her 2008 album, *Little Honey,* making it to number nine in *Billboard* magazine's rankings. She stuck with one label the whole time, the Lost Highway imprint that Mercury created specifically for Williams and other musicians like her. On tour, she routinely sold out midsized theaters, and by the time she was in her fifties, she was a musical heavyweight who transcended all of the categories that record company executives had struggled to place her in earlier in her career. She also overcame problematic-boyfriend syndrome and married a retail executive named Tom Overby, who became her manager and earned credit for adding a measure of stability to her career. It took far longer than she ever imagined, but Williams finally reached, and exceeded, the goal she had set in the early 1970s: She made a living playing music. A pretty good living.

When I interviewed Lucinda Williams, she told me, "You're probably not going to talk to too many other people like me." I knew that, but that's why I was interested in her in the first place. As somebody who had made an all-or-nothing bet on a music career, she was a case study in the cost and the reward of following your bliss. Most people can't afford to stick with something they love for twenty years if they're not earning a decent living at it, especially if there are kids to feed and a mortgage to pay. Going without those things was part of her tradeoff. But Williams also personifies the challenges that many people face as they hit decision points that force them to choose a direction in their career and try to get better at something they love.

Like a lot of people, Williams wishes she had learned a few lessons earlier in her career and been able to take advantage of them at a younger age. Some artistic purists equate commercial success with selling out, and while trying to get ahead, Williams was also fighting her own fears about compromising her integrity if she became too successful. That may have held her back in some of the record-company negotiations, when she refused to compromise on practically anything. It got easier as she became more comfortable aligning her artistic goals with the record companies' commercial ones. "The idea of being commercial has a negative connotation," she said. "I finally realized it was okay because I saw artists like Bruce Springsteen and Elvis Costello making great records and being commercially successful. So I knew it could be done." She also realized she wasn't doing herself any favors by showing up late all the time and being a difficult business partner. And while the turbulent relationships provided material for her songs, they also interfered with her creativity and made it hard to work. "It would have been really cool to be where I am now in my thirties," she told me when she was fifty-eight, "but in every stage of life you have to go through periods where you either accept it and move on, or let it drag you down."

Passion for her work helped Lucinda Williams overcome twenty years' worth of setbacks. But it took a lot more than that, and her long road to success also reveals the limitations of passion. Her passion didn't help sell records during the first two decades of her career. It didn't win over record companies or blaze a path to commercial success. What it did was keep her in the business long enough for her talent to mature and her persistence to pay off.

Williams knew she had talent, but even when she was young she also knew she had a lot of work to do if she ever hoped to convert it into musical success. "When I look back to when I was eighteen and nineteen and twenty," she said, "I mean, look at Bob Dylan when he first started out. And Hank Williams. They were kids, writing these genius songs. I wasn't anywhere near that. I was the opposite. People ask me all the time, Are you bitter because you didn't make it sooner? And I tell them, No! Because I wasn't ready. I didn't get good until I got older. It took me a while to get successful, but it worked in my favor."

Lucinda Williams didn't have to bounce back from one huge or daunting failure, the way some Rebounders do. Instead, she had to withstand a series of minor setbacks that were exhausting in their endlessness. For a lot of people, the slippery elusiveness of success can be just as withering as a single, spectacular flameout. It feels like time is running out or something always goes mysteriously wrong. Williams had to overcome the kind of doubt and frustration that sinks many others who simply give up before they're ready to succeed. It's probably safe to say that her career validates the 10,000-hour rule, or perhaps even a slow-motion variant, the 20,000-hour rule: It took her about ten years as a musician, while working a retinue of part-time jobs, to produce a record that garnered critical acclaim. Then it took another ten years to turn out a record that was a commercial success. But it took more than just time, and also more than just talent, for her to become successful. She allowed herself to take risks, living more or less unencumbered so she could go wherever it seemed like she needed to be to find the right opportunities. Her sweet, mournful songs show the ability to find meaning in lousy experiences, a handy characteristic for a songwriter. And modest goals made success seem attainable, providing a few earnest thrills among her many setbacks.

Like many Rebounders, she also had an accurate understanding of what she was good at and what she wasn't, a key component of resilience that helps distinguish Rebounders from unrealistic dreamers—and there are a lot of those in the music business. Williams knew there was a kernel of something special in her songwriting, partly because others told her so and partly because of what she calls her "inner wisdom." "I had something. I just knew," she told me. But Rebounders are able to balance healthy self-esteem with accurate self-assessment, identifying their own shortcomings without guilt or blame or all-or-nothing defeatism. That's how they learn effectively—and get the most out of those ten thousand hours. For Williams, in addition to becoming a better songwriter, that meant taking voice lessons, learning the nuances of singing, spending countless hours with other musicians exploring the intricacies of music, overcoming shyness that bordered on stage fright, and developing a more charismatic presence onstage. It took a long time to learn how to get a band to gel. And it took twenty years for the managerial part of her career—her manager, booking agent, and attorney—to fall into alignment with a good record label. "My talent got better as I got older," she said.

When younger musicians asked her for advice, Williams used to simply encourage them to keep playing and stick with it. But her own prolonged struggle made her a bit more circumspect. "I get a lot of CDs from people who want to know what I think," she told me. "If they're young and struggling and I can instinctively tell they have that *thing,* I'll encourage them, because I can see that they have enough time to get better." But when the drive or the talent seem to be missing, she keeps her mouth closed, because she knows they may not stay in the business long enough to reach the most important point of all: the moment when they're ready. Which sometimes comes a lot later than anyone wants or expects.

CHAPTER 6

WHEN TO QUIT

Tim Westergren had passion, drive, and talent, and he probably hit the elusive 10,000-hour threshold associated with high achievement at a fairly early point in his career. But after years of effort, all he had to show for it was a raging case of burnout and an empty bank account. So he tried something else for four years and struggled at that, too. In his third attempt at a career, Westergren founded the Internet radio site Pandora, which *The New York Times* described as a startup that spent most of its first decade on the "verge of death." That penchant for flirting with flameouts ultimately made Pandora one of the new dot-com darlings, and Westergren a multimillionaire.

Westergren's story provides an alternative view of persistence and shows that Rebounders follow no fixed template. Instead of sticking with one thing until he got it right, the way Jack Bogle and Lucinda Williams did, Tim Westergren quit one thing, then another, then tried something nobody had ever thought of after his first two efforts didn't work out. He didn't show the zealous, single-minded determination that some Rebounders exhibit. But he showed another trait that can be just as important: the ability to shift his goals and even change his mind when new circumstances arose. And there was consistency to Westergren's pursuits, because all along he was indulging something he loved—music. If he hadn't failed to make a living at it, Pandora probably wouldn't exist.

When Westergren graduated from Stanford University in 1988, he envisioned a career as a professional musician—and he started out with a lot more training than Lucinda Williams did when she first started performing. Westergren studied piano as a kid, and his training intensified in college. His musical ambitions competed briefly with the idea of becoming a doctor, which is why he started out as a premed major. But the rigors of organic chemistry made him rethink the medical profession, and he switched to political science, which interested him but also had another appeal: Of all the majors at Stanford, it had the lowest number of required courses. That freed him to do other things. He studied privately with a jazz teacher, routinely logging five or six hours a day at the keyboard. He also took electives on musicology and computer science—and devoted far more time to music than to his required courses.

After graduating, the obvious thing to do was form a band and aim for the big time. Jazz had been his specialty, but he began to play and compose rock music, settling into an indie-rock style influenced by jazz, folk, and country. Eventually he formed a six-person band called Yellowwood Junction, which did all the things a band needs to do to have a shot at commercial success. They started by playing small local clubs in northern California, where Westergren and the other band members lived. Since they barely got paid at first, and what they did earn got split six ways, they all had part-time jobs. The small gigs helped generate word-of-mouth interest, which led to bigger shows, and they started to tour in half a dozen western states, drawing three or four hundred people to midsized clubs. Then they signed an agreement with a small, independent record label, a preliminary step toward making a CD. It was a decent showing for a club band performing all of its own music. "There were times when I was sure we were going to be rock stars," Westergren told me years later, amused by the memory of his naiveté.

Touring was expensive, and costs ate up most of their earnings, so money remained a problem. But Yellowwood Junction enjoyed just enough success to keep the band members fueled on dreams of a breakthrough. "We bought into this narrative, like in *Almost Famous*," Westergren said, referring to the Kate Hudson film in which a raucous, dysfunctional metal band tours the country, groupies in tow, while on the verge of being discovered by *Rolling Stone.* "Getting in the van, getting on the road, man, booking five gigs in a row." Westergren also had the bulldozer mentality common to many people who think that persistence alone will power them through any obstacle. "When you're chasing a dream like that, you're just locked on the effort," he said. "You've got your arms around this thing and you're clinging to it. And you're just 100 percent, no doubt in your mind, hell-bent on making it work. That sort of manic commitment is what allows you to do it in spite of long odds and all the fear."

But sometimes, hell-bent manic commitment isn't enough. For all of the small, satisfying moments, Yellowwood Junction never made enough money to ease the financial stress on the band members, and tensions grew. Westergren was the de facto manager of the band, responsible for stoking creativity, keeping the peace, and driving the group's business efforts. While he had bought into the lifestyle tradeoffs required to be a musician, he got tired of relying on other people for his well-being. Looking back years later, Westergren realized that touring western college towns, as if tracing the early steps of the Grateful Dead, was a poor business strategy never likely to produce enough income for them to live on comfortably. Staying closer to home and concentrating on recording would have been a better way to scale up their efforts, with lower expenses.

After ten years of trying to make it in a band—just long enough to hit Gladwell's threshold for ten thousand hours—capitulation came abruptly. Westergren likens it to the "bonking" sensation endurance athletes experience when they hit their physical limit in a marathon or other long-distance race, and simply can't continue. "It's like one day you're tired, and you just can't keep doing this," he said. "Like running on a treadmill. If you slow down or stop, you're off the treadmill." But he didn't feel the kind of regret—or worse, guilt—that afflicts some people when they give up on something they spent years devoted to. "I remember the relief I felt when I decided one day I'm no longer going to do it," Westergren said. "In some ways, that's your compass."

For his next act, Westergren got into something equally competitive: composing film scores. He was determined to stick with music in some way, because that's what made him happy. So he figured that instead of butting heads on the road with a bunch of other musicians, he'd have more control over his work, and his future, as a composer responsible for his own projects. But so did a lot of other talented musicians. It took a while to get decent work, and his first big break also provided an insight that led him to rethink the film-composing business. A director hired him to be the sole composer for a full-length theatrical film—Westergren's first—and showed him all the other CDs that competing composers had submitted, in their own bids to get the job. The discs filled a table, stacked twenty high. "The director gave me about half a dozen to listen to," Westergren recalled. "They were just spectacular."

The project went well enough, and Westergren made plans to move to Los Angeles, the center of the film industry. Meanwhile, another idea had popped into his head. While analyzing different types of music to figure out what directors might want in their films, Westergren realized that he could create a mental map of hundreds of musical attributes. Those could define a listener's tastes much more accurately than simply lumping them into a category like rock, jazz, or classical. Most listeners, he realized, tended to prefer certain musicological characteristics—distinct elements of melody, harmony, tempo, instrumentation, rhythm, vocal style, and mood. Identifying musical attributes that a director preferred took some of the guesswork out of coming up with a suitable score for a film.

Then he realized that this idea—mapping all the individual characteristics of music, the way scientists had started mapping all the characteristics of DNA in the human genome project—might be the basis for a business. By then, music had become commonplace on the Internet. Westergren envisioned a service that might help music lovers and musicians connect more efficiently, much the way buyers and sellers of small items were beginning to find each other on eBay, the popular auction site. If you had a deep database of songs categorized by their musical attributes, you might be able to help listeners discover new music simply by identifying a few of their favorites songs. If you could isolate the musical attributes those songs had in common, you'd then be able to call up other songs with a similar blend of attributes. It might lead music lovers to songs they never would have heard on the radio, or found in a record store, and even help undiscovered musical acts—like Yellowwood Junction—find an audience.

Westergren bounced the idea off his girlfriend, who thought it sounded great and told him to chase it—an important endorsement, since they'd end up getting married a couple of years later. Since they lived in northern California in the late '90s, startup fever wafted on the air, more sensate than pollen in the springtime. Westergren shared his idea with a college pal, Jon Kraft, who had already become a successful Silicon Valley entrepreneur. Kraft liked it, too, and in no time they had drafted a business plan and started looking for investors. Westergren had never run a business, and Kraft knew nothing special about music. But such trifles didn't matter at the time, since venture capitalists were eager to fund almost any idea that might turn out to be the next technology breakthrough. They ended up with $1.5 million, and called their new firm Savage Beast, a cartoonish name that reflected their youthful moxie.

They were soon joined by a third founder, Will Glaser, and the eager entrepreneurs used the money to start hiring musicians—in ample supply around northern California—who would listen to thousands of songs and categorize each one according to a list of musical attributes that grew daily. Westergren dubbed it the "music genome project," which he described as the most comprehensive effort ever to create a detailed musical database. He and Kraft started trying to sell the service to music retailers like Best Buy and AOL, which could use it to power listening kiosks and online recommendation tools that would help their own customers search for music.

Savage Beast got started in early 2000, when the first Internet boom was at its peak. Within months, however, the dot-com bubble had burst, with hundreds of startups crashing and burning as stock values plunged and panicky investors shut their wallets. Westergren had been lucky to get funding when it was available, but with very little revenue in its first year, Savage Beast began to look like it would end up as another forgotten casualty of the crash. By the end of 2001, Savage Beast had fifty employees but no cash. Westergren spent most of 2002 firing his staff as the money ran out. To keep the company afloat, he persuaded some of his musician pals to work for free, with a promise to pay up once more money came in. Other employees said no way, and sued for back pay.

By the end of 2002, Savage Beast was down to four paid employees and a handful of unpaid ones. Westergren maxed out eleven credit cards and took out all the personal loans he could get to pay the rent, run the computers, and keep the company alive. All told, it amounted to about $250,000 in personal debt. The firm got just enough business to persuade Westergren he might be onto something—the way modest turnout had been just enough to keep Yellowwood Junction on the road—but the stress of keeping up became severe. "The intensity of that challenge dwarfed anything I had ever experienced before," he said. "By far. Add zeroes to it. I spent almost two years waking up at four in the morning every single night in a cold sweat."

I asked Westergren if there were moments of doubt when he wondered how he had gotten into such a mess. "Moments?" he answered, rising in his chair. "Months!" Westergren is a cerebral guy who still seemed impassioned and energetic at the age of forty-four, when I interviewed him. But he described the stress of the early years at Savage Beast with such rapid-fire ardor that he still seemed to be decompressing from it all. "It was emotional torture," he said. "It really was. I mean, I wasn't hungry. There are people who have much more serious challenges in their lives. But psychologically, it was very tough." He started losing his hair and even went to the hospital one night with symptoms of cardiac arrest that turned out to be a panic attack.

The break came in 2004. It took much longer than he had anticipated, but Westergren had gradually inked some strong deals with music retailers using Savage Beast to help their customers find new music. He had also made hundreds of pleas to investors, begging for money to keep his company alive. On the 348th attempt, he got what he was after. The dot-com bust was easing by then, and investors were starting to sniff around once more, although Savage Beast wasn't precisely the kind of company they were looking to fund. In Silicon Valley, at least, investors wanted to back companies that used new technology to gain a commanding lead over entrenched competitors or offer a compelling new service. There was an element of technology to Savage Beast's business plan, but it was also heavily dependent on the manual labor required to code thousands of songs and keep adding to the music genome database. For all of his passion, and battle-hardened experience, Westergren was fixed on a vision for the company that left investors unimpressed. In fact, the lead investor on Savage Beast's crucial second round of funding, Larry Marcus, later told *The New York Times,* "The pitch that he gave wasn't that interesting. What was incredibly interesting was Tim himself. We could tell he was an entrepreneur who wasn't going to fail."

The investors ponied up $9 million, which was enough to plug the huge hole in the ship and start running Savage Beast like a more professional company. The first thing Westergren did was use $2 million to honor back pay and get everyone out of debt. He rehired some of the talented employees he had been unable to keep back in 2002, and then recruited a CEO, Joe Kennedy, who had run successful businesses at E-Loan and General Motors' Saturn division. Westergren became chief strategy officer, happily relinquishing the top job to somebody with a longer résumé than his own.

Once onboard, Kennedy suggested that they might be wooing the wrong customers. Instead of selling their service to retailers, why not target consumers directly? It made sense. The music business was changing dramatically, with retailers like Barnes & Noble and Tower Records, which licensed Savage Beast technology, selling fewer and fewer CDs, and new online services like iTunes selling more digital tracks directly to consumers over the Internet. Since consumers were getting used to finding music through their computers, the new team decided to relaunch the company as something completely new—an Internet radio service that listeners could personalize. Users visiting the website simply had to call up a few songs they liked, and algorithms would identify an unlimited stream of similar music that would play over their computer speakers, as long as there was an Internet connection. For the relaunch, they decided to drop the name Savage Beast in favor of something more wry and elegant. They renamed the company Pandora, a reference to the ingenue in Greek mythology whose insatiable curiosity led her to open a container in violation of the gods' orders, ushering evil and chaos into the world and leaving just one thing left inside: hope.

The new strategy aligned Pandora with powerful consumer trends that were just starting to take off, and the company began to grow the way a hot new startup is supposed to. As it grew, it continued to adapt. At first, Pandora was a subscription service that users had to pay for on a monthly basis. But there seemed to be a better way, so it began to offer two tiers of service: one for free, with occasional ads running between songs, and a paid option with no ads. Most people chose the free service and tolerated the ads. That made advertising an important revenue stream, and Pandora had some basic personal information about its users—it knew what kind of music they liked, after all, plus their age, gender, and ZIP codes—that allowed the kinds of targeted ads that are most lucrative on the Web. If users wanted to purchase and download a song they heard on Pandora, they could click on a tab that would bring them to iTunes or Amazon, with Pandora getting a small cut for each purchase it helped originate.

By 2007, Pandora had seven million registered users and more than half a million songs in its database. It had swelled to one hundred employees, half of them part-time musicians coding songs, and was getting close to breaking even. But unforeseen problems are a fact of life at startups, and a new threat to the company emerged just as it seemed to be hitting its stride. With no warning, a government panel that regulates music royalties tripled the fee that online radio services like Pandora had to pay record companies every time they played a song. The higher fees would have dramatically raised Pandora's costs, forcing it to charge every user a fee that most would probably balk at, especially after getting used to the service for free. Westergren worried that it could sink the whole company. But threats to Pandora's existence were nothing new, and he had finagled solutions before. So this time Pandora hired a lobbyist in Washington and reached out to its users through an email campaign and notices on its website, asking them to protest the fee hike by writing letters to Congress. More than one million Pandora users contacted Congress, a remarkable outpouring for an issue that would otherwise be the kind of internal industry matter consumers rarely pay much attention to. The regulators, unaware that they might be pricing a popular new industry out of business, didn't give Pandora everything it wanted, but they lowered the royalty rates enough for Pandora to stick with its business model.

If you dodge enough bullets, there's a good chance the odds will turn in your favor sooner or later, and that's what finally happened to Pandora. The widespread adoption of high-speed broadband made Pandora a simple and effortless website to access, even on laptops connected to the Internet by a wireless network. Westergren and Kennedy had barely thought about mobile phones, but all of a sudden the iPhone and its many imitators offered a whole new opportunity: mobile streaming radio. When Pandora launched its first iPhone app in 2008, the company's growth rate nearly doubled overnight. As bigger mobile devices like the iPad and other tablets came along, it allowed Pandora to feature "cover art" and lyric notes in a much richer format than the puny CD inserts that were rapidly fading anyway. Pandora then began to ink deals with automakers to include the service in cars, which made it a competitor with the old AM/FM bands and satellite radio, in addition to the purchased music people carried on their iPods. And all of that came as the information revolution was overwhelming adult consumers, leaving even die-hard music lovers scarce time to research new artists. For many, Pandora was their musical salvation.

The user base hit twenty million, then fifty million, and Westergren began to talk of someday having billions of listeners worldwide. Instead of sleepless nights and unpaid bills, he now enjoyed wealth and adulation. *Time* included him on its 2010 list of the one hundred most influential people in America, putting him in the company of Lady Gaga, Steve Jobs, Barack Obama, and Sarah Palin. Investment bankers began to wine and dine him, anticipating a rich public stock offering that they wanted a piece of. Musicians loved Westergren and his service, too, because they made money when their songs got played and reached new listeners who may not have found them otherwise. In 2011, Pandora went public at a value of nearly $3 billion, turning a rich profit for investors who had put their faith in Westergren, and the few diehards who had stuck with the company from the beginning. More than a decade after hanging up his own musical career, Westergren had become a kind of rock star after all.

When I asked Westergren what kept him going during the gloomy days between 2002 and 2004, he didn't tell me what I expected to hear. He didn't say that he had unflinching belief in himself or that he knew he'd succeed if he only hung in there long enough. The main thing that kept him going, he said, was the cost that failing would impose on the people he had borrowed money from and everybody else who had a stake in his company. "I can't look myself in the mirror and say, I was just tough," he said. "I felt an absolutely crushing obligation to everybody around me. There was just no way I was going to give up. I was going to go down with the ship. I really didn't have a choice. At least I felt that way."

Instead of confidence, he talked about humility. "I'm in the church of humility," he said. "You can be bold and humble at the same time. Those are not incompatible. To me there are two important things about being humble. One is you listen. You believe you have something to learn from your experiences and from people around you. That makes you aware of your environment and how it's changing. You're much wiser about your decision making and your business. If you're humble, you also don't get caught up in the trappings of success, which can be very corrupting for most people. You can get drunk on that if you're not humble." His decision to hire a CEO, and then follow the new boss's advice about changing the business model, certainly show an ability to listen and overcome the not-invented-here syndrome that leads many mediocre people to reject ideas that aren't their own. Westergren also disputes the Nietzschean axiom about adversity making people stronger. "A lot of people say that once you've been through a stressful situation you're better at handling stress later on. I no longer believe that. I actually think it's the opposite. It's a little bit like a childhood fear. When I get stressed, which happens far less frequently now, it's an emotion I remember well."

Among entrepreneurs and Silicon Valley technologists, Tim Westergren and Pandora have become a fabled case study in persistence. But what I like about the story are two wrinkles that contradict much of the conventional wisdom about how to succeed. First, Westergren followed his bliss, but when he didn't like where it led him, he changed course. It was almost as if he made his bliss follow him. His core love was music, of course, but he also discovered that he didn't have to be a traditional musician to enjoy the satisfaction of doing something he felt passionate about. He found other ways. It took him ten years, but Westergren finally overcame his own preconceived idea about how to succeed in music, which is the kind of trait that allows Rebounders to recognize their weaknesses, learn from their mistakes, and continually improve. In her book *Mindset,* psychologist Carol Dweck describes the difference between a "growth mindset," which allows people to discard static ideas and think in new ways as they learn and discover, and a "fixed mindset" in which people stick with familiar ideas, almost as if they're dogma. Rebounders like Westergren succeed because they're able to discard ideas that don't work or don't seem as good as new ideas. Wallowers are the ones who rarely change their minds or try something new. They tend to overestimate their abilities, stick with what's familiar, pass up learning opportunities, and flail when something goes wrong.

By adjusting his thinking, Westergren found new ways to follow his bliss, until one of them finally paid off. He got comfortable with the idea of giving up the band, because working as a film composer—something he had never contemplated until the band started to flounder—seemed like a better way to make a living while staying connected to music. He was willing to give that up when another good idea surfaced, and people he trusted validated the idea. His original plan for Pandora didn't take off, but he agreed to change the business model several times, to adjust to circumstances. Westergren had one transformational idea—the music genome project—but if he had stopped at one idea, it probably would have withered like a beautiful plant that gets no water. It took a lot of flexibility and cultivation to build the idea into a successful business.

Westergren exhibits another core trait of Rebounders: He capitalized on his failures. He didn't know it at the time, but the years he spent with Yellowwood Junction as a dreamy twentysomething gave him distinct advantages as he was trying to get Pandora off the ground. First, the unique challenges of managing a band and its idiosyncratic musicians turned out to be good practice for running a startup. "It was great management training," he said. "Six people in a creative environment when nobody has any money, and everybody has to get along and row in the same direction." He also saw firsthand a niche that Pandora later exploited, to the benefit of everybody involved: quality music that for whatever reason never made it into the mainstream. As a film composer, an awareness of his own limited prospects led him to seek ways to distinguish himself, which became the germ for the music genome project. The jobs he left behind weren't just abandoned efforts. They were contributions to his personal database of knowledge, which finally became deep enough to persuade skeptical venture capitalists to invest millions in him.

As somebody who didn't have a defined career until he was forty or so, Westergren sees adaptability and self-sufficiency as core survival skills likely to become more valuable, not less. "People are going to have to do things, creative things, entrepreneurial things, that don't necessarily have a well-trod path," he said. "More people are going to have to make things up for themselves, kind of reinvent themselves. For a lot of people that's terribly unsettling. But if you need to start over and try something else, don't view is as a failure. It's just the next chapter." And there are usually more chapters than most people imagine.

CHAPTER 7

WHEN HARD WORK ISN'T ENOUGH

In May 2005, professional tennis player James Blake walked onto a tennis court in Tunica, Mississippi, wondering if he was becoming one of the down-and-outers who nurse their moribund careers playing for diminishing prize money in towns most tennis pros have never heard of. Just a few years earlier, Blake had been one of the top thirty men's players in the world, with a career that was gathering steam, not losing it. He played at all the big tournaments and had beaten Andre Agassi, then ranked number six in the world, en route to winning his first big tournament, the Legg Mason Tennis Classic in Washington, D.C. Blake's toothy smile and cheerful demeanor were making him a favorite with fans, and he had inked several lucrative endorsement deals. *People* magazine even named him one of their "sexiest men alive" in 2002, when he was a mere twenty-three.

Blake's downfall began in the spring of 2004, when he was playing a practice set while preparing for a clay-court tournament in Rome, Italy. With the set on the line, his opponent hit a loopy drop shot that nicked the net cord, rolled onto Blake's side of the court, and landed on the sideline tape—in bounds, and a tough ball to get. Blake raced after it, racket extended. It had rained earlier, and the clay was damp and clumpy, and as he lunged toward the ball, his feet got caught in the gathered clay. He lost his balance, tripped over the sideline tape, and before he knew it, he was airborne, heading straight for the steel post that anchored one side of the net. Blake turned his head to avoid a collision, but his neck smashed into the post, fracturing a vertebra—literally, a broken neck. Blake turned out to be lucky. Had he hit the net post head-on, doctors said, he could have been paralyzed. The fracture he sustained would take just two months to heal, and leave no permanent damage. It would force him to skip the upcoming French Open and Wimbledon tournaments, but by mid-summer he was practicing again, preparing for the U.S. Open—his hometown tournament, since he had grown up in Fairfield, Connecticut, just fifty miles from the famed courts at Flushing Meadows.

Blake never made it to the Open. Just as he was recovering from the fractured vertebra, he developed a puzzling and alarming rash that spread down one side of his head. Then the left side of his face became paralyzed. To open and close his left eye, he had to push the lid up and down with his finger. He also lost hearing in his left ear. That was followed by searing pain in his head, far worse than anything he had ever experienced, including the broken neck. After several visits to doctors, they figured out that Blake had contracted shingles, caused by the zoster virus that also causes chicken pox. Blake tried to play through it, but the virus threw off his balance and interfered with his vision, fouling up his entire tennis game. The doctors told him the virus would probably run its course, allowing him to fully recover. But he needed to write off the rest of the tennis year, and it might take as long as four years for the virus to fully recede, which was an eternity to a 23-year-old athlete in his prime, trying to compete against the best in the world. For most people who get shingles, it's a painful inconvenience that eventually dissipates, allowing them to resume life as normal. For Blake, it was a possible career ender that occurred at the worst possible time, just as he was hoping to progress from a promising up-and-comer to a contender for the top titles in tennis. It was a maddening comedown, and he was powerless to make it better.

Like most professional athletes, Blake had worked through injuries and other kinds of setbacks before. He had always relied on the doctrine of hard work, which he learned from his father. "You can't control your level of talent," his father always told him, "but you can control your level of effort." That's a common attitude among Rebounders and many ambitious people, who reason that they may not be able to outsmart or outperform their competitors, but they can surely outwork them. Yet as Blake tried to solve his problems by intensifying his effort, he realized that for the first time in his career, it wasn't working. He'd have to learn another way to succeed, or his tennis career might be over. "Hard work is almost a religion to me, because in many ways, it's the window through which I look for the answers to life's questions," he wrote in his 2007 memoir, *Breaking Back*. Waiting out the zoster virus, however, would require more patience than anything else. "The hardest things to do are those things that go against our own instincts, and by that measure, *not* working hard was actually going to be incredibly hard work for me."

As a kid, Blake had seen effort, diligence, and careful problem-solving pay off time and again. His father, Thomas Blake, was a soft-spoken tennis lover who worked for 3M selling medical supplies and taught his two sons—James and his older brother, Thomas Jr.— to avoid problems if they could, and fix them on their own if they had to. He seemed to embody that attitude in his own life. As an adult, he became a vegetarian who gave up drinking and smoking and worked out every morning like a young marine, even in his fifties. The Blake parents were a mixed-race couple—Tom was black, while his wife, Betty, was white—and their two boys stood out in Fairfield, a largely white suburban community. So the parents imposed weekend curfews, to prevent the two boys from being around trouble late at night, when they might be singled out if the police happened to arrive. If a problem did develop, the elder Blake was a fixer who always believed he could take care of it, given enough effort and determination. "My father craved details about any adverse situation so he could set about solving it," Blake wrote.

When Blake was thirteen—and a promising junior tennis player—doctors discovered he had severe scoliosis, which could become debilitating if left untreated. Surgery to straighten his spine was one option, but that would have limited his mobility and taken him out of competitive tennis. Blake's father began to research other options, deciding on treatment that included a brace his son would wear nearly all the time, except for a few hours between the end of school and bedtime. The brace was awkward and uncomfortable and made Blake, a shy teenager, even more withdrawn. But it kept him on the tennis court, helped him build confidence, and demonstrated the power of deliberately working through a challenge. Blake also slept on a plywood bed topped with a thin cushion, the flattest surface possible. And he made regular visits to specialists at the Shriners Hospital for Children in Massachusetts, who helped develop the customized treatment plan.

Blake and his brother Thomas were both talented tennis players, but there was never a serious thought of shipping them off to the kind of tennis academy where Andre Agassi and many other greats spent their teenage years. Blake never even thought he'd become a pro. But his tennis ability began to open doors. In 1997, it helped him get into Harvard, where he became the star of the tennis team, eventually becoming the top-ranked college player in America. The top ranking surprised him, and after his sophomore year, he and his family decided he should give it a shot and turn pro. The first two years were a struggle, but it started to seem like the right move. Blake cracked the top one hundred in 2001, ending the year ranked seventy-third worldwide. He got an agent with a prominent talent management firm, which led to endorsement deals and even modeling contracts. Blake was photogenic and bohemian looking, with funky Rastafarian dreadlocks and a cheerful grin that made him more recognizable—and marketable—than other players who ranked deep in the double digits. Landing on *People*'s sexiest man list in 2002 confirmed the judgment of the modeling scouts.

By the end of 2002, Blake was living a charmed life. In August he won the Legg Mason tournament, his first big victory. A few weeks later, at the U.S. Open, he lost a gutsy five-set match to Australian Lleyton Hewitt, then the third-ranked player in the world. The match would have been otherwise unremarkable, except that at one point a frustrated Hewitt accused a linesman, who was black, of making calls in Blake's favor because they shared the same skin color. The boorish complaint drew the boisterous Flushing Meadows fans, and the national media, to Blake's defense, even though he lacked the conditioning to endure a five-set match in the August heat and threw up on the court toward the end of it. Still, it pushed Blake into the national spotlight and generated sympathetic press. By the end of the year he had risen to twenty-eighth in the rankings. He was looking like a viable contender for the big titles and was making far more money than he ever imagined.

As happens in sports, however, the air came out of Blake's bubble the following year, for reasons nobody could explain. He began to lose matches by lopsided margins, even against comparably ranked players. He lost far too many games while serving, giving up the biggest advantage in tennis—using the serve to control the flow of play. He obsessed over what-ifs, a lethal confidence killer in any profession. He developed an unsettling routine in which he'd stay up all night after a loss, watching TV or playing online poker, to delay the inevitable moment when he'd have to turn out the lights, lay in the dark, and replay the day's mistakes in his head. "My mind was not in the right place to win matches," he realized. He wasn't "match-tough," a tennis phrase indicating you've honed your skills under the competitive pressure of live matches and are ready to draw blood on the court. For the first time, he went backward in the rankings, ending 2003 in the thirties.

He and his coach, Brian Barker, worked hard on his game, but Blake also had something more radical in mind: shaving his head. His agent, Carlos Fleming, gasped at the idea. Blake's dreadlocks were clearly part of his public appeal, conveying a kind of multiracial, Bennetonesque playfulness that people felt drawn to. If he ditched the dreads, there was no guarantee that sponsors like Nike would stick with him. But Blake didn't care. "I don't want to be known for my crazy hair," he told friends. "I want to be known for my tennis." So he asked a couple of friends to help with the barbering, and the dreads came off. When Blake called Fleming to tell him the news, the stunned agent immediately called sponsors to gauge their reaction. It wasn't good. Fleming estimated later that going bald had cost Blake a million dollars in endorsement money. It didn't matter. It felt like the right move, and friends told Blake that being bald made him look younger. He decided that a bald head would become his new signature look.

For a couple of months, it seemed like the shave, combined with hard work on the court, were having the intended effect, as Blake played deeper into tournaments before losing. Then came the collision with the net post in Rome. Despite the shock of the injury, Blake came to view it as a hidden blessing. For about a year, his father, whom Blake described as his Superman, had been fighting stomach cancer, and Superman was losing the battle. His father had handled the illness in typical ascetic fashion. He insisted that nobody fuss over him, and kept up his workouts as long as possible, determined to beat the disease. But he couldn't. The two months that Blake took off to recuperate ended up being the last two months of his father's life, and the hiatus allowed him to see his father as often as possible back home in Fairfield. His father's death, on July 3, 2004, triggered the kinds of realizations that hit many people after a life-changing event. Up till then, Blake and his family had relied on the doctrine of hard work and a fix-it attitude, which had proven itself over and over. But suddenly, the old habits failed. "All the days when we let optimism do our talking, putting the best face on, came bumbling down in front of us," Blake wrote in his memoir. "Our hope had gotten us far, a lot farther than it might have for most people, but it had not carried the day."

Within days of his father's death, the zoster virus, most likely caused by stress, put Blake on the sidelines, threatening his career. Blake had lived a privileged life until then, but the law of averages had started to even things out. Part of his challenge involved the basic maturity that occurs when many people in their twenties and thirties are forced to deal with new hardships for the first time. But there was more at stake for Blake than simply weathering his father's death and overcoming some health issues. Blake faced many of the challenges common to Rebounders—learning new ways to succeed, recognizing the limits of determination, adjusting his expectations— but he was under the time pressure faced by athletes in a sport where players routinely retire by the time they're thirty. He had to Rebound in a hurry, by unlearning the doctrine of hard work for a while, then relearning it when the time was right.

For a couple of months, Blake barely picked up a racket, as he waited for the pain, the rash, the facial paralysis, and the other symptoms of the virus to subside. Since he was living in Fairfield again, where he owned his own home, he had time to reconnect with childhood and high school friends. Blake typically traveled thirty weeks out of the year, and spent many of his off weeks training in Florida, while his hometown friends mostly worked nine-to-five jobs close to the town they grew up in. Blake had kept in touch with many of his friends, but he had no feel for the rhythm of their lives. While Blake was camped out in Fairfield, his house became a kind of central hangout where the group would gather to watch sports, play poker, chow wings and burgers, and shoot the breeze. Blake loved the camaraderie—except that his friends all had to go to work during the day. While they were gone, he'd kill time, worry about his future, and count down the minutes until the workday ended and his friends would show up again, which always eased his anxiety. Blake ended up getting far more support from the ordinary folks in Fairfield than he did from the pros and other people he knew on the tennis circuit. It made him feel humble, and as Blake adjusted to circumstances he couldn't control, he began to understand the potent wisdom of his idol, Arthur Ashe, who died of AIDS in 1993 after contracting the deadly virus through a blood transfusion during heart surgery a decade earlier. "If I were to say, God, why me? about the bad things," Ashe had famously remarked, "then I should have said, God, why me? about the good things that happened in my life." When Blake felt self-pity, he thought of Ashe's courage and honesty, and quickly got over it.

As Blake's symptoms improved, he began to stutter-step his way back into shape and start practicing again. The captain of the U.S. Davis Cup team invited him to play in an upcoming match, a show of confidence that Blake found moving. But he pulled a muscle during a warm-up and sat out the competition, feeling as disconnected from the game as ever. Once he recovered from that, he played a few exhibition matches, performing erratically and losing. It was like his early days as a pro, when he was a newcomer to the tour, losing frequently to more experienced players. Except now he was the more experienced player. Sometimes he'd feel powerful and poised on the court, as if well on his way to a comeback. But other times there was clearly something wrong, even when the dizziness and other overt symptoms weren't the obvious cause of his lackluster play.

Early in Blake's pro career, tennis legend Pete Sampras had told him that to succeed on the court, "You have to have a short memory. If you blow a point, or a game, or a set, just forget it." Sampras himself, who won fourteen Grand Slam titles and spent six years ranked number one, was notably unflappable, rarely showing frustration on the court, or any other emotion, for that matter. As simple as the advice sounded, however, Blake found it maddeningly difficult to pull off. It felt like his confidence was shattered. Losing a set or even a few games was all it took for Blake to start questioning his performance, at which point it was all but over. "Mental pillars were beginning to collapse," he wrote of one dispiriting match, in the 2005 Australian Open, in which he sprinted to a commanding lead, then started to make a few mistakes. By the third set, he yielded to the pressure, basically giving away the match.

That's how Blake ended up in Tunica, Mississippi. He had struggled before, during the first couple years after he turned pro, when he lost matches he should have won and wondered whether he even deserved to be a touring professional. Over time, he had built the confidence it took to become a competitive and popular player. So he figured he may as well do the whole thing over. That meant returning to the Challenger circuit, which was essentially the minor leagues of pro tennis, where promising young players spent some obligatory time on their way up, and fading old-timers not ready to retire continued to earn a few bucks on their way down. It was a humbling comedown for Blake. Compared to the immaculate courts and glamorous settings of the tour-level tournaments, Challenger events were more like a county fair. The ball boys stood out of position and made mistakes that would get them banished from one of the major tournaments. There were no big sponsors, and the players sometimes had to keep score themselves. The press rarely showed up. Instead of gathering at some trendy hotspot where the paparazzi were likely to be lurking, players in Tunica hung out at a Wendy's fast-food restaurant, where nobody paid them much attention.

The enforced humility worked, however. Blake won the tournament in Tunica, his first victory since 2002. He won the next Challenger tournament, too, coming back during a tense semifinal in which he nearly blew a comfortable lead. The French Open was up next, and to earn his way into the main draw, Blake would have to win three matches in the qualifying rounds that preceded the main event, a grueling pre-tournament tournament in which 128 lesser-ranked players competed for thirty-two open spots in the main bracket. He won those matches, along with his first-round match in the French Open. He lost in the second round, but felt it was a respectable showing for somebody who had spent eight of the last twelve months sidelined by injuries and illness.

Blake lost in the first round at Wimbledon a month later, but instead of berating himself, as he would have a few years earlier, he used the early exit to look back on where he had just been. Beginning with the Challenger tournaments, he had picked up his pace of play and racked up a few victories. For the first time since the zoster virus knocked him off-stride, he felt sure that his play was consistently improving. He also felt more relaxed, and instead of scrutinizing his ranking every week and replaying every missed point in his head, he was learning the discipline it took to look forward, not back. He was getting a second chance, and for that alone he felt grateful.

That summer, Blake made it to the finals of the same Legg Mason tournament he had won in 2002, losing to Andy Roddick. Winning would have been better, but still, he felt buoyant as he sailed through one round after another, dispatching players who would have shut him down just a few months earlier. The next stop was a new tournament in New Haven, Connecticut, just twenty-five miles from his hometown, called the Pilot Pen. Blake claimed it as his hometown tournament and ended up with his own cheering section, which spontaneously became known as the J-Block. Blake made sure to get tickets for all his friends, then asked for more tickets as his cheering section swelled. Their presence was naturally motivating—like a supercharged home-field advantage—yet Blake still faced several of those haunting moments when he fell behind and wasn't sure if he'd have the wherewithal to overcome the usual physical and mental barriers.

After losing the first set during one match, he sat in a chair during the break, toweling off and thinking of his father's frequent admonition: If you have a problem, fix it yourself. For all of the drilling and coaching, that's what tennis—and life, he realized—really came down to: each player, alone with his demons, summoning all the strength he could muster. Blake recovered to win the next set, then, in the third and decisive set, he slipped into a zone he described as, "that desirable sensation of leaving my body, of moving up to that plane of peak performance, of flow, of operating on pure instinct and desire." He won the match, the J-Block going wild, then won three more matches, coming back from a lost set and a potential collapse in each one, which made him the tournament champion. It had been thirteen months since the zoster virus had derailed his career, and if it was still there, he was no longer feeling it. He was match-tough.

The U.S. Open came next, and Blake rampaged through the first two rounds. In the third round he faced Rafael Nadal, the ferocious Spaniard who had just won the French Open and was ranked number two in the world. In front of twenty thousand rambunctious spectators, Blake won the first set but lost the second, pushing him into the danger zone where self-doubt could be as threatening as any opponent. But instead of obsessing over lost points, Blake concentrated on the points ahead of him, the ones he knew he needed to win. He was following Sampras's advice, finally, and it paid off. He beat Nadal, which put him into the fourth round, where he won again.

Blake was now in the quarterfinals, where he faced the legendary Agassi, who was thirty-five but still a powerhouse who had become one of the most entertaining players in the history of tennis. On any American court, Agassi usually had the crowd behind him, especially since his age made him an underdog in a game dominated by men in their twenties. But Blake's comeback had made him a favor-

ite of the fans, too, with *People* calling him the "Cinderella Man" of
the U.S. Open. Even Agassi said that if Blake were to beat him, "I
couldn't wish it for a better person." In one of the electrifying
late-night matches under the lights that the U.S. Open is famous for,
Agassi and Blake battled deep into a fifth set, and when they ended
up tied 6–6 at about 1:00 a.m., the delighted crowd gave them both
a standing ovation. Blake got out to a lead in the tiebreaker, but
Agassi, showing remarkable stamina that defied his age, scrambled
back, chasing down everything Blake tried to power past him. Even
the tiebreaker was a cliffhanger that went to 6–all, until Agassi hit
two winners in a row and won the match. He would go all the way
to the finals, where he'd lose to the red-hot Roger Federer.

For a quarterfinal loss, Blake's performance earned widespread recognition, since it capped the kind of irresistible, real-life comeback
that was ready-made for the media. Blake told his story on the David
Letterman and Oprah Winfrey shows, then made prime time when
60 Minutes profiled him. Blake felt intimidated at first by the heady
obligations that came with being the kind of role model that people
looked to for guidance and inspiration. But he got comfortable with
it and used his newfound fame to establish high-profile fund-raising
projects that pulled in money for cancer research and public tennis
programs. He also seized the moment to get started on his memoir,
which became a bestseller when it was published in 2007.

Blake also spent the latter months of 2005 improving the skills he
felt had let him down in that pivotal match against Agassi—mainly
his serve. He was employing the doctrine of hard work again, and
this time, the zoster virus didn't interfere. As 2006 began, Blake felt
a kind of confidence that was deeper than he had ever experienced
before. Mistakes didn't bother him that much. He didn't unravel
when he fell behind, and he knew he could dig himself out of a jam,
because he had now proven that he could. A couple of tour victories
and strong showings in several other tournaments pushed his ranking into the top twenty, then into the top ten. In one tournament he
lost a pivotal set to his nemesis, Lleyton Hewitt, who had beaten
Blake each of the six times the two faced off. But instead of surren-
dering his mental edge, as he had dozens of times before, Blake re-

covered to beat Hewitt and win the tournament. By the time of the
U.S. Open in the summer of 2006, Blake was ranked fifth in the
world—the highest-ranking American. He lost in the quarterfinals
to Federer, who went on to win the Open. But still, Blake was earning plaudits, fame, and money like he never had before. He ended
2006 with five tournament titles, more than he had won in his entire
career up till then, including victories over some of the highest-ranked
players in the world. He had also signed a multi-year endorsement
deal with Evian that was worth millions. He was dating a model and
was a regular presence at A-list celebrity events, such as Beyoncé's
birthday party. *Sports Illustrated* called him the "face of American tennis."

Blake's story didn't quite climax the way a Hollywood screen-
writer would have scripted it. The events of 2006, including the epic
five-set match against Agassi that he lost, turned out to be Blake's
high-water mark. He ended the year ranked fourth, and stayed in the
top twenty for most of the next three years. In 2007, he played on
the U.S. Davis Cup team and won several key matches that helped
the Americans claim the title. But he never attained the personal
glory that comes with winning one of the four Grand Slam
events—the Australian, French, and U.S. Opens, plus Wimbledon.
That was partly because Federer and Nadal had become unusually
dominant players who mowed down practically everybody they faced
in the major tournaments. But Blake also hit a kind of natural pin-
nacle in 2006, far exceeding his own career expectations. As the glow
of that success began to fade, Blake was once again dogged by media
critics and disappointed fans who complained that he was an "under-
achiever" who failed to play at his full potential. By 2010, when
Blake was thirty—an old-timer, in tennis terms—his ranking had
fallen below one hundred for the first time in five years.

Most of his critics, however, had never made it to the top ten in
anything, and Blake, mindful of how close he had come to bailing
out of tennis altogether in 2005, came to view his career as an unqualified success. "I definitely feel like I've reached my potential in
tennis," he told me when he was thirty-two. "My main goal when I
started playing was to have no regrets when I put my rackets down.

I don't have any regrets. I'm really happy with the way I've performed." His career stats may seem unimpressive compared to the likes of Agassi, Federer, and Nadal, but they're pretty good for a guy who wore a back brace for eighteen hours a day as a kid, broke his neck at the age of twenty-four, played with a paralyzed face for nearly a year, and never even thought he'd become a touring pro. By the age of thirty-two, Blake had won ten singles titles and been a finalist fourteen other times. He had earned more than $7 million in prize money, and a lot more than that in endorsements. Most of his accomplishments came after he contracted the zoster virus and faced the prospect of a short-circuited career.

Blake's comeback consisted of many intangibles, like any streak in sports. But he sees a direct connection between the hardships that nearly triggered his downfall in 2004 and 2005, and the updraft he enjoyed in 2006. "My greatest professional successes occurred after I had faced my most daunting personal challenges," he wrote in his memoir. "I used to think this was ironic; now I realize that my success flows directly from having cleared those hurdles." When I asked him to link cause and effect, he told me that simply spending time with family and friends, getting out of the bubble he had been in on the pro tennis circuit, made him more confident, because for the first time in years he was among people who didn't expect him to prove anything. "So much of my life up till then had been based around tennis," he said, "and my success or failure at tennis was the most important thing to me. I realized that these people didn't care if I won or lost a tennis match." At the same time, his coach, Brian Barker, was telling him that even if his career ended, he had accomplished a lot and would end up just fine. Like other Rebounders, he realized there was a Plan B, which relieved some of the pressure he felt to execute Plan A.

Blake also had to learn patience, something that many busy, ambitious people would rather not be bothered with. Taking time off, and waiting for the virus to run its course, was his last-choice option, yet it helped him become a more mature player. He learned there are times you have to wait, when pressing harder might actually be the worst thing you can do. In matches, he learned to pace himself better and wait for his opponent to lose momentum or make mistakes, rather than forcing an outcome or pressuring himself into even worse mistakes than he may already have made. That made it easier to follow Pete Sampras's advice: forget about what had already happened and play each point as if it were a brand-new game.

Blake also changed the way he thought about success. When he had been a teenager in high school, he got to know Mats Wilander, the Swedish star who stunned the tennis world in 1982, winning the French Open at the age of seventeen and going on to win six more Grand Slam titles. Wilander had told Blake not to worry about rankings. Just build a sound game, he said, and the rankings will follow. But Blake had forgotten that advice for a while. During the first few years of his pro career, everything revolved around his ranking and his match record. Then his ranking plummeted and he struggled to get the ball over the net, even in practice. So again, with no other choice, he had to find a new way to measure success, and decided that as long as he was getting better and could notice his own improvement, that counted as success. He was finally following Wilander's advice, and worrying less about the standardized measures of success turned out to be the very thing that helped him improve by those same measures. "I was playing without pressure," he said. "I had no fear of losing. I was just happy to be playing."

Blake's memoir, *Breaking Back,* which he wrote when he was twenty-six, is less boastful, less guarded, and more endearing than the typical sports tell-all. There are no gossipy revelations about other players, but plenty of insights about the author's own confidence crises, his moments of doubt, and personal failings. While it helped boost Blake's image as a likeable, down-to-earth celebrity, the memoir is also a guileless account of one athlete's genuine struggles. Part of what makes it seem genuine is the naiveté that comes across as a privileged professional athlete in his twenties comes to grips with death, hardship, disappointment, and even fear, universal challenges that afflict everybody and don't respect the Members Only sign posted at the entrance to the VIP tent. When I interviewed Blake just a few years later, however, he sounded like a wise old man of tennis, a veteran able to look back knowingly on his mistakes as a youngster. "I had an idealized vision of myself," he said of the way he lived and played in his early twenties. "There are so many times in life when you have plans, then things happen that are out of your control that change your plans." He made it seem like a gift to struggle young, learn vital things, and enjoy the insights that come with being a Rebounder while still young enough to do almost anything you want.

It's always desirable to hurry through the low points as fast as possible, and learn painful lessons with the minimal amount of pain. Blake turned out to be a fast learner who made the necessary adjustments in less than a year, in time to capitalize on the fleeting abilities that professional athletes must use, or lose. So I asked him a hypothetical but important question: Could he have become a better player without going through the ordeals that made 2004 and 2005 the worst time of his life? "I don't think that's the way it works," he told me. "In my twenties, I was stubborn. I didn't know as much as I thought I knew. I had to learn how to listen. I wish I didn't have to go through all that, but it gave me a better perspective. It helped open up all the advice I had heard." Speaking as an insightful veteran, he described watching some of the younger players who reminded him of himself in those younger years—brash, hurried, and playing every tournament that might help boost their ranking, while neglecting pace, fundamentals, and advice from more seasoned players. If it's a player he knows, Blake told me, he'll sometimes bestow a bit of the wisdom that others have given to him: slow down. Worry less about points and rankings. Let go of mistakes. Sometimes they heed his advice, but more often they don't. "If they don't listen, it's out of my control," he said. "I just smile. They'll live it and learn it."

CHAPTER 8

THE BRIGHT SIDE OF BURNOUT

Hard work can solve a lot of problems, but there are limits to what it can accomplish. James Blake discovered that he needed to learn some other skills when hard work wouldn't get the job done. Others have learned that hard work can leave them frayed and exhausted—burned out—without making them better off in any appreciable way. When burnout interrupts your career, what message is it trying to deliver? Should you stop what you're doing and try something else? Would taking a vacation suffice? Or should you barrel through the fatigue and discouragement in unrelenting pursuit of whatever's on the other side?

There's no formulaic answer, and people handle burnout in personalized ways, just as they handle any other kind of stress. But burnout surfaced as a factor in the careers of several Rebounders I interviewed or researched, so I wanted to learn more about how different people handled it. Tim Westergren felt burnout in his first career, as a touring musician, which is why he decided to do something else. Yet the strain of the early days at Pandora was far more severe, and he stuck with that. Why? The stakes were much higher.

He felt an obligation to other people who had cast their lots with Pandora and were dependent on him in some way. He owed a lot of money he needed to pay back. Plus, it was his third shot at a breakthrough career, and it wasn't clear how many more chances he'd get. Necessity focused his mind and boosted his resolve.

Majora Carter is an urban revitalization strategist whose résumé is filled with the kinds of achievements most people are happy to leave to somebody else. As a resident of the South Bronx, one of New York City's poorest and grittiest neighborhoods, she took on a city bureaucracy accustomed to using her home turf as a default location for noxious industrial projects nobody else wanted in their backyard. She opposed the construction of new waste facilities and got parks built instead. She helped bring jobs, growth, and greenery to one of the most blighted stretches of urban America, earning a slew of prestigious awards for her work. Yet it took several career restarts and burnout so severe that it threatened her health before she found her way to the work that would change her life. I wanted to find out if she felt she had been destined for the kind of urban-renewal work that she ultimately discovered, or if it was more of a fluke that made her an accidental, if happy, success.

Majora Carter grew up in a tough neighborhood, but she doesn't look back on herself as the stereotypical frightened child dodging bullets in an urban battlefield. She grew up in the South Bronx much the way other kids grow up in safer places, exploring her surroundings, testing boundaries, and enjoying freedoms as she found them. She figured out only later that some of the features of her environment were rough. There were occasional crimes, with bloodstains left behind to tantalize the neighborhood kids and provoke imaginations. Kids learned to recognize the local junkies and stay away from them. Then, when she was seven, her older brother Lenny—one of ten siblings, and her favorite—was shot dead in a drug incident. A couple of times there were stacks of cash in the house, which her dad, retired from his work as a janitor, explained by saying that it had been a good day at the track. Ornate furniture and other luxuries would fill the house for a while. But other times were lean, with little for dinner except rice and beans.

The attitude in the South Bronx was that if you wanted to live someplace nice, you'd move—most people didn't think about sticking around and fixing up the neighborhood. So Carter, who did well in school, left. She went to college at Wesleyan University in Connecticut, where she got interested in the arts. Filmmaker Spike Lee was just becoming famous, and Carter envisioned herself as a female Spike Lee, making movies that would stimulate and enlighten audiences all across America. So after graduating, she moved back to New York City—to Brooklyn, this time—to pursue a film career. Her plan was to get work in the various film projects around the city, then go to film school at New York University, just like Lee had done. She got the work, but not much pay. There were plenty of film shoots, but they were looking mostly for unpaid interns. She got a few paying jobs as a production assistant, earning $125 for each eighteen-hour day, but that work was always sporadic and temporary. So she took the usual filler jobs as a receptionist, office assistant, coat-check clerk, and, for one awful day, telemarketer. Meanwhile, she had student loans to pay and could barely afford her rent, even when piled into a boardinghouse. Film school would cost more than $60,000, which meant more loans, on top of the ones she was struggling to repay. Then she'd have to come up with another $100,000 or so to make her own film. The film career she had once felt so sure about began to seem prohibitively expensive. So even though she got into NYU's film school, she sidelined the dream.

On top of that, she got married and divorced in the space of two years, another dream dashed. Instead of film school, she enrolled in NYU's creative writing program, which was just as expensive but wouldn't require her to finance a high-budget project at the end. Instead of a filmmaker, she'd become a writer, and the degree would allow her to teach while she wrote the great American novel, which might then be turned into the great American film. She got the degree, but the economics still didn't work out. Part-time teaching jobs left her time to write, but she turned these jobs into full-time work, because the inner-city kids she was teaching needed far more help than she expected. She continued to run short of cash and tried every cheap living arrangement she could think of: stints with family, friends' couches, illegal sublets, sometimes in the worst, cheapest neighborhoods in town.

She finally made a decision she was dreading: moving back in with her parents. "It was a defeat to go home," she told me, looking back. "I was close to thirty, I didn't know what I was doing with my life, and I had to move back in with Mommy and Daddy." She'd try to arrange her day so that she left early in the morning and came home late at night, doing little more than sleeping at the house, pretending, in a way, that she didn't really live there. She continued teaching for a while, then finally decided she wasn't cut out for it. A local nonprofit called The Point Community Development Corporation, named for the Hunts Point section of the Bronx it served, was hiring, and Carter got part-time work that turned into her first permanent full-time job. The Point's mission was to bring arts and cultural activities to a section of the Bronx that artists and performers usually bypassed. Her film, writing, and arts background fit the profile, and staying with her parents afforded her the ability to live on the relatively low pay she was getting.

It was a job that turned into a calling. Unlike teaching, Carter found it stimulating to work on projects that made her hometown a better place to live. She became the kind of compulsive worker who doesn't notice that quitting time has come, the sun has set, and everybody else has gone home. "It was just that exciting," she said. "I was only paid for twenty hours per week, but sometimes I'd work ninety." It also put her in the hospital. One of the first projects she was responsible for was a film festival, which she never saw to completion. Just before the festival began, her sister paid a visit, and immediately asked why Carter had hives all over her face. If you met Majora Carter today, you'd find this hard to believe, because she's a stylish dresser with the blindingly white teeth of a model and the crisp appearance of somebody who takes pristine care of herself. But at the time, she barely looked in the mirror and avoided doctors because she didn't have health insurance. She admitted to her sister that she hadn't been feeling well, but she said she hadn't noticed the hives. Her sister took her to the hospital, where doctors admitted her and gave her antibiotics for an untreated infection that was probably triggered or exacerbated by stress.

Carter got interested in environmental issues, which were endless in the South Bronx, effectively creating a new environmental department at the Point and earning a reputation as a tenacious activist. She helped stop the construction of a waste-processing station in the South Bronx, which already handled 40 percent of New York City's commercial waste facilities. She helped develop a proposal to decommission an underused highway that ran atop Hunts Point, hoping to restore neighborhood access to a river she felt could be revived. When the state Transportation Department said no, Carter formed a coalition to keep the pressure on and develop economically viable alternatives to the highway, hoping to get it torn down one day. She had more success with a plan to build electrified truck bays at the gigantic Hunts Point Food Distribution Center, which allowed parked 18-wheelers to get power without idling their engines and spewing even more diesel fumes into the local air. She was idealistic, but she learned the value of pragmatism, too: It was easier to get things changed when you came up with solutions that made economic sense, as well as environmental sense.

Most residents of Hunts Point didn't know it, but a river flowed through their neighborhood—the Bronx River, which originated twenty-three miles to the north and emptied into the Long Island Sound, at the eastern tip of Hunts Point. It might seem incomprehensible that a river could go unnoticed, but the Bronx River, which was flush with beaver and waterfowl when European traders discovered it in the 1600s, had long served as a discharge pipe for the sewage treatment facilities, power plants, recycling centers, and other industrial businesses that lined its banks, locked up behind ugly fences. A few other lots were so overgrown with brush and debris that you couldn't tell they abutted the river—and wouldn't want to explore them even if you did know.

Carter was jogging early one morning with her dog, Xena, a German shepherd mutt she had rescued after finding it tied up in a neighbor's yard for several hours one rainy night. As they passed an abandoned lot, Xena darted into the weeds, as if suddenly on a determined hunt. She dragged Carter by the leash, past the typical detritus of an illegal dump: refrigerators, tires, oil drums, discarded roofing, and hypodermic needles left by junkies. Carter tried to lead

Xena back toward the road, but Xena was eighty pounds of muscle on a mission, and she dragged her master through the trash and weeds as if headed for a must-reach destination. After one last thrust through a tall patch of brush, there it was: a river, alive with swans and butterflies. Carter had known from looking at subway maps that there was a river nearby, but she had never gone to look for it. The sight amazed her.

In Middletown, Connecticut, where Carter had gone to college, there was a waterfront park along the river that ran past the town, and a wildlife basin just a few miles up the river. In Manhattan, where she lived briefly after college, miles of piers and old industrial areas along the Hudson and East Rivers had been reclaimed and turned into parkland or other public space. But the South Bronx enjoyed no such amenities. So back at the Point, Carter wrote a grant proposal that earned $10,000 in government seed money, to explore the possibility of turning Xena's abandoned lot into the kind of riverfront retreat that's common in more upscale communities. Volunteers began to clear the lot, local businesses and city agencies offered support, and residents claimed it as a de facto public gathering place. The seed money grew into $3.2 million worth of city funding, and seven years after Xena tore into the weeds, a park was born. A play area for kids featured a spray shower set in the middle of a faux fishing village. Seats shaped like conch shells added to the nautical theme. Tall poplars and English oak trees screened the park from a recycling plant on one side, and a huge truck lot adjoining the food distribution center on the other side. A small pier jutted into the water, attached to a boat ramp where kayakers and canoeists could put in.

Majora Carter showed me around Hunts Point Riverside Park one chilly January afternoon. It was clean, artful, and well-maintained, in better shape, even, than some of the parks in tony Manhattan. There was no escaping the urban surroundings, and downriver a couple of hundred feet, a small, abandoned sailboat was halfway sunk in the shallows, a reminder of the debris that surely littered the river bottom. But a separate park on the other side of the river compounded the greenery and enhanced the view, and the park clearly served as a pleasant respite from the concrete and asphalt that surrounded it.

A group of teenagers was hanging out on the little pier, laughing and doing nothing in particular while we were there. A photographer was with us, shooting some photos of Carter for a book she was to be featured in. The photographer told the kids that Carter had been the driving force behind getting the park built. "Do you own it?" one of the teenage boys asked Carter.

"You own it!" Carter answered. "We all own it."

"We come here more in the summer," the boy said. "We swim in the river sometimes." Carter advised against that.

"We need more of these in Hunts Point," a girl in the group said.

"I know," Carter told her. "You need to help with that." Then, as the teenagers wandered away, she yelled after them, "Take care, my loves."

After a couple of years at the Point, Carter was finding her way, paying off her student loans and feeling emboldened by her break-throughs as an environmental lobbyist. Her work was beginning to stretch far beyond the mission and limited resources at the Point, which was still an arts and cultural organization at its core. City council elections were coming up, and a new term-limits law meant that two-thirds of the seats would be open—the perfect opportunity for an ambitious newcomer like Carter. She figured she had done a pretty good job navigating the city bureaucracy so far, and one thing she had learned was that the city council had enormous power over land-use decisions and the other kinds of environmental issues she cared about. So she decided to run for city council and use that as a springboard to the next phase of her career. "I thought I'd be a one-term council person because I wanted to raise some hell," she said. "I figured I wouldn't get reelected."

Like many people with big plans, however, she hadn't yet stress tested her scheme, which began to unravel almost immediately. What she hadn't yet learned was that politics in the Bronx was a bare-knuckle business dominated by a couple of family dynasties that called the shots and made challengers feel mighty uncomfort-able. Carter had built a decent network of connections, but it was nothing like a political base. As she started to take on an entrenched political machine, she suddenly found she had fewer friends than she thought. Nasty rumors about her began to circulate. There were veiled warnings that she might be in danger, and one night Carter thought a goon had followed her home. A fellow community activist, older and more seasoned, insisted on driving Carter everywhere she went, since walking might be too dangerous. The stress became severe—and the hives returned. As the folly of running in such a bruising political environment became apparent, Carter quickly reevaluated. "It was beyond foolish," she told me later. "Not being a political animal, not understanding the process, being a little whippersnapper and goofy and naïve." She quit before officially declaring herself as a candidate. The day she did that, the hives went away.

Carter had thought she might start her own nonprofit after spending one term on the city council and gaining more visibility. But that part of the plan was no longer in the future. It was in the present. She had become an ardent and effective fund-raiser by then, and she asked various supporters what they thought of her idea to start her own advocacy group. The feedback was encouraging. Money seemed to be available. To her great surprise, many of the political operatives who had undermined her aborted run for city council supported her environmental ideas, so in 2001 she started her own nonprofit, called Sustainable South Bronx. Carter was the executive director, with a board of directors but no employees. The mission was to combine environmental improvement with economic development, focusing on projects that would create jobs while making the South Bronx a cleaner, greener, and more enjoyable place to live. After the city council flameout, it felt like an enormous breakthrough. "The way it happened was a beautiful education for me," Carter said. "Because the ones who tried to destroy me were the ones who had to help me start S.S.B.X. And do it fully on my terms."

The goal at Sustainable South Bronx was to take small, tangible steps that would transform the neighborhood from the "land of stepped-on dreams," as Carter called it, into a community that residents could take some pride in. She persuaded the city to hire locals instead of outside contractors to do basic cleanup work like clearing abandoned lots and planting trees, figuring it would engender local spirit, plus bring badly needed jobs to an area where the unemployment rate was close to Depression-era levels of 25 percent. She got grants to help train ex-convicts and other hard-luck cases in trendy skills like green-roof installation, brown-field remediation, and urban forestry, then find them actual jobs in the Bronx—and help them remain employed. She got funding for studies on how to reduce asthma and other illnesses related to air and environmental pollution. Sustainable South Bronx even helped incubate other startups that specialized in conservation or environmental improvements, and employed locals. In a field where bureaucracies move slowly and talk often trumps action, Carter developed a reputation for getting results and finding solutions that pleased businesses, politicians, and residents alike.

Carter's projects became the kind of model efforts that foundations could highlight for their own boards of directors, to show how effectively they were doling out grants. Her work began to draw national, and even international, attention, and she started to travel in order to share her ideas and see what other groups similar to hers were up to. So it seemed peculiar when funding began to dry up. "The more successful we got, the smaller my funding was," Carter said. It was as if she was being penalized for success. The more she asked around, the more she realized that funders figured she was so successful, she must be getting plenty of money from someplace else. So grants she might have gotten a few years earlier were going elsewhere.

Carter's body, meanwhile, continued to remind her of the stress she endured. At one point, she developed a neck pain that worsened until she was unable to get out of bed. Paramedics carried her to an ambulance on a stretcher, and took her to a nearby hospital, where doctors loaded her with potent painkillers but did nothing to treat the problem. It didn't help that Carter had bought health insurance for the three employees she had by then but hadn't gotten around to activating her own plan, which limited her options and may have led the doctors to neglect her. After two weeks at the hospital, friends intervened and took her to a proper doctor, who figured out what was wrong and treated it correctly.

In 2005, Carter received a surprising phone call. She had just returned to her office from the Longwood subway station, after a meeting downtown, and found on her voice mail a message from a British
woman asking her to please call the president's office. The president
of what, she didn't quite catch, as she jotted down the information.
She called the number and said, "Hi, this is Majora Carter. Who's
this?"

"Oh! Hold on one moment, please," the British woman answered.
A man got on the phone.

"Majora, I'm so happy to hear from you," he said, introducing
himself as the president of the MacArthur Foundation. She knew all
about foundations, and that MacArthur was a big one, known for
funding social justice programs and also handing out "genius" grants
every year to a select group of overachieving individuals. This is
great, she thought. Somebody I know must be getting an award.
Maybe they need a recommendation from me. "Are you in a private
place?" the MacArthur guy asked her.

That seemed like an odd question. "No, I'm in my office," Carter
said.

"Well, is your door closed?" he asked. She started to wonder what
was going on. "You should probably sit down," he said. She said
okay, and sat down. "Have you heard of the MacArthur fellows program?" he asked. She had. "Well, this year you're one of them."

She burst into tears, then had a terrible thought: It was a prank.
"Is this a joke?" she shouted at the phone. "Because if this is a joke,
it's a very, very cruel joke!"

"Majora, dear," he reassured her, "this is not a joke." The intense
black girl from the South Bronx, who had failed to make it as a filmmaker and moved back in with her parents, really was a MacArthur
"genius." She began to cry all over again. The official citation would
describe her as, "a relentless and charismatic urban strategist who
seeks to address the disproportionate environmental and public
health burdens experienced by residents of the South Bronx."

There was some confusion when she got another call from
MacArthur about the money. Like the other twenty-four MacArthur
fellows that year, Carter would get $500,000, in increments of

$25,000 every quarter for five years. She'd have to pay taxes on it, but other than that, there were no strings attached. MacArthur clearly hoped that such a rich reward would motivate its fellows to do even better work, and give them the means to do it. But recipients were free to blow the money on cars and vacations if they wanted to. When the director of the fellows program called her to arrange the financial details, she told him to send the checks to Sustainable South Bronx. "Majora, I don't think you understand," he said. "This is your money." She said fine, she'd provide her Social Security number for tax purposes, but then turn it over to her organization. "You really don't have to do that," he said. He was telling her to keep half a million dollars for herself, and the more she thought about it, the better it sounded. She was still in serious debt. Her father had died several years earlier, leaving so many bills that she had to max out her credit cards to get her parents' finances straightened out. That added up to about $80,000 in credit card balances. She earned $63,000 a year at Sustainable South Bronx, which was a lot of money in the Bronx but not all that much for an East Coast professional working long hours. So she decided to accept the money personally. She'd use some of it to pay off her personal debts, and give some to various causes she supported.

To people she knew in the Bronx, she was suddenly rich. Her boyfriend, James—whom she would later marry in a ceremony at Hunts Point Riverside Park—was a videographer unfamiliar with the dynamics of the nonprofit world. "Wow," he said, when he learned the news. "All those people who hate you, they're going to want to be your best friend now."

"No, baby. No," she corrected him. "You watch. Those who love me are going to love me more, because they recognize that I didn't just win this, because everything we hold dear just won this, and it's going to raise attention to this work like you can't believe. But those who hate me are going to hate me more." She was right. Carter had a Wikipedia page by then, and online vandals repeatedly added false and derogatory information to her biography. Fund-raising got even harder. "There was all this enmity and jealousy from other social justice groups, who felt I didn't deserve the attention," she said.

A friend knew a lot of the people in charge of funding at the foundations Carter was used to working with, and she sat Carter down one day for a talk. "Majora, listen," she said. "At many of these foundations, your work is lifted up as exemplary. And I know from talking to you that these are the same people that don't fund you."

"You've got to be kidding," Carter said. It began to dawn on her that there was a lot more to getting grants than simply doing good work and demonstrating results. "I wasn't looking for handouts," she told me later. "I was looking for investors. On some level that wasn't perceived as the kind of attitude a nonprofit leader should have. Since we didn't fit the profile, we weren't necessarily respected."

The MacArthur grant had given Carter a fresh advantage: high visibility, which tends to propagate itself. She went from being well-known in the relatively narrow world of urban activists to being a downright celebrity. She was invited to speak at a TED conference, renowned for the visionaries and game-changing entrepreneurs they usually featured, on "greening the ghetto." Her face began to appear in magazines and on popular websites. More awards followed, and she became a coveted public speaker, earning as much as $25,000 for some appearances. As traditional funding declined, she began to use speaking fees to fund Sustainable South Bronx and finance some of its projects.

But none of it was right. The attention she got was exciting, but Carter began to spend more time traveling and giving speeches, to keep the money coming in, and less time doing the work back home that she actually enjoyed. She was married by then, and wanted to spend more time with her husband, too. And the "petty social-justice slaps," as she called them, began to sting. A strange irony began to afflict Sustainable South Bronx. The assumption in the nonprofit community was that the organization was richly funded, because of its all-star leader, even as it got harder and harder to meet payroll and finance projects. At one point, Carter needed to hire a deputy, and many applicants assumed that the job paid a six-figure salary, which would have been far more than Carter herself earned, and nearly 10 percent of the group's entire budget. "Everybody felt I was getting more money than I was," she said.

A couple of years after winning the MacArthur grant, Carter was at a conference on climate change when a woman she had met a couple of times said to her, "Majora, I don't really know you, but I hope that you become a little more gentle with yourself."

"I burst out in tears," Carter told me. "I thought, oh god, if these people who don't know me can see this, I can only imagine what other folks are seeing. I was running myself ragged." She pondered what to do. Someone at the conference invited her to attend a leader-development retreat in Massachusetts a month later. While there, she was going through a few exercises with other participants, and her mind began to clear. Her role at the nonprofit she founded had become safe. She could do it forever if she chose, and keep earning accolades, but it wasn't what she wanted. She had actually started to hate her work and resent the groveling she had to do to get funding. There were unwritten rules about the way nonprofit directors were supposed to behave, with snubs and penalties for those who got too big for their britches. The hives hadn't returned, but she felt that heavy sense of burnout returning. "I realized that so much of what I was doing was not about me," she said. "It was not fulfilling me in any particular way and not helping me grow into a fuller human being."

She decided on the spot that she was going to quit. In one of the interactive sessions, she told the group, "I hate being an executive director," outlining the many things she disliked about her job. She mumbled it at first, not making much of an impression. But by the end of the session she was shouting it: "I hate being an executive director!" The group cheered, aware that it was a pivotal moment for Carter. She called her husband next, telling him that she was going to quit her job and start her own company—this time, a real company that didn't have to beg for funding. When she got back to the Bronx, she told her board that she'd be stepping down in six months. "My board had a heart attack," she told me. "But that was their problem. It was the best decision I ever made for myself."

In 2008, Carter started her own company, the Majora Carter Group, calling herself a "green-collar economic consultant." With a deep recession forming, it was a terrible time to launch a business, and there were plenty of startup snafus. When I met Carter a couple of years later, her company was still struggling to attract clients and get off the ground. There was a lot she didn't know, which had been the case every other time she tried something new. She and her husband, who quit his videographer work to become her marketing director, had jumped into it without a formal business plan, which forced them to devise one on the fly. They spent a lot of time learning how to run a business that relied on revenue, rather than grants, to fund operations. It had been tricky to package Carter's name, vision, and ideas into a marketable product that municipalities and businesses would pay money for. Carter was still funding the enterprise by giving speeches. And she realized it might have gone more smoothly if she had taken a few months off after leaving the non-profit world, to catch her breath and develop a strategic plan, instead of diving right into her own firm.

But one thing I had learned about Rebounders by then was that they don't wring their hands wishing they had done things differently, or tally their mistakes. Even when they realize that they've screwed up, Rebounders keep heading toward their target, no matter how far they've drifted off course. That's basically how Carter described her own instincts as we discussed the many directions her career had gone up until that point. "When you're in adversity and you don't quite know what it is, you just have to find a way to keep moving," she said. "You know that you've got to move through it." Her attitude reminded me of Walmart founder Sam Walton, who lost his first retail store in Arkansas because of a foolish mistake, and quickly opened a second store, the humble starting point for his retail empire. When asked how he reacted to mistakes, Walton indicated that he rarely wasted time on introspection or reflection. "I've always had a strong bias toward action," he said.

Carter, too, had a bias toward action, and whether she realized it or not, she had been moving nonstop since she was a kid. While dating James, she had told him about her life as a child, including the junkies, the neighborhood crimes, and her brother's murder. "You were raised in a war zone!" he told her.

"No I wasn't," she insisted. But as he pointed out all the difficulties that surrounded her, she realized that maybe he had a point.

Carter began to see a connection between the hardships of her childhood and the vicissitudes of her professional life. She had developed a comfort level for discomfort. A lot of Rebounders have that trait, which is why they're often able to make lifestyle sacrifices and put up with deprivation, as long as they believe it will help them accomplish something important. But Carter seemed to have a higher tolerance for pain than most, which might be why it took hospitalizations and physical manifestations of stress for her to recognize she had gotten on the wrong path.

Burnout, for her, was a catalyst indicating that she had to make a change. A lot of people know the sensation, but what made Carter's burnout different is that she acted on it, while still allowing passion to play a decisive role in her decisions. Like Tim Westergren, she followed her bliss until she didn't like where it led. Then she went in a new direction, and sure enough, her bliss followed her. She began by trying to become a filmmaker, then a writer, then a teacher, then an activist, and briefly, a politician. Instead of logging ten thousand hours at any one activity, she was going through a process of elimination until she found a calling that fit.

Hardly anybody goes into nonprofit work for the money, but for Carter, her first full-time job provided just enough income and stability to give her creativity and passion a fighting chance. It was passion, not cash, that motivated her to turn a decrepit riverside lot into a captivating park, which ultimately brought her international recognition. She burned out at Sustainable South Bronx when resentments and pointless barriers interfered too much with the work she loved. But that helped her discover another passion: running her own business. By then she had overcome so many setbacks that the challenges of making a startup succeed didn't intimidate her.

Like other Rebounders, Carter learned that passion wasn't enough, especially when she was defying the odds and pursuing a dream in the land of stepped-on dreams. When people ask her advice about following their own dreams, she quickly corrects the idea that simply doing something you love will be enough to make you successful. "People don't understand how hard following your dream actually is," she said. "They tend to think it's this linear path that gets you there. It's not. But part of the fun is getting stuck and figuring out, okay, how am I going to get myself out of this one?" It's a lot more fun looking back at the challenges, of course, especially when you've overcome them—and that's the tricky part. "People say all the time, You make it look so easy. And I say, Well, be with me at three o'clock in the morning on a Saturday night when you're out partying and I'm working."

Carter also learned to be selfish, and turn it into an asset. For a lot of people, selfishness is easy—so easy, in fact, that it's a major liability that prevents them from accurately understanding their own shortcomings. But Carter knew she did her best work when feeling most fulfilled—a well-known formula for success—and leaving the nonprofit world behind allowed her to shake off the guilt and resentment that had begun to interfere with her work. Rebounders often bounce back by channeling their efforts into things they can control, and by learning not to waste their energy on things controlled by others—especially by people with petty or manipulative agendas. By setting up her own firm, Carter wasn't just escaping the burnout she felt at her nonprofit, she was setting herself up for more fulfillment and even greater success. Majora Carter's critics may have been partially right when they argued that she was motivated by self-interest. They should have tried it themselves.

CHAPTER 9

HOW TO IMPROVISE

Most career advice focuses on setting goals, developing skills, gaining advantages, and overcoming other bad career advice you might have gotten. But many Rebounders, I discovered, also end up doing something else that gets a lot less attention: improvising. As a musician, Tim Westergren understood the art of playing notes that weren't written on any page, developing improvisational instincts that he ultimately applied to his own career. Majora Carter learned that there was no linear path to success, not for her anyway. To find fulfillment and stability, she had to keep trying new things and learn how to heed the signals telling her it was time to move on. There's mounting evidence throughout the workplace, in fact, that the kind of predictable, single-channel career that many baby boomers enjoyed will be far less common in the future. To be successful and turn change to their advantage, many twenty-first-century Americans will have to move quickly from one field to another, without much of a map to guide them.

I thought I might hear some entertaining insights about career improvisation by talking with John Ratzenberger, and I was right. A lot of people don't know Ratzenberger's name, but they know his work. If you're over forty-five or so, you probably know Ratzenberger as Cliff Clavin, the pompous, know-it-all postman who had something irrelevant to say about practically everything on the hit sitcom *Cheers,* which ran from 1982 to 1993. If you're younger, you may not recognize his face, but his unforgettable voice has animated characters in every Pixar film, going back to 1995, including Hamm the Piggy Bank in all three *Toy Story* films, P. T. Flea in *A Bug's Life,* and the villainous Underminer in *The Incredibles.* I tried to avoid Hollywood celebrities while researching the Rebounders for this book because the media slathers so much fawning attention on them already. But Ratzenberger is an unconventional celebrity. He considers carpenters, plumbers, welders, and other practitioners of the industrial arts to be "the might of civilization," while regarding actors like himself, plus sports stars and other celebrities, to be filling "nonessential jobs." Instead of supporting worthy but trendy causes like orphanages in Africa or disaster relief in Haiti, Ratzenberger put his modest celebrity weight behind organizations such as The Center for America, which promotes skilled trade, ingenuity, and the tinkering spirit. He's also an apostle of self-sufficiency, an underappreciated trait that's likely to make a comeback.

It will probably come as no surprise that Ratzenberger grew up in a blue-collar community, in Bridgeport, Connecticut, with a father who was a truck driver, a mother who worked in a factory, and two grandfathers who were carpenters. Some of the neighborhood activities when he was a kid were the types of things that today's parents are likely to find too risky or unstructured. Ratzenberger's mom would buy him old radios at yard sales, encouraging him to take them apart and put them back together, without fretting about the odds that he would get electrocuted. One of his fondest childhood memories is finding a storm-trashed wooden rowboat with his friends, washed up on the shore of Long Island Sound. They hauled it to Ratzenberger's backyard and spent weeks rebuilding it, learning how to measure and cut wood, hammer nails, apply caulking, and coax the neighborhood old-timers into lending a hand or contributing some supplies. That summer, a rowdy gang of seafaring nine-year-olds rowed the vessel out into the sound to play king of the boat, pushing one another into the water in a contest to see who would be the last boy standing, while the others swam. When they noticed a few mothers standing on shore, shouting and waving them back in, they pretended they were too far out to sea to hear.

After high school, Ratzenberger walked up to a local work site and asked if they needed a carpenter. An Italian guy with a thick accent was in charge, which Ratzenberger, the accomplished actor, emphasized in the retelling, forty-five years later. "You a carpenter, eh?" the boss said skeptically. "I show you a carpenter. You wanna work here, you come tomorrow, six A.M." Ratzenberger did, and spent the winter hauling boards and bags of cement around, performing little carpentry but proving his toughness by clomping around in the frozen mud for hours on end. Once spring arrived, the boss finally started to give Ratzenberger the work he had asked for. "Now, I show you how to hold a hammer," he told the teenager one day. Ratzenberger was sure he knew how to hold a hammer—who didn't?— but it turned out he didn't really know. There were all sorts of other techniques for handling a nail gun, wielding power tools, and cutting wood. As Ratzenberger did more of the skilled work, he'd hear that old-country voice from somewhere nearby every time he missed a nail: "John! Don't be sloppy! You wanna be a good carpenter or a bad carpenter?"

One hot summer day, Ratzenberger was helping to construct a roof, standing gingerly on exposed joists while hoisting up heavy sheets of plywood that would form the roof's base layer. While his hands were full of plywood sheets, he felt something on his boots, and looked down to discover Corky and Dana, two of the more experienced carpenters, nailing the protruding soles of his boots to the joists. Then they double-knotted his laces as tightly as they could, so he wouldn't be able to get the boots off while trying to keep his balance on the slanting, exposed beams. They were nailing him to the roof. Corky and Dana climbed down, and the whole crew got in their cars to go get lunch. "See you, John!" they shouted out the car windows, laughing. As they drove away, Ratzenberger tossed the plywood sheets down onto the ground, and took out a pocketknife that, luckily, he had tucked away. He cut the laces off his boots, with a smile on his face. "It was one of the happiest moments of my life," he told me, "because I knew I was accepted. I had passed the test. Otherwise they wouldn't have bothered. That was their way of saying, Welcome to the crew. After that we had a great time."

Ratzenberger became the first person in his family to go to college, enrolling at Sacred Heart University, in nearby Fairfield. He majored in English and got interested in drama, earning a role one year as the understudy to the lead in the Tennessee Williams play *Summer and Smoke.* The cringe moment happened one day before the play opened, when the lead actor quit. Ratzenberger was there as a lark. He didn't know the lines and hadn't even read the play. Since he was now the lead, he studied furiously the day of the opening, and got through the first act with the help of a script reader awkwardly mouthing the lines from offstage. By the second act, though, Ratzenberger was so lost that there was little he could do but improvise. Luckily, the audience wasn't very familiar with the play, and they didn't seem to mind as he turned a heavy drama into a farce of slapstick and ad-libs. The rest of the cast was ready to heave him off the stage, since he delivered none of the cues they needed to deliver their own well-rehearsed lines. But the audience laughed, and the louder their roars, the more Ratzenberger hammed it up. "When people started laughing, that's when I got the bug," he said. "It was that laughter. I was surfing it, and all of a sudden, the waves were getting bigger. So I just went for it." He learned his lines for the later performances, but the opening-night comedy act left the bigger impression around town. A local theater director who had been in the audience tracked him down afterward, and told him he had a genius for improvisation. "What are you talking about?" Ratzenberger asked, unfamiliar with the concept. "I was just making stuff up."

Encouraged by the praise, Ratzenberger thought he'd give acting a try, so he formed a small troupe in Bridgeport with a few friends, and joined another ensemble group after college. But there was no money in it, so he started to earn a living the best way he knew how: as a carpenter again. He was doing some work in Vermont, sleeping in the hayloft of a barn and enjoying the company of some of the most colorful characters he had ever met, when he decided to accept the invitation of a college friend who had moved to England. His pal was working as a social worker in London, and he kept sending Ratzenberger postcards describing how much fun it was, and saying come on over. Since Ratzenberger's carpentry work didn't seem to be heading anywhere in particular, he used the money from a tax refund to buy a one-way plane ticket to England.

He had figured that he could support himself practically anywhere as a tradesman, so one of the first things he did was take out a magazine ad offering the services of "John the Carpenter." He ended up working at a theater in London, helping build sets and keep the theater in good repair. Since he had little money, he ended up living in a series of "squats," abandoned buildings that the government let people move into, a practice that helped keep the rodents in check and prevent fires if somebody was taking minimal care of the property. Ratzenberger's fix-it skills made him popular among the squatters, and he began to get the best rooms (usually at the top floor of the building) in exchange for his efforts patching roofs, repairing plumbing, and getting the heat working. He got to know the local greengrocer, who would save the blemished, picked-over produce nobody else wanted for him. Ratzenberger would bring it home and cook it on a stove he had built himself, out of an old oil drum. I asked Ratzenberger if the subsistence living got irritating, and he practically mocked the question. "I never felt sorry for myself or felt like, oh, this is such hard work. I knew it was, but I expected it to be."

Ratzenberger still had an interest in performing, and while working on sets at the theater, he learned that the British government funded the performing arts more generously than the government back home, allowing stage actors to earn modest pay. The friend he had gone to visit was working as a social worker, but they had both been in the same acting troupe back in Bridgeport, and the two of them decided they could come up with an act at least as entertaining as the people they saw onstage—and earn a few quid in the process. So in 1971 they formed a two-man improv group, which they called Sal's Meat Market—the same name as their short-lived theatrical group in Connecticut. They started out by performing at the Oval House in South London's Kennington district, a fringe theater where amateurs could experiment with material and find their footing. Unlike the glittery theaters in London's famous West End, the Oval House was run by an avuncular, fringe-theater pioneer named Peter Oliver, who cultivated a joyful, carnivalesque atmosphere at the Oval House and didn't particularly care how much money his shows brought in. "He said, 'I'll give you an audience. Do whatever you want,' " Ratzenberger recalled. " 'This is where you can start.' " Around the time Ratzenberger started his stage act, film star Pierce Brosnan got his first acting jobs at the Oval House, and bestselling author Salman Rushdie gave readings there.

Each performance by Sal's Meat Market was 85 or 90 percent new material, with very little carried over from show to show. They'd put a collection of mundane props behind a black wall at the back of the stage, and build each night's show around whatever odds and ends they had collected that day: an old army helmet, different kinds of hats, a wrecked bicycle, and other interesting debris plucked from the trash. In their skits, they'd play various townspeople, dock workers, clowns, aliens, whatever popped into their heads. "It was very simple comedy," Ratzenberger said. "Laurel and Hardyish in a lot of ways." Since the Oval gave amateurs time to refine their acts, Ratzenberger and his partner were able to stick with it long enough to start drawing a crowd. One reason Sal's Meat Market became popular is that audience members knew they'd see something new if they came back a second or third time, which helped build a dedicated following and generate word-of-mouth buzz. They started to tour Europe and became popular outside the U.K., too. After six years, they were getting standing-room-only audiences when they went on tour, and people in the streets of Amsterdam or Copenhagen would recognize them. "Within the fringe theater, we were the 400-pound gorilla of comedy," Ratzenberger said.

Sal's Meat Market eventually ran its course. Ratzenberger's partner was married, with a son, and touring became a family strain. Besides, they had gone about as far as they could, with little chance of breaking into the more lucrative West End scene. Neither man had gone to Oxford or Cambridge, the traditional breeding ground for England's favored performers. They weren't even British, which meant they didn't have the network or connections to springboard into the mainstream London theater. But Ratzenberger's work at the Oval opened doors nonetheless. Many casting directors who worked on British film productions had seen Sal's Meat Market, or heard of it. After a few years onstage, Ratzenberger had realized that he was rolling the dice as an actor, especially since he wasn't developing any other kind of career. So he decided he'd better get a bit more serious about his profession. He hired an agent, got some professional glamour shots made, and put together a portfolio highlighting his work. That helped when casting directors called, and call they did. Military films were popular in the late seventies and early eighties, and Ratzenberger was the right age, with the right build, to convincingly play a man in uniform. He got bit parts in the 1977 classic *A Bridge Too Far,* plus a few other less memorable military films. Then came roles in *Superman* and *Superman II, The Empire Strikes Back, Reds,* and *Ghandi.* They were small parts, sometimes uncredited, but Ratzenberger was astonished that he was being paid to travel to exotic places like India, Malta, and many corners of Europe, all while learning a "trade," as he called acting. "Never in my wildest imagination had I thought this was a possibility," he said. The takeaway seems obvious, but if you happen to be an egomaniacal, self-consumed celebrity, here's the point: Humility is a winning trait.

A few of the films he got roles in were being made by world-class directors, including Richard Attenborough, John Schlesinger, and Milos Forman. Ratzenberger was one of the least-known members of the cast, but that was no reason to waste the opportunity by being obsequious or acting awed by the very presence of famed filmmakers. So he asked questions, probing why they might be filming a certain way or doing things he didn't understand. During the filming of *Yanks,* a 1979 release about the buildup of American troops in England during World War II that starred Richard Gere and Vanessa Redgrave, there was a long lull in the shooting. Ratzenberger wondered what the delay was, so he walked up to director John Schlesinger, famous by then for *Midnight Cowboy* and *Marathon Man,* to ask what was going on. "Wow," Ratzenberger said. "You've got a couple hundred people standing around waiting. Why are you holding everybody up?"

"Well, John," Schlesinger answered, "you should be able to separate every frame of a movie, put a frame around it, and hang it on the wall. Because every frame is a painting. It's visual." They were filming on farmland in the English countryside, and Schlesinger explained that he was waiting for a prop crew to put some snow on the roof of a barn, which would be a minor change in the background but would nonetheless help bring out the other colors in the shot. "What I'm doing now is painting," he told Ratzenberger, who was sufficiently impressed, and convinced he was working with one of the best directors ever.

Ratzenberger's work at the Oval also helped him get hired as a TV writer for the BBC. Then he partnered with an American comedian who also happened to be in London, Ruby Wax, to write a late-night TV show for CBS. It was supposed to be about the Roman emperor Nero, who was mad and murderous and whose life, CBS thought, might be the basis for an entertaining TV comedy. Ratzenberger and Wax wrote the script, and CBS liked it so much, they considered turning it into a prime-time show. The two writers flew from London to Los Angeles to negotiate with CBS, arguing that the changes required to tone down the material and comply with the rules for prime-time programming would gut the script. "We got a lecture," Ratzenberger recalled. "These executives told us, Listen, we know what we're doing. American humor's different from English humor. So we said, Okay, if they pay for it, they can have whatever they want." But when they turned in the revised script, the network executives no longer thought it was funny. The project died.

While getting opportunities, Ratzenberger was still an obscure talent with few connections in the show business firmament clustered around Los Angeles. He was in his mid-thirties, with no formal training as an actor, no career breakthroughs, and no immediate prospects. I asked if he got discouraged. "Are you kidding?" He laughed. "This was all indoor work. I was working with funny people, traveling the world. Every day was a blessing." He told me about reading the novels of James Fenimore Cooper as a kid, and being fascinated with the Natty Bumpo character, best known by his nickname Hawkeye in *The Last of the Mohicans.* "These people back then," Ratzenberger said, "they would pack their powder and their musket and just go off into the woods, without knowing where they were going or how to get back or what they would come up against. I felt the same way on the journey through New England, fixing broken things, then going to Europe for ten years. It was just a great adventure. That's all it was." In a way, Ratzenberger cast himself as the protagonist in a mythic drama, similar to the way Jack Bogle did.

The breakthrough that led to his role on *Cheers* could be a case study in serendipity. While in Los Angeles for the doomed CBS project, Ratzenberger met a guy who repaired VCRs, the video machines used before digital downloads and DVD players became common. He'd help fix the machines, tinkering, basically, as a way to relax and pass the time while he waited for the writing project to develop. The VCR handyman told Ratzenberger that he ought to get an L.A.-based agent, and that he happened to be fixing a VCR for an agent he'd be happy to introduce Ratzenberger to. He did, and it turned out the agent knew that NBC was conducting auditions for a new show called *Cheers,* to be set in a Boston bar. The agent thought Ratzenberger might be a good fit. He called one day and said, "You're from New England, aren't you?" Ratzenberger said yes, but explained that he was heading back to London in just a couple of days. "Look," the agent said, "there's no way the American public is going to accept a show in a bar. It will go five, seven episodes at the most. If you get something out of it, go back to London, buy yourself some nice furniture or a car or something." Ratzenberger had done okay up till then with small, temporary roles, so he figured sure, why not.

When he got to the audition, he expected it to be like the casting calls he had been on back in London. They were never actual auditions, with the actor reading lines and showing off his talents, because the casting directors did all the work ahead of time, vetting the actors and making sure they'd be right for the part. So when Ratzenberger had gone to meet the producers or directors, mostly they'd sit in a room and talk about the movie, the director's vision for it, Ratzenberger's background, and how he might approach the job. Then they'd thank him for coming in. The *Cheers* audition turned out to be totally different. When Ratzenberger got to the room, he noticed there was no place for him to sit, and he started to look around. "What are you looking for?" one of the producers asked.

"My chair," he said.

"You're not here to chat," the producer said. "You're here to audition."

That's when he knew something was wrong. "The blood rushed from my body," he recalled. "I stumbled through whatever it was they had written. I just wanted to get out the door." He was unprepared for an audition, and he also knew he was embarrassing the casting director who had invited him in. "It was a horrible audition," Ratzenberger said. "I was literally leaving, sure that my eight-by-ten was already wafting into the wastebasket. My dignity was in tatters all over their carpet." Then, right before they shut the door on him, he stopped. "I had done some really good work in Europe for close to ten years," he recalled. "I didn't want to leave without them knowing I had been in that office. The writer part of me took over."

With one foot out the door, he turned around and said to the producers, "Do you have a bar know-it-all?"

"What are you talking about?" one of them asked.

Ratzenberger explained that in New England, every corner pub had one character who sat at the end of the bar and fielded every random question that came up. Whether the answers were right or wrong didn't matter. "As long as he says it with enough authority, nobody cares," Ratzenberger told the producers. "He's the arbiter of everything, and every single bar has one of these guys. There are never two. They're like gunfighters. You're not going to have Wyatt Earp and Kit Carson sitting at the same bar. It's one or the other."

He was improvising now, and he was on a roll. Smiles on the producers' faces indicated that the audience was warming to him, as they had when he ad-libbed over the bungled lines in *Summer and Smoke,* and when he hammed it up with a pith helmet or the mangled carcass of a bicycle at the Oval House. He began to create the character of Cliff Clavin on the spot, using the same thick New

England accent familiar to anybody who has seen an episode of *Cheers.* "Hey Bud," he said, mimicking a bartender trying to enlist the know-it-all to mediate a barroom disagreement. "What's the length of a whale's intestine?"

"Baleen or blue whale?" the know-it-all answers.

Ratzenberger devised another question for the know-it-all, about the origin of the telephone: "Well, you know the, uh, telephone was originally devised by American Indians talking into coconut shells. . . ."

After a bit more improv, Ratzenberger told the producers, "Good luck with your show." Then he left.

"They knew Ratzenberger was in town," he told me, looking back. "Whether I got hired or not wasn't important. What was important was that they knew I knew what I was doing."

Ratzenberger never made it back to London as planned. The producers added the bar know-it-all to the lineup, casting Ratzenberger in the part. They shot the initial seven episodes, but instead of offending viewers and folding, as many had expected, *Cheers* drew enough viewers to survive a rocky first year—and then it caught on. Over eleven years, the sitcom earned twenty-eight Emmy Awards, generated some of the most memorable characters in TV history, and spawned another hit show, *Frasier.* Virtually every actor on the show—Ted Danson (bartender Sam Malone), Shelley Long (Diane), George Wendt (Norm), Woody Harrelson (Woody), Rhea Perlman (Carla), Kirstie Alley (Rebecca), Kelsey Grammer (Frasier), and Bebe Neuwirth (Lilith)—enjoyed the kind of status after *Cheers* that opened doors to plum roles and created career freedom that anybody would envy. As for Ratzenberger, he stayed with *Cheers* for all eleven seasons, got married in 1984, had two kids in Los Angeles, went on to the Pixar roles, created a series for the Travel Channel called *Made in America,* and seemed to have a lot more fun—even with small, forgettable roles—than most of the privileged actors and actresses who grab headlines.

Ratzenberger didn't exactly fail at something before he succeeded. But he's a Rebounder because he turned humble circumstances to his advantage, changed his thinking when he had to, and never clung to a scripted plan that prevented him from discovering better opportunities. In that regard, he's similar to Thomas Edison, who changed his whole priority scheme if an experiment or discovery was more promising than expected. Improvisation is obviously an apt metaphor for Ratzenberger's career, because he had the creative energy to extemporize in his choices, much as he did onstage. He "surfed the wave" when he encountered it, and even generated the wave when he auditioned for the role of a lifetime, on *Cheers*. Some of his choices were whimsical, but Ratzenberger was also able to take risks in his career because he knew he'd be okay if they didn't pan out. He learned early on to be comfortable with discomfort—whether on a frozen construction site in the winter, in a run-down squat in London, or on a stage where he might bomb. Over the years, he honed the improvisational skills that gave him the presence of mind and the courage that allowed him to lunge for what might have been the best chance he would ever get—seconds before it was about to expire. Many ambitious people find themselves on some kind of stage from time to time, with a fleeting chance to demonstrate their talents. As they do at many other pivotal moments, Rebounders have an edge. They know that if they flop, they'll still land on their feet.

CHAPTER 10

WHAT COULD GO WRONG

Reed Hastings thinks about failure every day. For much of his career, that must have seemed a peculiar obsession, since his company, Netflix, was one of the most storied startups in America. Since founding the video-rental firm in 1997, Hastings had built it into a powerhouse that changed the way people rented and watched movies and drove its top competitor, Blockbuster, into bankruptcy. In 2010, *Fortune* dubbed the Netflix CEO its "Businessperson of the Year," ranking him above Steve Jobs, Warren Buffett, Facebook's Mark Zuckerberg, and dozens of other dazzling business leaders. By mid-2011, the company's stock was a legendary investment that had soared by roughly 4,000 percent since the day Netflix went public in 2002, compared with a mere 20 percent gain for the overall stock market during the same period of time.

Hastings reveled in that success, but he was wary of it, too. He frequently studied promising startups that collapsed, such as Web portal AOL, which squandered a huge lead in a new industry by clinging too long to its founding technology, dial-up Internet access, while competitors embraced high-speed broadband and rapidly overtook AOL. Netflix, too, could become a victim of corporate hubris if it didn't stay on its toes, Hastings often warned. In June, 2011—at a time when everything seemed to be going right for Netflix—Hastings confessed his fear that Netflix could become "slow and stodgy," like other dominant firms that lost their edge. "You hear about companies getting long in the tooth," Hastings said. "All of these innovations are going on every day, all around you. One day, someone could overtake you."

When Netflix finally stumbled, however, it wasn't because a new competitor turned out to be smarter or faster. It was because Hastings's own fear of obsolescence led the company away from its roots too quickly. Netflix had gotten its start in 1997 by allowing its customers to choose rental movies from a website, with the DVDs delivered by mail. The clever new service saved viewers a trip to the store, as long as they planned in advance, with no late fees or other annoyances that were common among video-rental chains at the time. The service relied upon lightweight and durable DVDs that were easy to mail, but Hastings knew that DVDs would eventually be replaced by video streaming over cable lines and the Internet. His goal with Netflix was to use the technology of the present, DVDs, to gain a foothold and be ready when the technology of the future arrived. That's why he named the new firm Netflix, instead of Mailflix or DVDs by Mail. And while building a huge base of DVD-rental customers, Netflix also began to offer TV shows and movies streamed instantly to desktops, laptops, tablet devices, and TVs equipped for streaming.

By the middle of 2011, Hastings felt sure that the technology of the future was finally poised to displace the technology of the present. It was the equivalent of broadband overtaking dial-up, and he was determined not to repeat AOL's mistake. So Netflix devised a new strategy meant to steer customers away from DVDs, which were costlier for Netflix to offer, and encourage them to do more streaming, which is where Netflix planned to invest most of its money in the future. The DVD service became a separate company called Qwikster, which required a separate account. The main company would focus mainly on streaming. Customers who wanted both services would have to pay about 60 percent more. Hastings and his fellow executives expected some cusomers to complain, but they were moving boldly into the future, and a revolution like the one under way in video entertainment couldn't be stopped by a few stragglers clinging to the comfortable but obsolete routines of the past.

The present, however, didn't yield to the future nearly as readily as Hastings had expected. Instead of a few mild protests, there was a revolt among Netflix customers. In the twelve months prior to the announcement of the new strategy, Netflix had added more than ten million new subscribers, with explosive growth fueling the soaring stock price and keeping the company's outlook buoyant. But in the three months following the announcement, the company lost more than 800,000 U.S. subscribers. With its growth suddenly arrested, everything changed. Wall Street analysts—whose gushing praise had helped send Netflix stock into the stratosphere—now saw deep flaws in the firm's business model and began to question whether the whole enterprise was sustainable. The stock plunged, falling 75 percent from its peak by the end of 2011. Some shareholders called for Hastings's ouster. The lower stock price made Netflix vulnerable to a takeover by a larger competitor, which might also lead to Hastings's departure. Qwikster became a symbol of corporate folly, the New Coke of the twenty-first century. Slow and stodgy, it turned out, would have been better.

Hastings, lionized just a year earlier as an innovative genius, was now a corporate goat. It took a few uncomfortable weeks, but he finally acknowledged that Netflix had screwed up. The company killed the Qwikster scheme. It kept the price hikes intact, but reunited its DVD and streaming websites and publicly apologized for its dismissive treatment of customers. Hastings later joked that the Qwikster fiasco had been a "head fake," adding that, "It's unfortunate that we did this to the DVD subscribers."

The whole strange episode left customers and shareholders wondering why a CEO at the top of his game would sabotage his own company. But Hastings knew something many of his critics didn't: Playing it safe is often the worst possible thing you can do, and it is better to struggle through mistakes every now and then—even big ones—than to get comfortable with an old strategy. He hadn't just read about it. He had seen it up close early in his career then made mistakes of his own at the first company he started, before Netflix, that ultimately helped him become a far better business leader. Hastings had learned that anticipating curves and potholes helped keep you at the front of the pack. If you drove aggressively, there might be times when you took a turn too fast. But by the time of the Qwikster episode, Hastings had recovered from several other strategic mistakes in his career, learning how to regain control and make up lost ground—lessons that might help him regain control now. The arc of Hastings's career, in fact, illustrates how Rebounders are sometimes able to take the risks needed to outpace competitors because they know they'll be able to recover if something goes wrong.

Hastings grew up in Belmont, Massachusetts, a comfortable Boston suburb, and Washington, D.C., where his father, a lawyer, served a stint in the Nixon administration. He went to a pricey Massachusetts prep school and, like John Ratzenberger, began to improvise his way through life once he was on his own. After high school, he spent a year selling high-end Rainbow vacuum cleaners door to door, stretching a summer job into a yearlong franchise because he enjoyed proving to skeptical housewives, through a vacuum test on their own carpets, that his Rainbow machine was superior to whatever they were using. After that, he went to Bowdoin College in Maine, where he majored in math and won a couple of prestigious math prizes. Hastings believed in serving his country, and considered joining the Marine Corps but decided it might be too rigid for his inquisitive personality. The Peace Corps seemed like a better fit, so he enrolled right after college.

Hastings spent three years with the Peace Corps teaching math at a high school in Swaziland, sleeping on a cot in a thatch hut with no electricity. He made just one trip home the whole time he was there, for his sister's wedding, and took another short trip to Mbabane, the capital of Swaziland, to take the graduate school entrance exam. He wanted to study computer science at MIT but didn't get in. Stanford was his backup, and he arrived there in 1986 knowing little about California except that Stanford was supposed to be comparable to the Ivy League schools back East. He quickly felt at home in California, and after graduating, went to work for one of the technology startups that were popping up all over the area, turning Silicon Valley into a famous place known for its groundbreaking blend of technology and entrepreneurship. In his first full-time job out of grad school, he helped develop software for a thirty-person firm hoping to sell its product to big companies, which is where the money was. But the money would only materialize if companies bought the product, which they didn't. The startup flopped, giving Hastings an insight similar to what the young Tom Edison figured out after his first patented invention fizzled 130 years earlier: If you're going to build something, make sure it's something people want to buy. "We had spent two long years building software that no one cared about," Hastings told *Fortune.* "The big lesson? If you are a great people leader, you had better not lead them into a box canyon from which there is no escape."

Software engineers like Hastings were in high demand in Silicon Valley, and his next job was for another startup developing telecommunications software. But Hastings had a bigger idea: He had personally created a debugging protocol that would make many types of software, in a variety of industries, run more smoothly. Today, software bugs are little more than a nuisance that might occasionally require a system reboot, on machines that automatically back everything up, so little or no harm is done. But in the late 1980s and early 1990s, software bugs were a major problem, especially since airplanes, automobiles, medical equipment, and many other types of indispensable machines were beginning to rely on computers to work properly. Processors and memory chips routinely crashed as they got overloaded, and corporate programmers were constantly writing software patches and troubleshooting problems to keep the systems running.

Hastings figured out a solution. During nights and weekends, he worked late into the wee hours devising software that would seamlessly and automatically fill the memory leak that occurred in many commercial programs, preventing them from crashing. The company he worked for was run by an entrepreneur named Audrey MacLean, who realized that Hastings might be on to something big. She encouraged Hastings to cut back his hours at her own firm, while spending more of his time developing the debugging software. Hastings thought about licensing his software to another company that would commercialize it, market it, and pay him royalties, but a friend suggested he forget about that and start his own company. Unlike a lot of beginner entrepreneurs, Hastings got excellent advice. His talent and instincts had led him to the right place and the right people at the right time. So in 1990, he founded Pure Software, to sell the debugging tool that would purify code written by others. Even though he had never managed anybody or handled a balance sheet, Hastings would be the CEO.

He had a compelling product, but Hastings needed investors and was unschooled in the art of building a company. "He was not a slick pitchman," recalled Paul Holland, a friend of Hastings who later became a prominent venture capitalist. "Reed's pitch was very aboriginal, very homespun. He'd take quotes from developers who were his friends and embed them in his business plan, saying, 'This is better than sliced bread.' " Investors heard him out, but most lumped him with the 99 percent of projects they took a pass on. Companies built around software tools, like Hastings was developing, had a spotty record of going public and earning back the investors' money. Plus, a recession was under way, damping much of the startup fervor of a few years earlier. Still, Audrey MacLean, his boss, invested $20,000. Fellow engineers who understood the importance of what he was working on invested small amounts of their own money, as did family members and other friends. Hastings scraped together the rest himself, and a couple hundred thousand dollars was enough to get Pure Software off the ground.

Hastings never wanted to be CEO of his own company, or of any company. He wanted to be the product guy, building great software, while letting somebody else worry about business strategy. But with limited funding, he couldn't afford to hire a CEO. He had only enough money to bring on a few sales and technical people, so he ended up running the company during the day and programming software at night. He had gotten used to an intense, work-till-you-drop culture in Silicon Valley, with demanding hours that would test anybody's devotion to their work. "That was what I loved," Hastings told me. "The hard-ass culture." He scheduled a weekly staff meeting at 6:00 A.M. Monday mornings, a way of signaling his aggressive attitude. Others followed the boss's lead, working long hours on nights and weekends. His employees nicknamed him Animal, for his ferocious work habits. His tour in Swaziland had given him a high tolerance for discomfort, and he lived with his wife in an unheated cottage in the woods south of San Francisco, where it was cheaper to live than in other parts of the Valley.

Pure Software had one big thing going for it: The product was dynamite. "It was lightning in a bottle," Holland said. "It improved the quality of software everywhere." Hastings still needed venture capital, and the odds improved as customers bought the software and revenue poured in. As the firm became profitable, Hastings finally persuaded investors to provide several million dollars' worth of new capital, which would allow the company to hire more people, expand, and develop a deliberate growth strategy.

Hastings continued to have misgivings about his own role as a CEO. He was extremely self-assured when it came to the area in which he had genuine expertise—software engineering. But he lacked the skills and experience that other CEOs had. He didn't have a business or finance degree, or the huge force of personality that Steve Jobs or Larry Ellison at Oracle had. Compared to people like that, he was a geek whose rightful place was in front of a computer screen, tapping code into the machine—not in front of investors or clients or the press.

His shortcomings weren't just theoretical. With the additional funding, Pure built a strong staff of engineers, marketers, and product developers. But the sales department struggled, mainly because Hastings repeatedly hired the wrong people to run it. Sales was something Hastings had never done himself, except for the year he spent peddling vacuum cleaners to housewives. He knew practically nothing about the skills, connections, and personality required to sell software to corporate clients. Hastings hired one sales director after another who made a strong first impression and seemed great on paper, but inevitably left in less than a year after underperforming or clashing with the company culture. Each changeover generated turmoil and left the company without a coherent sales strategy. "I was over my head and absolutely struggling to do a good job," Hastings recalled, nearly two decades later. "It was like trying to run a race and being really out of shape."

Hastings even tried to fire himself. Twice, he went to his board of directors, composed mostly of investors who had committed money to the firm, and offered to resign as CEO, while taking a different role in charge of engineering and product development, which he knew he was good at. "The guilt of the mistakes was tearing me up," he said. "Those mistakes in the sales channel created a lot of chaos at the company. We could have grown a lot faster." During a couple of quarters, the company even missed its revenue targets, because the sales team was floundering. The board members recognized the problem, but they also saw qualities in Hastings that he didn't see in himself. "Reed had the ability to explain complex things in simple terms," said Andy Rachleff, one of the venture capitalists on Pure Software's board. "He forced me to think at a high level because he thought at a high level. Reed instinctively knew that in technology, if you don't take risks, you inherently take more risks. If you play not to lose, you will lose." Years later, at Netflix, Hastings would express those same sentiments many times, to explain bold steps that others didn't quite understand. But as the young CEO at Pure, he still needed the more seasoned Rachleff to help calm him down and convince him that the company didn't need a new leader. It just needed to work through mistakes and give the salespeople more structure, more guidance. "You have to learn how to forgive yourself for mistakes," Rachleff told Hastings. "Trust the board. We'll replace you if it's appropriate."

Hastings's awareness of his own limitations became one of the very things that helped others develop deep confidence in him. Paul Holland had gone to work as one of the salespeople at Pure by then, and the continual turnover of sales directors affected him directly. Yet instead of bolting for a more stable firm, he stuck with Pure, largely because of his faith in the boss. "Recognizing your own flaws is one of the hardest things to do," Holland said. "There are very few people with the presence of mind to do that. When Reed sees a weakness, he'll work and work and work till he overcomes it. He'll read every book on a topic that he doesn't know well, introduce himself to experts, get meetings, do whatever it takes to learn something. Reed has probably read more about leadership and how to be a CEO than most people teaching at Harvard Business School." Psychology experts agree with Holland about the importance—and rarity—of people with the deep self-awareness it takes to acknowledge their own flaws and failings. Howard Gardner, who developed the idea of emotional intelligence and many other groundbreaking concepts, wrote in his book *Extraordinary Minds* that exceptional individuals have "a special talent for identifying their own strengths and weaknesses." An accurate understanding of your own contribution to a problem is often essential to solving it. For many Rebounders, self-awareness provides a key edge that helps them recover quickly from setbacks and keep getting ahead.

To outsiders, Pure Software seemed to be in good shape. The product was so good that sales doubled each year, masking the turnover problems and growing pains. The company expanded its product line and Hastings came up with innovative ways to boost revenue, one reason the board supported him. In a preview of what he would later do at Netflix, Hastings tried different pricing schemes, ultimately settling on a subscription model that amounted to a price hike for many customers. There was considerable risk that some customers would balk, forcing Pure to backpedal, which could cut into revenues even more. But that didn't happen, and Hastings's gamble turned out to be a smart one. Sales kept climbing. By 1994, Pure's sales were $16 million, with a net profit of $2.6 million—an impressive 16 percent profit margin. Pure was starting to look like a good candidate for a public offering, which would handsomely reward all the early investors in the company.

But as Pure grew, Hastings's job got harder, and he never felt like he hit his stride as the boss. He still stayed up late doing coding, and the strain of the hard-ass culture that he once thrived on began to wear him down. With a staff of more than one hundred, he now spent considerable time on personnel issues, on top of everything else, keeping the team in sync and helping people solve problems. One day he popped into the office of an employee who had stepped out, and was appalled to see pornography on the man's computer screen. Since it was still the early days of the Internet, there were no pictures, just raunchy stories. Hastings backed out of the office, too embarrassed to confront the employee directly. But he imposed a set of controls that governed what people could do on their computers during the day. "I was trying to manage by the stick, not the carrot," he recalled. "Telling employees what they shouldn't do was a typical but immature response." Once a nimble, freewheeling startup, Pure was becoming a bureaucratic corporation with rules for everything.

Hastings's first child was born in 1994, and there wasn't enough time in the day to be a hands-on CEO, a software engineer, an attentive husband, and an engaged father. "I was a lousy husband and a bad dad and I felt guilty about doing a bad job at Pure," he told me. "I'd say that I'd be home at seven, and then some employee would walk in my office with a problem, and instead of saying, Hey, I've got to go, I'd sit down with the employee for an hour or two and then get home at eight-thirty. Of course my family would be mad at me, and I'd be mad at them for not understanding the sacrifice." He was hardly the first parent-boss to struggle with the competing demands of work and family. Like many Rebounders, he invoked the doctrine of hard work, trying to do more of everything. It had paid off before, but this time, it didn't—there simply wasn't enough time in one day to squeeze in two or three days' worth of duties.

Hastings and his wife finally saw a marriage counselor, who helped him realize that something had to give. "That got me to see that in my own head, I could fail at my marriage, because people get divorced and in a way that's acceptable," he told me. "But failing at work was somehow a deeper wound. Just being able to articulate it at the time helped me say, You know, that's not really who I want to be or how I want to live. It comes back to that theme of forgiving myself." Hearing that twice—once from his board, and once from a marriage counselor—gave it more impact. Hastings established new boundaries at the office, saying no more often. "I found a different way to accept that I couldn't simply work harder to make things better," he said.

Pure kept heading higher, helped along, unexpectedly, by prominent bugs in Intel's Pentium processor and in software published by Microsoft. Suddenly, everybody using computers became aware of the damage that bugs could cause, which boosted demand for the type of products Pure sold. Pure acquired another small company in the spring of 1995, enlarging its portfolio. It unveiled new products that could be used over the Internet, which was just coming into common usage. Then, in August, Pure Software went public, with the stock soaring from its offering price of $17 to $30—setting the market value for Hastings's startup at about $80 million. Hastings and about a dozen other early Pure employees became instant millionaires. Hastings celebrated by buying an $80,000 Porsche, a nouveau-riche impulse he later regretted. His family moved from the unheated cottage in the woods to an oceanfront home in Santa Cruz. The CEO who had twice offered to resign was suddenly a hot commodity.

Despite the big payday, Hastings continued to take risks as CEO, using the proceeds of the stock offering to acquire a couple other companies and grow rapidly. The company, which became Pure Atria after one acquisition, was no longer a boutique firm with a lucrative niche more or less to itself. Pure's growth had made it a mainstream software developer competing with a lot of other firms, including goliaths like IBM and Oracle. The company got unwieldy and became "less fun, less inventive," according to Hastings. The acquisitions turned out to be a lot bumpier than the CEO expected, and sales were no longer surging the way they had been. Each acquisition created duplicate staff, and workers began to worry more about protecting their jobs than performing them. Key salespeople left, leaving others to sell products they barely understood. The turnover and turmoil impaired profitability. In 1996, Pure Atria lost $6.6. million. In the first quarter of 1997, the company lost $42 million. The poor performance dented investors' confidence in the firm. The stock sank, and the weakened position left Pure Atria a takeover target itself. Two years after Pure went public, a rival company, Rational Software, bought it for about $750 million. The Pure name dissolved, and many of the Pure employees, including Hastings, no longer had jobs.

They had a lot of money though. The Rational buyout netted Hastings more than $40 million, enough for him to become an investor himself in a few Valley startups. In less than a decade, he had turned a great idea into a marketable product that grew into a vibrant company that employed hundreds of people and generated a lot of wealth. But he wasn't dancing in the end zone. He had been forced to sell his company because he overreached, and as he got a glimpse of how his rival and suitor, Rational, did business, he felt humbled. "It was so different how they operated," he told *Fortune*. "The level of trust and the quality of interaction between them was impressive." His own company, by contrast, had become a place where the hard-ass culture of his own making led to a combative and chaotic atmosphere that interfered with profitability.

When Hastings started Netflix in 1997, he had many of his own mistakes in mind, and was determined never to repeat them. Creating a startup was no longer a blood sport to him. There was no need for manhood competitions over who could work the most hours, and there would be no "Animals" at Netflix. Despite his fresh fortune, Hastings was learning how fragile success could be. He realized how lucky he had been at Pure, because he survived the kinds of mistakes that sink many others. By then, Hastings had also been steeped in the "fail fast" mentality prevalent among venture capitalists, who knew that many of the startups they funded wouldn't succeed. Their goal wasn't to avoid failure, but to recognize failure quickly if it was bound to happen, fix what was fixable, junk what wasn't, and try again, smarter and shrewder. So while others sought to mimic the many success stories to be found in Silicon Valley, Hastings started to study the failures, to make sure he never became one of them. A continual focus on what could go wrong would become the guiding ethos at Netflix.

Hastings got the idea for Netflix after renting the movie *Apollo 13* on videocassette, misplacing it, and getting hit with an infuriating forty-dollar late fee. There had to be a better way, he reasoned. DVDs were just catching on, and since they were light and compact, Hastings wondered if it would be plausible to send them to subscribers by mail. To test out the idea, he mailed himself a few music CDs one day. They arrived in perfect shape. "That was the big excitement point," he told *Fortune*. Even then, Hastings was anticipating what could go wrong. As a technologist, he knew that DVDs were just a placeholder until the bandwidth was in place to support video streaming. But that was still in the future. Renting DVDs through the mail would be novel enough.

Netflix had a much rockier start than Pure Software. Instead of taking off right after it launched in 1997, the upstart firm muddled along with a strategy that wasn't quite right. The original service consisted of a website where people could order movies by mail and pay a fee each time. Interest was tepid, with many people wondering why they should wait two or three days for a movie, when they could pick one up at the local rental outlet any time they wanted. So in 1999, Hastings rolled out a subscription model (like he had at Pure) that allowed members to pay a set fee each month, for as many movies as they wanted. That caught on, and the familiar red-and-white envelopes began to arrive in mailboxes all across America. Still, Netflix endured many threats to its existence during its first decade, as most startups do. The company went public in 2002, which Hastings later felt had been too soon, because it gave competitors too much information about its strategy and finances. There were early problems getting movies to customers in the timely fashion Netflix promised, proving how difficult it could be to manage an inventory of thousands of films and operate a nationwide distribution system. Netflix didn't become profitable until 2003, six years after it started. Once it became popular, it had to fight off incursions by entrenched competitors that already had millions of customers, like Blockbuster, Walmart, Amazon, and Apple. As online streaming finally became commonplace, cable and phone companies launched their own on-demand video services. There were many opportunities for Netflix to fall behind the competition, turn a tactical misstep into a strategic blunder, or simply lose its nerve.

For most of its first fifteen years, however, Netflix stayed ahead of the pack, largely because of Hastings's relentless focus on how companies, and the people who run them, fail. At Netflix, he fixed the things he didn't get right earlier in his career. Instead of the hard-ass culture with top-down rules that had sucked the fun out of Pure Software, Hastings instituted a set of "freedom and responsibility" policies at Netflix that became the envy of corporate America. Employees could take as much vacation time as they chose, for instance, as they long as they got the job done. There was a limited corporate hierarchy, with few formal titles. Those were ways of guarding against the excessive control he had tried to exert at Pure, where he had badly overreacted when one employee marginally misbehaved by downloading porn onto a company computer. "Yeah, people are going to do some dumb stuff sometimes," Hastings said. "People say, How can you have no vacation policy? Aren't people going to abuse it? But as long as we focus on inventiveness and creativity, that's okay."

Before the Qwikster "head fake," there were several other moments when Netflix could have become the next AOL, by holding on too long to doomed technology, simply because it had invested heavily in it. But at least twice, Hastings killed video-player devices that Netflix had developed, because the advent of YouTube and other types of technology turned out to be better and easier for customers to use. He was failing fast, but fixing what didn't work and moving on to the next thing. At the same time, Hastings's near-compulsive fear of complacency led him to continually seek ways to make Netflix better. The company offered a $1 million prize, for example, to anybody who could improve the software that came up with movie recommendations for users, similar to the way Tim Westergren's music-genome project programmed music for listeners based on their likes and dislikes.

Netflix's biggest rival, Blockbuster, proved that Hastings was right about the dangers of complacency. As Netflix snatched market share and began to transform the movie rental business, Hastings and his team worried obsessively that Blockbuster, with its huge customer base and deep pockets, would muscle in on their growing niche. It took the nationwide chain so long to compete directly with Netflix that Hastings had started to think it would never happen. But in 2004, Blockbuster launched its own movie-by-mail service, giving Netflix the biggest battle of its young existence. Blockbuster eliminated late fees and copied Netflix's strategy, including video streaming, with the added advantage that its customers could combine the mail option with retail service at three thousand Blockbuster stores. Netflix couldn't match that, since it didn't have any stores. Many analysts predicted Netflix's demise, and its freshly minted stock took a temporary nosedive. But Netflix had some advantages, too. Its customers turned out to be more loyal than those at Blockbuster, where unforgiving late fees had left a deep legacy of bitterness, even after they were rescinded. And Netflix wasn't chained to a costly, outdated retail infrastructure, which turned out to be Blockbuster's undoing. Even though Blockbuster was run by sharp and experienced businesspeople, it clung too long to what it knew and ended up overcommitted to a failing strategy. Six years after Blockbuster first lunged after Netflix, it was Blockbuster's stock that crashed, as the once dominant movie chain drowned in debt and careened toward bankruptcy. When Blockbuster declared bankruptcy in 2010, Netflix became the leading firm in its industry.

By the middle of 2011, Netflix was becoming much more than a movie rental business. It was making distribution deals with Hollywood studios and expanding internationally, and starting to invest in original programming, almost like a TV network. Hastings now considered HBO a top competitor, along with a born-again Blockbuster emerging from Chapter 11 and companies operating low-tech video vending machines placed near many retail stores. It was amid this tumult of an industry being torn down and rebuilt that Netflix blundered into its Qwikster scheme. As Netflix struggled to quell the uproar, Hastings insisted that streaming was still the technology of the future. Netflix had simply moved too fast and forcefully, while badly misjudging what its own customers wanted. "We got overconfident," he said several months after the flap. "We berate ourselves for that lack of insight. But in three or five years we're not going to remember it."

Maybe. Hastings had learned to forgive himself and fix mistakes as quickly as possible, while staying alert for the next thing that could go wrong. He hoped to avoid future stumbles but knew there would probably be some. He might not even be running Netflix in three to five years. But he had learned that Rebounding wasn't something you did once, it was something you did whenever necessary. It was also a skill that made the risk of mistakes more tolerable, and therefore, perhaps, more likely. As Rebounding becomes more familiar, the challenge, sometimes, is convincing everybody else it's not that big a deal.

CHAPTER 11

WHAT TRUMPS PASSION

If you happened to be in Los Angeles in the early 1990s and you shopped at upscale grocery stores like Gelson's, you may have encountered a rangy, intense man in a white chef's apron peddling gourmet olive oil from a small table at the end of one of the aisles. There'd usually be a baguette cut into small chunks, with a toothpick sticking out of each piece, for easy dipping. The oil, called Evo, came in a handsome, wide-shouldered bottle with a cork—not a screw-on cap—sealed with wax and decorated with a fancy ribbon. If you asked where it came from, the man in the apron would enthusiastically explain that he blended it himself, traveling regularly to northern California to taste and select the best oils. Most customers who tried the oil balked at its twenty-dollar price, but if you were one of the splurgers who bought a bottle, you were unwittingly patronizing a culinary master who some food critics would regard a few years later as the best chef in America.

Thomas Keller reinvented fine dining when he opened the famous French Laundry restaurant in Napa Valley in 1994, to be followed by an equally esteemed sister restaurant in New York called Per Se. Food lovers waited months for a reservation to sample dishes they had never imagined, such as salmon tartare topped with crème fraîche and tucked inside a cracker that resembled a miniature ice-cream cone, and "macaroni and cheese" made with orzo pasta, mascarpone cheese, and lobster. The food was so captivating that diners paid upward of $300 per meal, usually with an ecstatic grin on their faces. Keller eventually built a prominent collection of restaurants around his luxe cuisine, with locations in Napa Valley, New York, Las Vegas, and Beverly Hills, a line of high-end knives and dinnerware, several bestselling cookbooks, and lucrative endorsement deals. Keller even created the namesake dish for the 2007 Pixar film *Ratatouille,* about an anthropomorphized rat in Paris who aspires to become a great chef. And the Thomas Keller Restaurant Group became a training ground for many future culinary stars, such as Grant Achatz in Chicago, Corey Lee in San Francisco, Jonathan Benno in New York, and Eric Ziebold in Washington, D.C. Keller accomplished all of that without a college degree, culinary education, or even a formal cooking class.

Yet his career as a chef was so zigzaggy for the first twenty years that before opening The French Laundry, Keller ended up unemployed in Los Angeles, with a limited set of options that made him feel grateful to be peddling olive oil to food shoppers. Over two decades in the kitchen, Keller had developed a rich and unique set of skills as a chef. But he had also flamed out half a dozen times, both as a hired chef working for others and as an entrepreneur running his own restaurant. From practically the day he started cooking, Keller never failed to make remarkable food that wowed the people who ate it. But he struggled to keep costs under control, manage his temper and impatience, balance his emotional love of food with the pragmatic requirements of business, and simply find the right outlet for his talents. Through recurring setbacks, Keller developed many of the finer attributes that other Rebounders learn. He began to understand the limits of his abilities, which made him more humble. He adjusted his thinking and began to contemplate possibilities he had once dismissed, which opened up new opportunities. He learned to keep moving when he hit a roadblock, instead of spending his time figuring out whom to blame or criticize.

For some Rebounders, such trials provide all the edge they need.

But for Keller, success still required an additional crucible that would test how badly he wanted to reach his goal. Starting The French Laundry required so much effort and determination that he might not have done it had he been able to visualize the whole ordeal in advance. By then, he had taken enough risks and burned through enough chances that he knew it might be his last shot, that he'd lose credibility for good if he made promises to partners and investors and failed one more time. When The French Laundry succeeded, he finally realized what differentiates high achievers from unfulfilled dreamers. "It's not about passion," he told me. "It's about desire. Passion ebbs and flows. I see the first stalk of asparagus in the spring, and I'm passionate about that. But at some point passion diminishes. What continues to drive you? What makes you look at that bundle of asparagus three weeks later, after the passion has diminished, and deal with it the way you dealt with the first bundle? It's desire. You wake up in the morning with that desire. When the passion's not there, it's desire that gets you through."

Keller had to learn whether he had desire himself, before he could tap it to help him become one of the most celebrated professionals in his field. He started in the restaurant business the way a lot of teenagers do—at the bottom, in the dish room. He was enchanted from the outset. "Putting dirty dishes in the rack, sliding them into the dish machine, and then forty-five seconds later they would come out clean. To me, that was magical," Keller told interviewer Charlie Rose in 2005. "It was so gratifying and satisfying to actually see results, immediate results from what you did." Keller's parents were divorced, and he lived with his mom, a restaurant manager in Florida who got him and an older brother cooking jobs at the various eateries she managed. After high school, Keller enrolled briefly in college, choosing psychology as a major—an inclination reflected throughout his career in his cerebral approach to food. But he left school when the chef abruptly quit at a Palm Beach restaurant that his mom was running, and she urgently needed a replacement. He took over the kitchen, despite limited experience, which is why he often says that he was a chef before he was a cook.

The restaurant business is notorious for rapid turnover and the nomadic lifestyle of those who enlist in it, and Keller began his culinary journey with the same improvisational wanderlust as many chefs before him. Keller left Florida for a while to check out New England, where he ended up spending a couple of summers cooking in Newport, Rhode Island. He was there to party as much as to cook, and it seemed like no big deal when he got fired from one position, then hired at another. But it turned out to be one of several serendipitous developments that would guide his uncharted career. He ended up working at a private club where a French chef, Roland Henin, became his mentor. Henin lent Keller a copy of the French cookbook *Ma Gastronomie* by Fernand Point, a legendary chef who opened one of France's landmark restaurants after World War II. *Ma Gastronomie* was as much a philosophical discourse on food as a guide to cooking. It contained no conventional recipes with the kinds of precise instructions common today—"sauté for 4 minutes in ¼ cup of melted butter on medium high"—but instead mixed cooking instruction and culinary history with Point's views on how food relates to life. Keller's girlfriend at the time noticed the borrowed book that he was reading and bought him his own copy, which he ended up taking with him everywhere. *Ma Gastronomie* became required reading for the chefs at Keller's restaurants, and Keller even had the bar top at Per Se inscribed with a quote from Point, translated from the original French: "One must read everything, see everything, hear everything, try everything, observe everything, in order to retain in the end, just a little bit."

Grand concepts were still far in Keller's future when he was working in Newport, however, and he returned to Florida with plans to team up with two others and open a restaurant in West Palm Beach that would capitalize on the growing popularity of jai alai, the fast-paced Spanish sport that features players in a three-walled court playing a game similar to squash, with glovelike wickets for catching and throwing the ball. Keller and his partners opened a restaurant called the Cobbley Nob close to the city's bustling jai alai complex, offering pricey, sophisticated food similar to what Keller had seen in Newport's upscale tourist restaurants. It was the wrong menu. The jai alai fans wanted burgers and hot dogs and draft beer, not steak Diane and sole Veronique and an extensive wine menu. The restaurant earned good reviews but folded after several months. Keller had put little money into the place, because he didn't have any, but he felt the pain of the failure nonetheless. He was the chef, after all, and the restaurant's closure meant his food had flopped. "I didn't have any equity in the restaurant, but I certainly had a lot of heart in it," he told me. "It's the heart part that is the most fragile. Money is one thing, but emotions are something else. That's where you really have to say, Is this really what I want to do?"

He got over it, and his growing reputation led him back north, where he worked summers running the kitchen at a small restaurant in Catskill, New York, and the rest of the year cooking with name-brand chefs at a swanky hotel in midtown Manhattan. He was gravitating toward French cuisine, and decided he needed to go to France to learn more. He lucked into a three-month job at Taillevent, the renowned Parisian establishment that had earned the Michelin Guide's rare and coveted three-star rating ten years in a row. He spent another eight months rotating among several other restaurants, learning techniques and sensibilities that would become hallmarks of his own cooking: Pay fanatical attention to detail. Use the freshest ingredients you can get your hands on, no matter how costly or inconvenient. Provide a delightful and memorable experience for the customer. They were the very things Fernand Point had written about in *Ma Gastronomie.*

Keller returned to New York a rising star, becoming the first American chef at La Reserve, a fixture in the city's growing lineup of world-class French restaurants. His ego, however, was swelling in equal proportion to his ability, and Keller insisted on a more contemporary interpretation of French cuisine than the owner wanted. A simmering disagreement developed between the two men, and when the owner appeared in the kitchen one evening, disrupting the flow of food preparation, Keller threw him out. Not surprisingly, it was Keller who was out a few days later, fired. Looking back, he regrets his arrogance but stands up for his principles. "I was a cocky twenty-eight-year-old," he said. "If everything goes well, the guest gets what he wants and it's a great day. If the cook burns a piece of fish, a waiter drops a plate, or the owner is in the kitchen, that's what makes me emotional, because there's some distraction."

Despite getting fired, Keller's reputation was growing, and after La Reserve, a successful New York restaurateur named Serge Raoul asked the talented, temperamental chef if he wanted to partner on a new restaurant. It was Keller's dream to own his own place, and he jumped at the chance. So in 1985, the two men opened Rakel—a combination of their last names, Raoul and Keller—a pricey, eighty-seat eatery where Keller was free to concoct the kinds of French-inspired masterpieces he envisioned. His food began to earn national acclaim. *Food & Wine* magazine named him Best New American Chef, and local reviewers gloried in the delectable and carefully architected creations that emerged from Keller's kitchen. But Rakel's business plan had a few holes in it. Its location near Manhattan's West Village neighborhood was meant to capture financial-industry foodies, advertising executives, and other big spenders able to foot the hefty bills at Rakel, and for a while it did. But the 1987 stock market crash shrunk a lot of Manhattan wallets, and an expected migration of well-heeled firms to the area never happened. By 1990, Raoul had decided that Rakel needed to become a lower-priced bistro, to appeal to a broader base of customers. He suggested renaming it Café Rakel or something similar, to signal that the prices had fallen and the food had become more approachable. That made financial sense, but Keller wasn't interested in turning out glorified pub food, so he parted ways with Raoul. Rakel ended up as a critical success but a financial failure, like a beloved novel that doesn't sell or a sleeper film that critics love but moviegoers can't relate to.

For Keller, it was a comedown that revealed the limits of his own abilities. Cooking, he knew. But there was far more to running a successful restaurant than turning out great dishes. "There are so many things that impact a failure," he told me. "I may have been overanxious. The other mistake I made was that all of the responsibility and hopes and dreams were laid on my shoulders. As a chef, my singular focus should be on the kitchen. I shouldn't be concerning myself with the financials on a day-to-day basis or running the dining room.

To support a restaurant you need an accomplished, knowledgeable chef, a really good bookkeeper or accountant, and, of course, somebody capable of running a dining room." As Keller became successful, he looked back on his many setbacks as parts of a continuum that helped him find his way. But failures are never stepping-stones just because they're failures. They point forward only if you're able to learn from them and resist the natural impulse to direct blame and indignation at somebody else. Like other Rebounders, Keller got better after failures because he recognized his own limitations, and improved on them.

Leaving Rakel was a pivotal career decision, the kind that many people confront when faced with a choice between something safe and predictable, and something exciting but risky and undefined. Keller could have stayed at the new incarnation of the restaurant and compromised his ambitions, but instead he chose to keep following his true desire—to create sublime, original dining experiences—even though he had nowhere to go. "The choice was to do bistro food or move out," he said. "I could have stayed, but I would have compromised my true goal, my true vision, which was fine dining. I'm a Francophile, and I really wanted to do that model of fine dining that I've studied all my life." Keller's desire and vision landed him in a rut. He wanted to start over at another restaurant and fix the things he had flubbed the last time. But it was the early '90s, in the middle of a recession, when money was scarce for a risky venture like a restaurant. Keller had also developed a reputation as a spectacular but emotional chef who couldn't control his food costs, and investing in him didn't seem like the wisest move in a weak economy. Instead of landing another restaurant deal, Keller consulted for a couple of restaurants, making more money than he ever had but finding the work miserable, because there was no pride of ownership and he wasn't creating anything or satisfying anybody other than a few people writing him checks. It felt like mercenary, soulless work.

Since arriving in New York, Keller had figured it was the only place in the United States where a committed chef could turn out food on par with the culinary masters in France. But he couldn't find the right opportunity in New York, so he had to rethink that.

Through his many jobs in New York, he had gotten to know dozens of restaurateurs who operated all over the country, including Los Angeles. He also had a few friends who had recently moved to California, and they urged him to come out west and give cooking a try there. A boutique hotel called Checkers in downtown L.A. needed an executive chef, and Keller fit the bill. He had won several awards by then and was known for his inspired French cuisine, which would help draw food lovers to a hotel that mainly catered to business travelers and could use more local buzz. For Keller, it seemed like a chance to capitalize on some of the things he had learned from Rakel's demise, since he'd be responsible for managing not just the food in the restaurant, but the room service, private parties, and everything related to food service throughout the hotel. He'd get deeper management experience, which would help him better run a restaurant of his own someday. So in 1991 he moved to Los Angeles.

Like Rakel, his gig at Checkers seemed to go well for a while. His food earned strong reviews and did, in fact, draw diners from outlying areas. But it soon turned into another painful learning experience he would have preferred to avoid. As executive chef, he spent a lot of time in meetings talking about occupancy rates, linen costs, and other stuff that had little to do with food. Despite some positive word of mouth, the hotel struggled. A big construction project was going on next door, with pile drivers, dust, and traffic barriers forming an industrial cloud around the hotel's intimate ambience. On the other side of the hotel was Pershing Square, which had become a hangout for homeless people. Despite the great food, Checkers had trouble drawing locals interested in a relaxing meal. The hotel owner who had hired Keller finally sold the property to a German consortium that wanted to slash costs and had little patience for a finicky chef insisting on the best of everything. When the Germans tried to short-change some of the artisanal suppliers Keller had come to rely on for lobsters, foie gras, produce, and many of the other items in his kitchen, it offended his sense of integrity, and he let them know it. They fired Keller within a few months, but if they hadn't, he probably would have quit.

Another flameout. Up until then, every setback in Keller's career had been explainable in some specific way. The location wasn't quite right. The economy was on the fritz. There was a strategic disagreement between owner and chef. The staff didn't gel. He could explain away this failure, too, if he wanted. But as he neared forty, Keller put it all together and knew he was hitting too many dead ends. He realized that ignorance played a role in all of his stumbles. At the Cobbley Nob, he had poorly predicted what potential customers would want. At La Reserve, the fancy French place in Manhattan, he had misjudged the owner. At Rakel, he had overestimated his skills as a restaurateur because he dismissed the importance of management and accounting. Now, he had gone to Los Angeles seeking opportunities he couldn't find in New York, while failing to foresee the tedium of the job and the vulnerabilities of his employer. "I needed something I could sink my teeth into," he recalled. "I'd had situations in my career where part of it was my fault and part of it was just circumstances. I could have survived the stock market crash and stayed with Serge, I could have been more amenable to the Germans on discarding these purveyors. But I always felt I needed to maintain my integrity and my standards, and if I started to compromise those, then I'd have nothing left."

He didn't have all that much left as it was. On the plus side, Keller could count some modest savings, a big stack of glowing press reviews, and a powerful vision for the food he wanted to create. But he was also unemployed in a city where he didn't know that many people. Keller decided to start the olive oil company to generate some income and bide his time. He got to know the distributors in northern California and bottled the oil himself, setting up a one-man production line in a part of a warehouse offered by a friend who rented the space. The business was modestly successful, and Keller added vinegar to his little product line, while also cooking at private parties to bring in extra cash. He earned enough to get by, since his rent was relatively cheap, he drove a fifteen-year-old BMW, and he didn't have a family to support. But it was hardly the career Keller envisioned for himself. The risks he had taken were not paying off, and there were many times when cooking bourgeois bistro fare for steady pay, back in New York, seemed like it might be pretty good work, compared to the magnificent, but imaginary, cuisine he prepared in his dreams.

Keller still plotted his fine-dining scheme, however, and he spotted an opportunity during a trip to Napa Valley to visit his friend Jonathan Waxman, a celebrated chef who operated successful restaurants in New York and Los Angeles and was building a Napa restaurant called Table 29. Waxman mentioned to Keller that there was a little place for sale in nearby Yountville called The French Laundry, operated as a popular, comfort food joint by a couple named Don and Sally Schmitt. The property had actually been a steam laundry once, which is where the name came from. Don Schmitt had been mayor of Yountville, and the restaurant became a kind of homey mixing place where locals would go to catch up on area news, and tourists would stop by to absorb some local flavor. Keller checked it out on a Sunday, when the restaurant was closed and the Schmitts weren't there. But he didn't need persuading. "The stars aligned," he said. "This was the place I'd been trying to get to. It was perfect. Small. Sixty seats. A beautiful property. It had so much potential. I said, I can really do this."

He called the Schmitts and asked if they'd sell it to him. They said sure—for $1.2 million. Keller had no business partners at the time, and practically no money, so when he met with the Schmitts in person, he explained his background, showed them all his press clippings, and told them about his olive oil company. They were impressed, but the price was still $1.2 million, which Keller didn't have. So he asked them to give him some time to form a business plan and see if he could raise it. The Schmitts were planning to retire and move a bit farther north, but they were in no hurry, so they said okay, they could wait a couple of weeks while he looked into financing.

While Keller raced home, his mind raced faster, formulating a business plan that would get the ball rolling before somebody else jumped on his irresistible property. He put some slides together in a binder and anxiously showed the rudimentary business plan to two friends, both of whom owned Napa Valley wineries and were successful businessmen. His restaurant would feature elaborate food bordering on culinary sculpture, with contemporary twists on the classic French cuisine he had studied and practiced for years. Ingredients would come from the best possible sources and be meticulously prepared. There would be playful, inventive variations on traditional American dishes, like peas and carrots and peanut butter and jelly, that would surprise and delight his customers. They'd leave craving more. There was no need for a clever new name, because the existing name, The French Laundry, nearly perfectly evoked the elegant and rustic Old-World ambience he was after. As for prices, they'd be set to cover costs, and if they were high, well, they were high.

One of Keller's friends told him it was a terrible idea. The food would be too fancy and expensive, even for Napa Valley, and he'd end up losing all the money he invested. Keller's other friend told him he might have a shot, and suggested ways to refine the plan, which, of course, is what Keller wanted to hear. Keller's reaction typified the phenomenon that psychologists call confirmation bias—he rejected the rejection and eagerly put his faith in the point of view that aligned most closely with his own. More often than not, that's a mistake that allows people to overestimate their own abilities and discount risks that eventually do them in. But in this case, it turned out to be a pardonable sin. Emboldened by the positive feedback, Keller committed to his quest, calling the Schmitts and telling them he'd put down a deposit, which normally, in a real estate transaction of that size, would be 10 percent, or $120,000. But Keller had nowhere near that much. He asked if they'd accept $5,000 and give him ninety days to come up with the balance. It was unorthodox, but they agreed. Something about Keller and his infectious enthusiasm convinced them.

It was the quality that Keller would later identify as desire, and he would need it more than ever before. Keller had done a terrific job of educating himself, refining his skills until they rivaled those of the best chefs anywhere. He had overcome his own preconceptions to go where the opportunities seemed to be. He took risks and didn't wallow in regret if his bold moves fizzled. He learned from his mistakes instead of blaming others and changed his own behavior when it seemed to be holding him back. But all of that wasn't quite enough to reach the goal he had set. There was one final challenge: raising the money to open The French Laundry, without the network of bankers, wealthy friends, and financial enablers who typically fund such projects. Keller knew he was at a crossroads that would determine the rest of his career. "It was my last chance," he said. "I told myself that if I don't make it on this one, I'll go to Tahiti and live on the beach. It's not going to work for me."

Keller hastily built out his business plan until it was three hundred pages long. One of his chef friends introduced him to a prominent lawyer, Bob Sutcliffe, who specialized in startups and venture funding, and after hearing Keller's plan, he said he could help—for $60,000. Keller opened his briefcase, took out a bottle of his Evo olive oil, sat it on the lawyer's desk, and said, "I don't have any money. But what I do have is this olive oil." While Sutcliffe contemplated Keller's sanity, the chef explained that he was running his tiny one-man company to help fund the restaurant. He was religiously committed to The French Laundry, and the olive oil was a token of that commitment. Keller then asked Sutcliffe to help him on a contingency basis, with his fee paid once the business was up and running. The lawyer relented, and said he'd do it, for $5,000 up front. Keller made judicious use of his credit cards and drew cash advances over the next two weeks, finally presenting Sutcliffe with the money. Sutcliffe condensed his business plan to a fraction of its original size, getting it into a shape that would be presentable to investors. Then the salesmanship began.

Despite all his experience with restaurants, Keller knew next to nothing about how to finance one, and most of his professional connections were people who handled food, not money. He had only a few thousand dollars himself, plus about $25,000 he was able to borrow on credit cards. The plan was to raise $600,000 from private investors, and $600,000 from banks, so Keller began to call everybody he knew, and everybody they knew, looking for backers. A few of his closest professional contacts said sure, they'd invest, and Sutcliffe found some investors, too. But that still left Keller short of the total amount he needed. He quickly sped down the list of people he knew, and ended up cold-calling friends of friends and others he heard of who might be inclined to help fund a restaurant. One share in The French Laundry would cost $20,000, and he'd break shares down into any fraction necessary to suit investors. One person agreed to pony up $500—one-fortieth of a share—which Keller happily accepted. As he slowly rounded up investors, the initial ninety days the Schmitts had given him came and went. They agreed to another ninety days, then another.

Such a big chunk of money turned out to be awfully hard to come by for a chef with a spotty record of success, and the pressure built. One day Keller read a motivating article in *The New York Times,* so he clipped the headline and taped it to his desk. "Having the Dream Is Hard. Living It Is Harder," it read. It wasn't about restaurants, but that, in a way, was the point: No matter what your dream, attaining it could be damn hard work, and that was what made strivers different, because they understood the price of success and didn't expect shortcuts. I asked Keller if the whole process made him feel discouraged. "I wasn't discouraged," he said. "I was terrified. The terror motivated me. Every morning I would get up with such anxiety, thinking, I have no money. I'm struggling. There are a dozen chefs I know who would buy that restaurant in a second. So every morning I'm just dying to get this deal done and find some security. And that phrase was right there. Every day I'd call people and I'd be looking at that, knowing that this is my dream and it's really difficult. If I don't show determination and desire, it's not going to happen."

A wealthy investor approached Keller one day with an offer that would neatly finalize the deal. He said he would finance the whole operation, with no need for banks or dozens of other investors, on one condition: He wanted half of the take from anything Keller did in the future. Keller didn't like the idea at all, but he had been trying to raise funds for nearly a year and asking the Schmitts for an extension every few months. They were getting antsy to retire by then, so he felt obligated to tell them about the offer, which would let him close the deal promptly if they needed him to. The Schmitts had taken to Keller and his quest by then, and decided to give him more time to do it his way. That motivated Keller more. "They really believed in me," he said. "They went out on a limb for me. I didn't want to disappoint them."

While trolling for investors, Keller applied for a bank loan for the other $600,000, bringing his business plan and his portfolio of press clips to the loan officers at Bank of America and giving them the same pitch he had given the Schmitts early on. The bankers checked his background and found that Keller was liable for $90,000 in back taxes, due to a payroll issue from his days at Rakel. Keller wasn't even aware of that, but he called his old partner, Serge Raoul, who eventually took care of the tax liability, absolving Keller and allowing the bank loan to go forward. To create a cushion and allow for a few renovations, on top of the purchase price, Keller applied for a Small Business Administration Loan, which turned out to be immensely complicated since he had to account for fifteen business partners at that point, plus a commercial bank loan. The paperwork almost suffocated him, but by then he felt like a humbled Hercules carrying out his twelve labors, so he plowed through it and got the loan.

In the spring of 1994, Keller got a phone call he had begun to think would never come. A Sacramento allergist named Garland Stroup had been to one of the open houses Keller hosted on Sundays at The French Laundry (which the Schmitts still owned), to taste Keller's salmon tartare cornets, drink some of the wine donated by Keller's winery friends, and hear the determined chef's vision for the restaurant he wanted to open. Stroup had thought it over, and decided he was willing to invest. He ended up purchasing four shares, investing $80,000, which put Keller over the top. He had his $1.2 million, plus a little bit more to renovate the place before opening the restaurant. To reach his target, Keller had called four hundred potential investors and ended up with fifty-two partners, whose investments ranged from $500 to $80,000. Finally, he had learned something about financing a restaurant. The whole process had taken eighteen months, far longer than he ever imagined. It would never have happened if not for the Schmitts' patience and commitment, Serge Raoul's forbearance, and dozens of lesser serendipitous events that had led Keller toward Napa Valley since he first picked up a spatula in Florida. Ignorance had been a liability in some of his earlier ventures, but it became a blessing in Napa Valley, because Keller never foresaw the whole torturous road that led to The French Laundry; his vision extended only to the next hairpin turn, which he thought he could manage, and then to the turn after that. "Ignorance caused us to lose our business at the Cobbley Nob," he said. "But ignorance isn't always a bad thing. Ignorance can be bliss. It helped me gain The French Laundry."

On July 6, 1994, Thomas Keller's The French Laundry opened for business. A lot went wrong. Keller hadn't cooked in a restaurant in more than two years. He had been able to finance minor renovations, but was mostly working with the kitchen as the Schmitts had left it. There weren't enough pans. The rhythm in the kitchen was more like slapstick than the ballet Keller has seen during his sojourn in France. The service was spotty. But one important thing went right: No critics showed up on opening night. They started to come on the second night, however, when Keller and his crew were ironing out the kinks and starting to put on a glorious show. And the critics were mightily impressed. John Mariani of *Esquire,* one of the first critics to sample Keller's Napa fare, declared The French Laundry one of the ten best new restaurants of the year. Many similar accolades followed. The James Beard Foundation named Keller the Best Chef in America in 1996. Influential critic Ruth Reichl of *The New York Times* told her readers that The French Laundry was "the most exciting place to eat in the United States." When the vaunted Michelin Guide began rating American restaurants, The French Laundry earned the top three-star rating immediately, as did Keller's Per Se restaurant in New York, which opened in 2004—making Keller the only chef ever to operate two three-star restaurants in different cities. Perhaps the most emphatic evidence of Keller's success were the prices at The French Laundry, which started at a relatively modest $49 for a five-course prix fixe dinner in 1994. Keller eventually expanded that to a nine-course meal that cost $270. Nobody complained, and it became even harder to get a reservation.

Thomas Keller obviously has many things in common with other Rebounders, and to his own mind, the most important quality of people trying to accomplish difficult things is desire. But there's another key requirement that's a corollary of desire: time. Food critics and fellow chefs clearly regard Keller as a culinary genius. But that wasn't nearly enough to make him successful. If the 10,000-hour rule applied, then Keller would have succeeded at Rakel in the 1980s, because by then he had been cooking full-time for more than ten years straight, continually learning more and apprenticing himself to the some of the best chefs in the world. But that wasn't enough either. By the time Keller got fired at Checkers, his experience, in fact, probably amounted to twenty thousand or even thirty thousand hours. And yet, there were vast amounts he still didn't know about the very thing he dreamed of doing: opening and running a top-shelf restaurant.

Like Lucinda Williams, Keller simply had to keep plying his trade, and keep getting better, until he was ready. Like a lot of people, he thought he was ready before he really was, which helped keep him going because he was always sure success was right around the corner. It was fortunate that he didn't know how many corners he'd have to turn before he found it. But who does? Shortcuts to success might be satisfying, for those able to pull them off. Longcuts, however, are often the only way. People who take the scenic route don't always arrive as quickly as they would like, but they usually look back on the journey with fond memories.

CHAPTER 12

OWN THE SUCK

Sometimes a setback is an inconvenience. Sometimes it's a major disruption. Sometimes it's even bigger than that. Severe hardships can be the toughest tests we face in life, capable of neutralizing ambition and wrecking years of careful planning. People who overcome traumatic adversities often do it by applying habits learned through lesser setbacks. In the same way that small triumphs can help build incremental layers of confidence and toughness, overcoming major hardships can generate newfound capabilities that may not emerge any other way.

One day toward the end of 2004, 36-year-old Tammy Duckworth awoke in a hospital room, wondering where she was and what had happened. As consciousness came and went, she heard doctors and nurses talking about a helicopter crash. It came back to her in fragmented, terrifying snapshots. Iraq. Heat. Sky. Dust. A deafening flash. Screeching machinery. Blood. Fear. Something terrible had happened, and she had been in the middle of it. For days, in the hospital, she felt an overwhelming sense of dread as she grasped at comprehension. But over the following months, Duckworth would transform shock, horror, pain, and a crippling new disability into an intensified sense of purpose. Modest goals grew into more ambitious ones. Her pace of accomplishment accelerated. Barriers to advancement that had once seemed imposing no longer got in the way. Above all, Duckworth developed the confidence to try bold and difficult things because the risk of failing no longer intimidated her.

Captain Tammy Duckworth, call sign Mad Dog 06, was a Black Hawk helicopter pilot assigned to the Illinois National Guard's 106th Aviation Battalion when it was sent to Iraq in 2004. Her unit was based northwest of Baghdad, near the notoriously dangerous Sunni Triangle, during a time of intense fighting. The Black Hawk was a utility helicopter used for transporting troops and supplies, and it could be vulnerable to ground fire if hovering or flying at low altitude. It was the same type of chopper that got shot down during the Battle of Mogadishu in Somalia in 1993, an event that inspired the book and movie *Black Hawk Down.* By late 2004, Iraq had become far bloodier than Mogadishu, with more than thirteen hundred American troops killed and ten thousand injured in the campaign that had begun with the U.S. invasion the year before. As Duckworth's unit arrived in Iraq, the violence was getting worse. American forces had become engaged in an open-ended war against insurgents and terrorists who were hard to identify and maddeningly difficult to stamp out. The Sunni Triangle, a swath of desert the size of New Jersey, had become the hive of the insurgency, with brutal urban combat in cities like Fallujah and Baqubah.

Duckworth knew the risks. When first sent to Iraq in March 2004, she figured she'd either come home at the end of her one-year tour completely intact or die in the line of duty. Surviving an injury wasn't a possibility she thought much about. "My biggest fear was that I was going to burn to death in my aircraft," she told me. "In aviation, throughout the course of your career, you're going to know people killed in accidents. I had friends who had burned to death, being trapped in their aircraft. You don't usually survive an accident." Through the first eight months of her tour, she had been fired on a few times, but never hit. She spent more time than she preferred on the ground, helping plan and oversee missions, which reduced her exposure to hostile fire. But she had gone to Iraq to fly, not to give briefings in a fortified command post. So she was enthused when assigned to fly an all-day mission on November 12, 2004. As a captain, she'd be the senior member of her four-person crew.

Duckworth and her crew started flying around 7:00 A.M., ferrying troops and supplies around Baghdad in support of a big battle raging near Fallujah, about forty miles west of the Iraqi capital. Everybody was on high alert, but the day had been uneventful until late afternoon, when the crew wrapped up the last of their logistical runs and began heading back to their base. When they were just ten minutes from landing, Duckworth heard the alarming metallic sound of small-arms fire strafing the side of her aircraft: *tat-tat-tat-tat-tat.* Almost simultaneously, a blinding fireball tore through the floor of the helicopter's right front quarter, where her feet were, and blew straight through the top of the aircraft. Duckworth later learned what it was: a rocket-propelled grenade, powerful enough to disable a tank and destroy a helicopter if it hit in the right place. Duckworth instinctively tried to press the foot pedals that controlled the helicopter, to get it on the ground. But the pedals had been blown off. So had most of her right leg, and her left leg below the knee. Her right arm was shattered and useless. Body armor had protected her vital organs, and while her face was somewhat burned, the ballistic shield affixed to her helmet had deflected much of the heat and shrapnel from the RPG, possibly preventing her from being blinded.

Somehow the Black Hawk continued to fly, but it wasn't Duckworth who was flying it anymore. The pilot in the left-hand seat, Chief Warrant Officer Dan Milberg, had taken over the aircraft. He had been scorched by the blast but was otherwise unharmed, and the RPG had missed the helicopter's rotors and other vital machinery, even though it wrecked the avionics. Milberg quickly landed in an overgrown field. Tall elephant grass suddenly poked through the hole in the bottom of the helicopter, filling the cabin on Duckworth's side. Insurgents would often race to capture the crew of an aircraft if they managed to shoot one down, since Americans were prized—and usually doomed—captives. But the crew of a second chopper that was part of the same mission immediately called for help, and two more helicopters quickly arrived and began providing cover overhead. Duckworth's other two crewmates, Staff Sergeant Chris Fierce and Specialist Kurt Hannemann, were injured, but Fierce started putting out fires as Hannemann got into defensive posture, in case any ground attackers arrived. It took just a few minutes for the crew of the second chopper to land in the field, get Duckworth and her crew onboard, and head toward the safety of the base.

Duckworth spent the next eight days heavily sedated, as doctors worked to save her life. After emergency surgery in Iraq, the army transported her to the Walter Reed Army Medical Center in Washington, D.C., which had become a huge convalescent ward for soldiers recovering from injuries sustained in Iraq and Afghanistan. Duckworth's husband, Bryan Bowlsbey, was a fellow Army National Guard officer who happened to be in Maryland for his brother's wedding, and he was there to meet his unconscious wife when she arrived. Duckworth's father had recently suffered a heart attack and was in the hospital in Hawaii, where her parents lived, but her mother flew in, and other friends and relatives began to show up. Bowlsbey began emailing updates on her condition to dozens of friends and colleagues. When the requests for information became overwhelming, he started to post updates to a website that friends and family could monitor.

As Duckworth fitfully regained consciousness, she didn't know she had lost her legs, partly because of phantom pains in appendages that her brain thought were still there, even though they weren't. Her husband and one of the doctors told her the awful truth as soon as she seemed awake enough to comprehend it. "She received the news with poise and stoicism," her husband wrote on the website. Though she struggled to express it, something bothered her even more than the news about her legs. During brief, foggy moments of awareness, she heard doctors and nurses refer over and over to a crash. To aviators, the word crash suggests that an aircraft got destroyed because of poor flying or a mistake by the pilot. That was a devastating thought. Duckworth knew her helicopter had been hit by hostile fire, and she remembered landing. But everything else was fuzzy. If the helicopter had truly crashed, that meant she must have screwed up somehow, making her responsible for a blown emergency landing. Her crew chief, Sergeant Fierce, had been seriously injured, nearly losing one of his own legs. She felt it was her fault. "I was devastated," Duckworth recalled. "The worst thing any soldier can find out is that they let down their buddies. It meant that I had failed as a pilot. That I didn't do a good job flying, and crashed the aircraft. That was probably the furthest down I've ever been in my life."

While coming to terms with her injuries and everything else about her condition, Duckworth tried to conceal the shame she felt about the helicopter crash. But it leaked out. One day in the intensive care unit, tears were rolling down her cheeks, and her husband quickly tried to console her. "Honey," he said, thinking she was mourning the loss of her legs, "everything's going to be fine. You're alive. They've got all these therapies now. We've got lives in front of us."

"I'm not worried about that," she said, sobbing. "I let down my guys. I crashed the aircraft. It's my fault. How am I going to face my crew? How am I going to face myself?"

"What are you talking about?" Bowlsbey asked, perplexed.

She explained how she didn't remember all the details, but figured that while landing, she must have rolled the aircraft, causing her own injuries and hurting her crewmates as well. Her husband explained that the facts were quite different. The RPG had destroyed the controls on her side of the helicopter, and while she might have thought she was flying it after the grenade hit, she wasn't. The other pilot, Dan Milberg, landed the chopper, which didn't roll. Then Milberg carried her out of the chopper and into the field. Fierce had been injured by the blast from the RPG, not by a crash landing. He was likely to recover. To completely convince her, Bowlsbey emailed her unit back in Iraq, and they sent a photo of the wrecked helicopter, showing the extensive damage caused by the projectile. When Duckworth saw that, she realized that Fierce's wounds and the lost aircraft weren't the result of poor performance in the cockpit.

A few weeks later, the army official who had been running the Baghdad emergency room where Duckworth underwent her first surgery tracked her down at Walter Reed, when he made a trip there. She didn't remember him, but he had a vivid memory of her. "You came into my emergency room giving orders," he told her, "propped up on your one arm, saying, 'I want the status of my crew.' And, 'How are my men?' I had no idea how you could be alive and awake and talking to us, because you had no legs and you were white as a sheet and you had no blood in you. And I put you out. I just wanted you to know that."

Duckworth had no recollection of that, but hearing it made everything easier. "That was a defining moment," she told me. "Knowing that until I died, literally, I was doing my job, looking after my men. I was living up to the codes and standards of being a soldier and an officer. I didn't let my men down. The relief was tremendous."

Duckworth had never experienced personal trauma or anything remotely close. But she still felt like she knew what she needed to do in order to recover. When she was finally able to speak, after waking up in the hospital, the first thing she said to her husband was, "I love you. Put me to work." Like James Blake, Jack Bogle, and many other Rebounders, she had learned early on that hard work was a reliable formula for overcoming challenges, even when she lacked other skills that might have made success easier. Duckworth and her brother Tom had grown up overseas, in places like Jakarta, Bangkok, and Singapore. Her father had been a career serviceman who landed on Okinawa during World War II as a terrified sixteen-year-old marine, and later transferred to the army, where he became an officer and fought in the Vietnam War. For most of her life, Duckworth had called her stoic father "Sir," even after he retired from the military and worked as a civilian for the United Nations and several multinational companies. Her mother was an ethnic Chinese woman who had grown up in Thailand, and was a "tiger mother" long before the term became trendy. She insisted that her daughter excel, even though she wasn't a naturally gifted student. Duckworth earned mostly As in school—but mainly because she did four to five hours of homework every night. As a kid, she learned how to work through intimidating challenges by setting a series of manageable, intermediate goals—breaking a thick schoolbook down into several ten-page segments, for example. That simple habit stuck with her when she joined the army. During road marches, she'd sometimes volunteer to carry the unit's radio or its M-60 machine gun, along with her own weapon and thirty-pound rucksack, just to prove she was as tough as her male colleagues. Since she weighed only about 120 pounds, the heavy load would leave her struggling. "I was never the fast finisher," she said. "I would tell myself, Okay, I'm going to go to that tree. And when I get to the tree, I'm going to go to the next thing. I'd usually finish in the rear of the formation."

That stepwise mentality helped her get through flight school and, ironically, put her in the cockpit of the doomed Black Hawk years later. When she got to flight school in 1993, Duckworth knew she needed to get assigned to the Black Hawk, the army's frontline helicopter, if she wanted a career as an aviator. But only a few of those slots were available. Most of the students would get assigned to the UH-1 "Huey," an older and less capable chopper the army was phasing out. She asked the sergeant major in charge of assignments what it would take to get one of the Black Hawk slots. He ticked off all the technical material she'd need to master and told her she'd also need to demonstrate crack flying skills and graduate at or near the top of her class. So in addition to the training missions and classroom instruction, Duckworth logged three or four additional hours in the flight simulator every night, racking up more simulator time than anybody who had gone through that particular flight school. She scored highest in her class on the check ride, the detailed flight test that comes at the end of a key part of the program, earning the coveted Black Hawk assignment. Duckworth was the only woman in the class, and when another student suggested that she must have curried favor with the instructors, the class leader—a grizzled veteran who had commanded a tank company during Operation Desert Storm—shut him up. "She's been in the simulator every night," he snapped. "If you'd been in the simulator every night, you'd get a good score, too. So back off."

Duckworth relied on that old habit of setting attainable, intermediate goals almost from the moment she awoke in the hospital. A few days after the attack, she developed an unusual allergic reaction to the morphine that doctors were giving her. One of the doctors told her husband that he had read about patients who were "narcotic-naïve," which meant their bodies rejected opiates, such as morphine, typically used as painkillers. The doc had never seen such a case, though; most people had some exposure to narcotics—often through recreational use—that conditioned their bodies to the kinds of chemicals administered for medical reasons. Duckworth, however, was so straitlaced that she had never tried any kind of drugs—even though she went to college at the University of Hawaii and had friends who grew pot in their closets. "I should have smoked a few joints in college," she joked later. "I would have had a better time."

It was anything but funny, however, when she had to switch to a different painkiller, because she had to be completely weaned off one medication before doctors could administer another. That forced her to endure five murderous days when she'd essentially be on no pain medication at all. "I went through five days of extreme, excruciating pain," she told me. "It took literally everything I had to breathe and to keep going. I wasn't sure I was going to make it through each day." But she broke each day down into smaller segments, and she felt sure she could make it through each minute, so she battled the pain by looking at a big clock on the wall and counting to sixty as each minute ticked by. At first, she counted "one dead Iraqi, two dead Iraqis, three dead Iraqis. . . ." But then she realized she was yielding to rage, and besides, it wasn't a typical Iraqi who had shot her legs off with an RPG. It was a bloodthirsty militant who may not even have been an Iraqi. So she counted "one dead mujahideen, two dead mujahideen . . . ," but that wasn't right either: The mujahideen were a brand of Islamic fighters from an earlier era, not from Iraq. The whole tiring thought process drained her anger a little, and she just started to count "one one thousand, two one thousand. . . ."

That worked well enough, except there were still moments when the pain was so crushing that it took all of her strength just to breathe. At one point, she knew that even counting to sixty might sap her of the energy she needed to stay alive. "Unless I shut down, I was going to die," she recalled. "I couldn't last another sixty seconds.

So I looked at my husband and said, 'I'm not going to make it if I don't shut down. I'm circling the wagons and I'll be back.' " Her panicked husband thought she was giving up and telling him she was about to die. But Duckworth did as she promised, conking out for a while, then waking up a few hours later.

Duckworth began taking the other small steps that would help her recover while still in intensive care. One of the nurses told her she needed to start rehabilitation right away and asked what parts of her body she was able to move. At the time, Duckworth didn't even have the strength to push the electronic button that would deliver more painkiller if she needed it. But she figured out that she could move her left wrist. So that became her first rehabilitation exercise. She'd move her left wrist, in three sets of ten repetitions, the same sort of regimen as if she were lifting weights or doing pushups. When she left the ICU after a couple weeks, she began to work intensively with physical therapists—known as "physical terrorists" to the many wry patients at Walter Reed—even though doctors were still rebuilding her right arm and she had several more surgeries to endure. Some goals were modest, like regaining enough use of her right arm to tie a ponytail. She had to learn how to get into an electric wheelchair, motor around in it, and get in and out of the shower. She wanted to drive again. And right away, she wanted to know what it would take to pilot a helicopter with artificial legs. The answer started with a lot of mundane, and often painful, exercises. She welcomed them, doing four repetitions if the therapist told her to do three, and adding weight or resistance on her own whenever she felt she could move to a higher level. The sooner she recovered, the sooner specialists would be able to fit her for prosthetics, and that was the path back toward the life she wanted. "Rehabilitation was my new mission," she said.

Duckworth asked her husband to hang a copy of the Soldier's Creed, a statement of principles the army requires all soldiers to memorize during basic training, near her bed. It's common to hear members of the military, brimming with can-do determination, insist that "failure is not an option." But the Soldier's Creed contains a different idea. It says, in part, this:

I will always place the mission first.
I will never accept defeat.
I will never quit.
I will never leave a fallen comrade.

The creed, notably, doesn't say, "I will never fail." Instead, it says, "I will never accept defeat," no doubt because there are many failures in military affairs, which is often the art of accomplishing the difficult. Defeat would be yielding to those failures and giving up. Duckworth read the creed often, especially during agonizing moments when she was on the verge of blacking out from the pain. It helped remind her that her recovery was her new mission, and that soldiers don't quit. "There were a lot of times when I couldn't even read down that list," she said. "You've got to find your personal motivation, and that was mine."

The atmosphere at Walter Reed helped Duckworth overcome moments of despair and stay focused on rebuilding her life. The army fit amputees with prosthetics more quickly than most civilian care centers, as part of the emphasis on purposeful action that's meant to raise the odds of a successful rehabilitation. Within six weeks she got her first set of artificial legs and started doing the intense training it would take to learn how to walk on them—part of her ongoing mission. She also benefited from the camaraderie with other patients, many of them fellow amputees. Injured soldiers practiced the same edgy banter in the hospital as they did in the field, and it was oddly comforting. For a while, the patient in the therapy bed next to Duckworth was a triple amputee who had lost both legs and an arm. If Duckworth had a down day, he'd chide her: "What, you feel bad because you have no legs? Gee, you call yourself an amputee? You've only lost two limbs." Others would joke about the doctors messing up their tattoos when cutting off their legs. Duckworth got into the spirit of the macabre humor, sometimes wearing T-shirts that read, "Dude, where's my leg?" Or, "Lucky for me, he's an ass man." When humor didn't lift her spirits, she'd look around the ward and realize there was always somebody worse off, like brain-injured patients or others who had been even more incapacitated than her. "On the days when you were just exhausted and you didn't want to do any more and you were grumpy and whiny and bitchy, all you had to do was look over and there was somebody else struggling," she said. "You'd realize, I just have to shut up and do this."

Walter Reed also had "peer visitors" who would show up voluntarily to chat with the patients and give them a glimpse of life after recovery. She got to know Tom Porter, a Korean War veteran, who was tall and confident and erect and usually toured the ward with his wife, Eleanor. Porter would make small talk, and after earning a bit of trust, he'd reveal that he was a double amputee standing on artificial legs. "I lost my legs when I was twenty," he told Duckworth. "I've had a family. I've had a business. I have grandkids and great-grandkids. I got this pretty thing here"—pointing to Eleanor—"to marry me after I lost my legs. I've lived more without my legs than with my legs, and my life has been great."

Those fellow survivors helped Duckworth believe that she, too, could have a rich life, whether disabled or not. "My peer visitors showed me that there was a way out," she explained. When you first wake up with the amputations and the pain, you're in this hole. Your peer visitor, your buddy, climbs into the hole with you and basically says, I know the way out. He doesn't carry you. He shows you the way out and you walk out with him."

As she recovered, Duckworth got drawn sporadically into the klieg lights of official Washington. Senator Richard Durbin, from her home state of Illinois, invited her to be his guest at the 2005 State of the Union address by President Bush, one of the most important events on the government's annual calendar. She met top officials from the Pentagon, who occasionally stopped by Walter Reed to visit with injured troops, and impressed them with her intelligence and courage. The veterans affairs committees in the House and Senate invited her to testify about the issues facing injured veterans, and amputees in particular. Her poise and visibility made her a natural magnet for the press, which led to several moving newspaper and magazine articles about her. Duckworth had studied political science at the University of Hawaii in the 1980s, then in 1992 earned a master's degree in international affairs from George Washington University, less than ten miles away from Walter Reed. She was well schooled in public issues and comfortable talking about them with the potentates in Washington.

Senator Durbin, a Democrat, became a kind of mentor. Duckworth also got to know Barack Obama, who at the time was the other senator from Illinois. After about six months in Washington, Duckworth was well enough to go home, so she and her husband returned to Hoffman Estates, the Chicago suburb where they lived. Since Duckworth had been a "weekend warrior" with the National Guard, she also had a full-time civilian job, as a manager with the community organization Rotary International. She figured she'd return to that, but Durbin urged her to consider a new career in politics. She had a kind of public charisma, and her military record would be a major asset. The idea appealed to Duckworth. Seeing the struggles of so many injured soldiers at Walter Reed had made her passionate about the needs of veterans, and she'd have more power to help them if she were part of the government. Plus, a congressional seat was opening up in Illinois's sixth district, where long-time incumbent Henry Hyde, a Republican, had decided to retire.

The idea of running for office also terrified Duckworth. She was comfortable taking on tough challenges, as long as it was in the incremental, familiar manner that had helped her excel at flight school. But doing something new and risky—improvising, basically, like John Ratzenberger—was something she had always dreaded. "I was all about other people's approval," she told me. "Getting my dad's approval, getting my mother's approval, getting the gold star at school. It was always about living up to an expectation or a standard." Running for office would be daring voters to express their disapproval, as some of them surely would. It was the kind of challenge she would have veered away from just a few years earlier. But after a year of living without her legs, she had become more comfortable with discomfort. She had never imagined coming home from Iraq badly injured, but facing so many unforeseen obstacles had left her less intimidated by the unfamiliar. Learning how to adapt to life as an amputee had been an abrupt new challenge she had no obvious training for. But she turned out to be better prepared than she ever would have guessed, and was accomplishing things she had never envisioned. "I had a new sense of fearlessness," she said, "because now, even on my worst day, nobody was shooting at me. And I wasn't laying in a hospital bed counting to sixty." She decided to run.

That congressional race, in the 2006 midterm elections, ended up being one of the key battles in a momentous political year. Both houses of Congress, then controlled by Republicans, were at risk of swinging to the Democratic side. Every race mattered. Duckworth started out with a lead in the polls, her military experience giving her strong credentials on the important issue of national security. But as election day neared, Republican party officials decided that the sixth district was one where they had a fighting chance to stave off a Democratic victory. Money flooded in during the last couple of weeks, allowing Duckworth's opponent to boost his TV and radio advertising. Republican supporters mounted an aggressive last-minute phone campaign, highlighting their candidate's tough stance against illegal immigration—an issue that Duckworth had downplayed, underestimating voter concerns. For all of her pluck, Duckworth was still a political novice, running as a Democrat in a district that was largely Republican. The Democrats ended up taking over the House and Senate without her: She lost the sixth by a narrow 51 to 49 margin.

It was just the sort of rejection she had long feared, and for a while, it felt crushing. Despite the support of her state's two senators, Duckworth had been unprepared for the hardball tactics of national politics. She felt her opponent had played dirty, and she took it personally. "Losing that election definitely felt like a failure," she told me. "I wasn't able to counter the last-minute tactics quickly enough to turn stuff around." For a few days, she dodged friends and supporters and nursed the psychological wounds. "I'd sit in the tub," she said, "because it was the only place my cell phone wouldn't ring. Wonderful people were calling, saying it was a great run, and I'd sit in my bathtub and cry." But three days after the election, Illinois's governor offered her another job, as director of veterans' affairs for the state. She jumped at the chance. And on November 12—her "alive day," two years after she had lost her legs in the attack on her helicopter—she flew to St. Louis to see the three crewmates who had helped her survive. "So even though the race was a failure," she said, "I woke up on November 12 knowing that if it had not been for my buddies, I would be dead."

The risk she had taken by running for Congress continued to pay off in ways she didn't anticipate. She campaigned for Barack Obama when he ran for president in 2008, and after he won, Obama appointed her to be one of the top officials in the Department of Veterans Affairs, in Washington. Part of her assignment there was to tackle the problem of homelessness among veterans, which had mushroomed as the recession intensified in 2008 and 2009. The army often discharged disabled veterans like Duckworth, but she lobbied hard to stay in, and the army agreed, so she continued to serve with the National Guard. She couldn't fly helicopters anymore, but she was still a trained aviator, fully capable of staff work, like helping run a command post. She got promoted to major and then lieutenant colonel, and did regular rotations at the National Guard's operations center in Washington. Duckworth also enjoyed the supercharged motivation that turns some injured people into inspirational overachievers, completing the Chicago marathon in the wheelchair division, relearning how to scuba dive without the benefit of her once powerful legs, and even getting certified as a private pilot, which was less demanding than flying a military helicopter.

Still, her injuries were an ongoing struggle, and there were constant reminders of lost privilege. She nearly lost her damaged right arm to a persistent infection. When she returned to a Black Hawk flight simulator to test her piloting abilities with artificial legs, it was so demanding that it made her feel like she was back on her first day at flight school. Walking on her artificial legs could be exhausting, so she got in the habit of reserving them for speeches, presentations, military duty, and other times when it was important to project what the army calls "command presence." And she learned to allow herself the occasional mournful moments that came with the loss of small joys. "There are times when I want to be able to look pretty for my husband," she said. "I want to wear heels again. The reality is, it sucks."

Being in Washington gave Duckworth the opportunity to become a peer visitor herself back at Walter Reed, where she'd often visit female amputees like herself, or pilots with serious injuries. She gave it to them straight. "I can only tell people that it's going to suck," she explained. "You're going to have really bad days. Days when you can't stop crying. Days when you wish this hadn't happened to you. You have to recognize those things for what they are. You have to acknowledge them. But you can't let them overwhelm you.

"In Iraq," she continued, "we had this phrase: 'owning the suck.' It sucks being over there. It sucks being deployed. You're out there tromping, and you've got your gear on, and your feet are blistered, and it's raining on you, or it's freezing, and you're lying in the mud with your weapon on guard duty. Know that it sucks. Acknowledge the suck. Own it. But keep doing your job. Because you have to do your job. So I can only tell people that it's going to suck. It's going to hurt. And it's your pain, whether it's a physical pain or a sorrow. It's yours and nobody else's. Just own it. Take command of it. Don't let the pain or the sorrow own you. You own that suck. It's yours."

Sometimes, when she delivered that message at Walter Reed, she could see a flash of recognition on a young soldier's face. She'd walk in wearing her artificial legs, the way Tom Porter had, to demonstrate that a crumpled but determined survivor could build a vigorous and accomplished life. Wearing one of her smart-alecky T-shirts—like, "It's just a flesh wound"—could help break the ice. But some soldiers didn't want to hear it, and Duckworth knew that a few of them would never own the suck. The suck would always own them. She could usually tell, because they were the ones wallowing in self-pity. And she struggled to come up with a convincing reason why they shouldn't feel that way. Some were still teenagers. Their lives were wrecked. She couldn't plausibly tell them otherwise. She was there to offer encouragement, not to judge anybody. But she also knew that self-sufficiency started with one small step, then another, and the toughest cases were the ones without a sense of mission about their own recovery. Sometimes that happened when parents or other loved ones helped too much, taking the sense of mission away. "If your parents are there saying, Oh, my poor baby, let me do this for you, it takes away your strength," Duckworth told me. "The tough thing is to struggle and learn how to do it yourself. Sometimes we have to step in and encourage the moms to let them struggle. Some respond well, but some never get it and their loved ones are the worse for it. Sometimes they'll take their child out of the hospital and move him someplace and isolate him even further. Those are the guys we have a really rough time with."

Duckworth acknowledged many moments of despair in her own life as she struggled to recover from her injuries and learn how to live with them. But when I asked if she ever felt sorry for herself, like some of the troops she encountered as a peer visitor, she said no. "I earned my wounds," she said proudly. "I earned these amputations. This wasn't an accident. I didn't get drunk, drive down the road, and crash into a tree. These wounds are the equivalent of wearing a medal on my chest. I earned these wounds because I served my country. So I don't ever feel sorry for myself."

After serving more than two years in the Veterans Affairs office, Duckworth left in the middle of 2011 to prepare for another run for Congress in the 2012 elections. This time she'd have stronger advantages. She'd be running in a newly created district more hospitable to her political party. She'd have better name recognition, which would help with fund-raising and voter appeal. She'd be more experienced at politics and the peculiar ways of Washington. She'd also have a deeper sense of empowerment, which had accrued to her since 2004 as a collateral benefit of struggle. Losing again, she knew, would suck. But she also knew that if it happened, she would own it.

CHAPTER 13

FROM WALLOWER TO REBOUNDER

The Rebounding skills demonstrated by Tammy Duckworth, Majora Carter, Tim Westergren, and everybody else in this book are things nearly everybody can learn. Decades of research into the quality known as resilience make that clear. But that doesn't make it easy to do in real life. Rebounders don't always know they're Rebounders. Usually they've never even thought about it. Tammy Duckworth never did. Hardly anybody spends the early part of their life deliberately building resilience, in case something terrible happens later on. Parents are better situated to help their kids develop coping skills and "stress inoculation," but there are a lot of reasons why that doesn't always happen, either. By its very nature, adversity is unpredictable and frightening. It challenges us because we don't know it's coming, and if we did know it was coming, we'd try to avoid it. It's common for Rebounders to think they'll never be able to handle some intimidating challenge that suddenly looms before them—and then to end up surprised when they do.

Anybody who doubts their potential as a Rebounder should learn about the transformation of Joe Torre, the professional baseball player and manager who led the New York Yankees to six American League titles in the twelve years he spent managing the team, and four World Series championships. To do that, Torre had to manage and assimilate some of the biggest and baddest egos in the history of sports, while also appeasing one of the world's most demanding bosses: George Steinbrenner. That required a deft touch that came from years of experience in baseball, but also from a series of personal failures and even the taste of humiliation. When the Yankees hired Torre in 1995, he had the hallmarks of a has-been: He was in his mid-fifties, with a career losing record as a manager, plus, he had been fired from each of the three teams he had managed before. That was hardly the kind of pedigree Yankees fans were used to. The *New York Daily News* dubbed Torre "Clueless Joe," while sneering that he was "naïve at best, desperate at worst" and nothing more than a whipping boy for Steinbrenner. A year later, as Torre was leading the Yankees toward victory in the World Series, the same *Daily News* columnist offered a "retraction" and said that Clueless Joe ought to be named Manager of the Year. In fact, he was. Torre went on to become one of the most successful and popular managers in baseball history, attaining the rarified status of a sports coach able to give the nation's CEOs some advice: His 1999 book, *Joe Torre's Ground Rules for Winners,* became a business-list bestseller.

But Joe Torre didn't start out as a Rebounder, or even as a winner. In fact, as a kid growing up in Brooklyn, New York, he was a self-described mama's boy, the baby in a family of five, who struggled with a turbulent upbringing that easily could have made him a lifelong Wallower. His father, a New York City police detective, was a rageful bully who terrorized his family with his temper and frequently struck Torre's mom. When something wasn't right with dinner, he'd throw his plate against the wall. He'd shout at his wife over trivial matters, leaving everyone in the house cowering. Torre himself never endured physical abuse, but his father routinely browbeat and humiliated him. One time, when he was about eight years old, Torre looked on as his sister Rae defended their mom with a knife. As his father reached for a drawer where he kept his revolver, Torre snatched the knife from his sister's hand, most likely preventing a violent episode. When Torre was eleven, his brother Frank, who was eight years older, finally led a family intervention and forced the old man to accept a divorce and move out. The household became more peaceful, but nobody ever explained to Joe why his father had been so angry or what had really gone on. He heard his older siblings and his mom whispering, and thought he had done something wrong. Torre struggled for much of his life with the fear and anxiety seeded during those early years. Loud noises always frightened him, since they brought back the savagery of his father's outbursts. He desperately avoided confrontation. Torre wouldn't even talk about the ugly family secret until he was in his mid-fifties and had two failed marriages of his own to look back on.

Not surprisingly, Torre's mother doted on him, practicing the kind of "helicopter parenting" that psychologists today blame for an epidemic of narcissism and a generation of fragile, self-absorbed kids. His mom was a traditional Italian cook, and she filled her son with pasta and other comfort foods, making him one of the plumper kids in the neighborhood. Torre was already a shy boy, probably on account of the anxiety and guilt caused by his truculent father, and as he gained weight he became even more withdrawn. By the time he got to high school, he seemed more like a forgettable wallflower than a future World Series champ. "I had no confidence in myself," Torre wrote in his 1997 memoir, *Chasing the Dream*. "I didn't do anything, join any clubs, or anything like that. I was a champion of self-defeat."

He loved baseball though, motivated partly by his brother Frank, who became a major leaguer with the Milwaukee Braves in 1956, when Torre was fifteen. Frank looked out for his kid brother, paying for him to go to prep school. Torre joined a local sandlot team, the Brooklyn Cadets, which helped him build enough confidence to join his high school team, where he played first and third bases and pitched occasionally. He was often the heaviest player on the field, but he worked hard to get better. One summer, when another brother, Rocco, arranged for free access to the batting cages at Coney Island, Torre swung at so many pitches that his hands bled. Despite being slow and heavy, he became a skilled and powerful hitter. He crushed one soaring home run for his high school team that cleared the fence and smashed through a window in a building beyond the field, the kind of memorable shot that people talked about. His senior year, he batted nearly .500, getting a hit every other time at bat. Torre began to develop hopes of playing professionally, just like his brother. But when the big league scouts—often nudged by Frank—came to see him play, they were startled by his stout physique. They decided he was too heavy and slow to have a chance as a major leaguer.

So when Torre graduated from high school in 1958, he got a job on Wall Street as a page with the American Stock Exchange. He continued to play baseball as an amateur with the Cadets, however, and Frank came up with a new idea. He had long felt that his kid brother was too soft and pampered, and he could be blunt about it, sometimes calling Joe a "fat slob" who embarrassed the family. "He thought I was a candy-assed kid who needed toughening up," Torre wrote. "He hated the fact that I was the baby of the family, whom my mother constantly coddled, calling me 'my Joey.' " So Frank helped his brother become the Cadets' catcher, which was the grittiest position on the field. Frank felt that squatting in the dirt, getting bruised by foul tips, and facing down runners barreling full-speed toward home plate would make a man of his baby brother. It would also give him a different angle with the scouts. Catching was the least popular job in the majors, with the fewest number of players competing for slots. It was also the one position where speed and agility didn't matter that much. So Torre made the switch and found he enjoyed catching, since it made him feel less self-conscious about his weight. Sure enough, scouts began to take another look at him, and as a catcher, he seemed like he might have a better baseball future. St. John's University offered him a baseball scholarship, but Torre was unenthused about books, and when his brother's team, the Braves, offered him a contract in 1959, it was an easy choice. Torre's Wall Street career ended abruptly, while a prolific baseball career that would span more than fifty years had begun.

Torre spent a year playing for one of the Braves' minor league teams, traveling between small cities in the upper Midwest, where the team played most of its games. He got called up to the majors for a couple of games in 1960, and in his first professional at-bat on September 25, 1960, he ripped a single up the middle. Then, because Torre was so slow, the manager immediately took him out of the game, replacing him with a pinch-runner. Torre started 1961 back in the minors but got called up to the Braves when the starting catcher got injured. Torre batted a respectable .278 that season and came in second in the voting for National League Rookie of the Year. By 1963, Torre won the job behind the plate for good. He steadily improved, batting over .300 for the first time in 1964, when he made the National League All-Star team. The following year he earned a Gold Glove Award for his strong defensive play as a catcher. Torre had become a dependable major leaguer—bordering on a star—and he was making good money, too. The only real disappointment was that he never played a season on the same team as Frank, whose seven-year career was winding down by the time his little brother's was heating up. But they remained close, with Frank mentoring and informally coaching his increasingly accomplished brother.

Torre's prowess on the field, however, was matched by a swelled head and pompous attitude. Professional athletes in the 1960s weren't quite the deified multimillionaires they are today, but there were still frequent opportunities for a cocksure twentysomething to misbehave, and Torre passed up few of them. He did, in fact, act like the pampered prima donna his brother worried he'd become. In 1963, he married a twenty-one-year-old Playboy bunny he met at the Playboy Club in Miami, where he and Frank had stopped in one night. His family disapproved, so he didn't invite any of them to the wedding— not even his mom. The marriage unraveled quickly and would have ended in a shotgun divorce, except that Torre's wife got pregnant two months after they were married, so they waited until their son, Michael, was born in 1964, and then split. Torre got custody of the boy, but since he was never home—and he was an immature twenty-three-year-old—his mom and sisters agreed to raise him, back in Brooklyn. Even so, Torre became dismissive of his family and drifted away from them, entranced by the charms of big league life. Frank got so disgusted that he didn't speak to his brother for a year.

"I'm embarrassed to think of how I acted then," Torre wrote in his memoir. "I was a kid in a candy store, thinking I should have anything I wanted without attaching any responsibility to it."

In 1966, the Braves left Milwaukee and moved to Atlanta. Torre was delighted, because Milwaukee had little nightlife compared to the lively bars and clubs on Peachtree Street, where he ended up spending a lot of time and cash. Torre boasted to one reporter that he saved hardly any money, since he spent practically all of his disposable income on clothes, meals, and bar tabs. In 1967, a year Torre later referred to as "the height of my irresponsibility," he and another player bought an Atlanta bar where many of their fellow players—known as the "playboys of Peachtree Street"—hung out and drank. In 1968, Torre got married for the second time, to a pretty blonde woman he had spotted in the stands during batting practice before a game one day. He didn't invite his family to this wedding, either. Later that year, Torre was driving home one night after several hours of dining and drinking when cops pulled him over, arrested him for drunk driving, and tossed him in jail (while asking several times for autographs). It was all over the news the next day, with fans and the press hammering the popular player. Torre convinced himself it wasn't his fault. "I blamed the cop for not letting me go," he wrote. "Looking back, I was so spoiled that I easily placed blame on other people but never on myself."

At this point in his life, as he approached the age of thirty, Torre had few of the qualities that typically characterize Rebounders. He lacked humility. While obviously a skilled ballplayer, he had an inflated sense of his talents off the field and a poor grasp of his limitations. Though he had suffered from adversity early in his life, he hadn't learned much from it. Others had opened doors for him, reducing his need to learn how to do it himself. He gave himself too much credit for his early success, without fully acknowledging how his brother and others had helped him. When he did fail—as in his first marriage, or his drunk-driving episode—he blamed external factors instead of probing his own contribution to the problem, which led him to repeat the same kinds of mistakes instead of improving his performance.

In 1968, Torre suffered a career setback when he got hit in the face with a pitch, which broke several bones and took six weeks to heal. The incident dented Torre's confidence—a problem that still nagged him, when things didn't go quite right—and he ended up with a so-so season. The Braves began to cool on him, and after a contract dispute they traded him to St. Louis—the first time a major league team had rejected him. "That was a gut check," Torre told me. "It felt like a failure." The players and team executives in St. Louis were happy to have him, however, and there, he found his groove again. In his first season with the Cardinals, in 1969, he batted .289 and drove in 101 runs, while moving over to first base, since the Cardinals already had a strong catcher, Tim McCarver. Torre developed deep friendships with McCarver and a few other players, including the legendary pitcher Bob Gibson and shortstop Dal Maxvill, who would end up as the Cardinals' general manager after he retired as a player. In 1971, Torre had a career year that turned out to be his high-water mark, batting .363 and driving in 137 runs, which earned him top honors as the National League's Most Valuable Player. To his own surprise, the Cardinals named him team captain, seeing leadership qualities in Torre that he didn't see in himself.

The disparity between Torre's on-field success and his personal failures continued, however, mainly because his second marriage was failing. Torre and his second wife, Dani, had a daughter, Cristina, plus Dani's daughter from a prior marriage, Lauren. He tried harder to fix the trouble than he did the first time, agreeing to move to New York, for instance, where Dani was from, so she could feel closer to home. But nothing worked. Torre spent less and less time at home, shutting out his family so he could focus on the one thing he was good at: baseball. Ordinarily, trouble at home begets trouble at work, but Torre enjoyed the best years of his career at a time when his family life was miserable. When I asked him why, he explained that baseball had become his respite from all the other things that weren't going right. "I'd hide in the game," he said. "Nobody could get at me when I was between the lines. When I was out there, I never wanted it to stop. It was really the only thing that made me feel good or gave me any confidence." Torre also began to realize that he couldn't take success on the field for granted anymore, especially after he turned thirty, in 1970. He started to work out more and pay closer attention to his diet, dropping twenty pounds. He had also become a more mature player, thanks in part to all the time he had spent catching, which involved a lot of strategizing with the pitcher and the coaches.

After his killer season in 1971, Torre played three more years with the Cardinals. His numbers were decent, but he never again approached the form of his MVP year, and the comedown felt like a major disappointment. He avoided home and there were moments of despondency when the bad marriage got to him. Plus, it started to seem like he would never make it to the World Series. The Braves had never even gone to the playoffs while he was on the team, and while the Cardinals had gone to the Series in each of the two years before Torre joined, winning once and losing once, they had become a middling team that would never finish higher than second in their division throughout the 1970s. Torre knew his career was on the downslope, and since he was highly paid, on account of his MVP season, it was more noticeable when he underproduced. When the Cardinals brought up a promising young first baseman, Keith Hernandez, there was no room left for Torre. At the end of the '74 season, they traded him to the New York Mets, who had made it to the Series the previous year, and lost, but were on their way to becoming one of the weakest teams in baseball.

Torre wound out his playing career during three forgettable seasons with the Mets, from 1975 through 1977. He had the worst year of his career in 1975, batting .247. In one game, which Torre called "an especially humiliating night," he grounded into four double plays, tying one of the league's more ignominious records. "For the first time in my life, I dreaded going to the ballpark," he wrote. He felt like maybe it was time to quit, but didn't want to go out after such a lousy year, so he trained intensely over the winter and recovered somewhat in 1976, batting .306. But he had become a part-time player by then, with just thirty-one runs batted in that year. As the 1977 season opened, there was talk of trading Torre to the New York Yankees or offering him a new job managing one of the Mets minor league teams, which would give him a chance to start a new career as a manager. Then, with a big shakeup in the organization under way, the team surprised Torre, asking him if he wanted to manage the Mets. He lacked experience, but he had name recognition that would help in New York, which, after all, was his hometown. Torre had also developed an easygoing rapport with the press, and he was comfortable in the spotlight, which was important in a city where the glare of media attention could be disorienting. So he jumped at the chance, since it felt like a natural extension of what he had been doing as a catcher and then as a team captain.

The lackluster Mets may have been the only team in baseball that would have hired such an unproven manager, and Torre's tenure with the team coincided with one of the most dysfunctional periods in Mets history. One of the owners' first big decisions after Torre took over was trading away some of the team's most talented players—including pitcher Tom Seaver, a future Hall of Famer—a move the press dubbed the "Midnight Massacre." Torre got off to a slow start and barely sped up. In his first year, which began about six weeks after the season started, the Mets' record under Torre was 49–68, a dismal winning percentage of .419. The team finished last in its division, as it would for the next two years. When new owners bought the Mets, Torre knew they probably wouldn't want to keep the old manager around, which was typical. His final season managing the Mets, 1981, was nearly as miserable as 1975, his worst year as a player. The season was marred by a strike that canceled nearly one-third of the games. The team went 41–62, a .399 winning percentage. Torre ended his Mets tenure after the 1981 season with a weak .405 winning percentage over five years. On top of that, Torre's marriage finally ended for good, forcing him to move out and accept another failed relationship. Sticking it out that long, and trying to work on improvements, had only delayed the inevitable.

Five seasons as the Mets' manager, however, had begun to finish the job that Frank Torre started two decades earlier, when he got his kid brother transferred to catcher, to toughen him up. There was nothing in the Mets' performance under Torre's command for him to be cocky about. He had put aside thoughts of making it to the Series or even winning the division, instead setting small intermediate goals and seeking ways to keep players motivated when the team's performance was pitiful. Just keeping a sense of humor could be difficult. But he must have shown some capability, because right after the Mets dropped him, his old team, the Atlanta Braves—now owned by the "Mouth of the South," the colorful and combative Ted Turner—hired him. Torre did better there. The Braves started the 1982 season by winning thirteen straight games, the longest opening winning streak ever in baseball. They went on to finish first in their division, then lost the National League playoffs. It was a good season, but Turner never settled for good enough. Over the next two seasons, the Braves came in second and third, and Turner, determined to win the Series, started to lose patience. Torre liked Turner, but also clashed with him. After one loss, for instance, Turner screamed at Torre in front of several other team employees. It was the kind of hostile confrontation that reminded Torre of his abusive father and made him feel humiliated. So the next day, after winning a game, Torre told Turner that sure, he was the owner, and he had the right to scream at the manager any time he wanted. "But don't you ever, ever yell at me in front of a bunch of people again," Torre told his boss. "Don't do it in front of an audience."

Turner fired Torre after that season. His record as the Braves' manager was a respectable 257–229, with one division title. But Torre felt bitter after his departure from Atlanta. This time he had been fired outright, whereas the Mets had simply declined to renew his contract while in the midst of a complete change of regime. And despite his improved performance as a manager, Torre was now damaged merchandise. No other teams came calling. So Torre inquired about a broadcasting job with the California Angels, where he ended up as the color commentator with play-by-play man Bob Starr, then spent a year in the booth with Joe Garagiola and Reggie Jackson. He enjoyed the work but missed being on the field with the players. A few teams called when they were looking for a manager, but none of those nibbles led to bites. By the late 1980s, Torre figured his career as a manager was probably over. There was one consolation. In 1981, he had met a twenty-four-year-old student named Alice, who went by Ali, and the two started dating. The romance developed more slowly than before. Torre got to know Ali's parents, who were concerned about their daughter being involved with somebody seventeen years older than her. Eventually, they took a liking to Torre. When the two got married, it was six years after they had met. Torre's mom had died by then, but for the first time Torre made sure to invite the rest of his family to his wedding, including his three children, whom he managed to be close with even though they remained in New York while he moved around the country chasing baseball jobs. Once married to Ali, home began to seem like a peaceful and relaxed place, instead of a tense and turbulent pressure cooker he sought to avoid.

In 1990, Torre heard from his old St. Louis teammate Dal Maxvill, now the Cardinals' top executive, that their manager was about to quit. Would Torre be interested in the job? It was the opportunity Torre had thought would never come, and he said yes right away. He hadn't managed in six years, and it was a risky move by the Cardinals. Torre took over a struggling team two-thirds of the way through the 1990 season, and the squad limped to a 70–92 finish that landed them in the basement of their division. The next season was better, with the Cardinals going 84–78 and coming in second. They had a winning record each of the next two years but came in third each time, and then Torre started to have trouble with the owner, August Busch III, just as he had with Turner in Atlanta. Busch had taken over the Cardinals in 1989, when his father, Gussie Busch, died, and while he was a tough businessman, he wasn't that interested in baseball. He felt the team had been too deferential to players and managers and needed to lower costs. Torre knew he faced trouble in the summer of 1994 when Busch fired Maxvill, his main advocate in the front office. A 234-day players' strike started in August 1994, canceling the rest of the season and carrying into the '95 season. Torre sympathized with the players, which enraged Busch, but he was contractually obligated to manage the rogue's gallery of replacement players the team fielded, which made the regular players resentful when they returned about a month into the season. Torre couldn't please either side, and in June 1995, Busch fired him. It was a frustrating end, at the hands of another imperious owner. This time, Torre figured, his managing career was probably over for good. He felt disappointed, but also relieved.

After getting fired, Torre and his wife moved to Cincinnati, where Ali had a large family that they planned to enjoy spending time with. Torre followed the rest of the '95 baseball season as a spectator. At the end of the season, however, he began to get a few phone calls from executives with the New York Yankees, who asked if he'd be interested in the general manager's job. Being a G.M. was demanding front-office work, requiring year-round engagement, and Torre declined because of the strain it might place on his family. Soon after, however, the Yankees lost their popular young manager, Buck Showalter, after a row he had had over the coaching staff with the Yankees' volcanic owner, George Steinbrenner. Would Torre be interested in moving back to New York to manage the Yankees? As a kid, Torre had rooted for the New York Giants—who left New York for San Francisco in 1958—so the Yankees weren't exactly his favored team. But New York was home nonetheless, and he wasn't as fed up with managing as he led himself to believe after the Cardinals fired him. His brother Frank advised against taking the job, since it would just amount to more hassle. But the more Torre talked about it, the more he wanted another chance to see if he could turn in a winning performance. Ali supported the idea, so Torre told the Yankees yes. He'd earn less than he did in St. Louis, but he didn't mind. Being back in the game was an opportunity he didn't expect.

Torre was a curious choice for the Yankees. He was fifty-five when they hired him to replace Showalter, who was a mere thirty-nine. He had a career losing record as a manager of 894–1,003, and on top of that had been fired from every managing job he ever had. Torre could rationalize each flameout one-by-one, on account of the changing of the guard at the Mets, Ted Turner's epic impatience at the Braves, and the ugly strike that poisoned the atmosphere when he was at the Cardinals. But it all added up to a mediocre career at best, which is why the press lampooned Steinbrenner's choice. The press reported that the Yankees had offered the job to others before Torre, each, supposedly, with better credentials. They all said no, probably because of Steinbrenner's history of raucous and short-lived relationships with managers; since buying the team in 1973, Steinbrenner had changed managers fourteen times in twenty-three years. There were even rumors that Steinbrenner was trying to lure Showalter back, at the same time that he was inking a deal with Torre. The press delighted in the controversy, and Torre did, in fact, seem somewhat clueless, as if he was the butt of a joke but didn't know it.

Torre might have been a bit naïve, but somewhere along the way over the prior thirty-five years, he had also become a Rebounder, which made the humbling elements of the Yankees' offer perfectly tolerable to him. Shortly after accepting the Yankees job, Ali asked him to join her at a self-help seminar in Cincinnati. That was hardly Torre's style, but Ali was eight months pregnant with their daughter Andrea, who would be Torre's fourth child, and Torre was in an accommodating mood, so he said sure, he'd go. It was a four-day symposium, and Torre figured he'd just keep his mouth shut and nod benignly until it was over. But Ali was no fool, and she knew her husband held some ancient emotional demons under lock and key. For the first time, they sprang free. By the third day of the seminar, Torre was fully engaged, with tears running down his face as he told complete strangers about the awful feelings he still had from the years he had grown up in a violent household. He realized he was saying things he had never told anyone, and others told him they had endured similar difficulties. He wasn't the only one. It felt liberating. So he went back to New York and asked his two older sisters to tell him what they knew about their father's violent urges. They told him that their father had pushed their mother down a flight of stairs when learning that she was pregnant with their fifth child—him. He had bashed her head against a wall numerous times. Their mother had lived a terrified life while she was married—but, of course, she never wanted her Joey to know anything about it. Torre never entered deep counseling or tried to resurrect repressed memories, but he didn't need to. Just articulating the things that bothered him and learning the full story from his sisters felt like a flood of relief. "I was able to connect the dots," he explained. "I always had these fears and sensitivities. If something went wrong, I felt I had caused it. Now, I knew where the feelings came from."

Torre figured out that his self-absorption in the early part of his career was an antidote to guilt and anxiety that had become so in-bred he didn't even realize those feelings were unusual. His swagger as a rising, well-paid major leaguer was a disguise meant to hide a fear of failing instilled in him during his father's frequent rants. When he got arrested for drunk driving or there were other prob-lems, he blamed others because his outsized sense of guilt prevented him from taking responsibility for his own mistakes. He was lucky to have talent as a ballplayer, but that talent also gave him the excuse he needed to flee from off-the-field problems and to dismiss insights he didn't want to hear, such as the protestations from his family over his first two marriages, which turned out to be legitimate.

A lot of people struggle with guilt, fear, blame, arrogance, and dismissiveness, which are textbook resilience busters. Some of them get therapy, learn humility, rebuild their confidence, or find other ways to purge their afflictions. But many don't, and they become lifelong Wallowers who never understand the things that hold them back. They deny or excuse their failures instead of learning from them, and struggle to get ahead. Torre started out that way, but over time he became a Rebounder able to turn failure to his advantage. He learned to recognize his own limitations and steadily improve the things he wasn't good at. The seminar in Cincinnati was a breakthrough experience, but there were many other moments—including some of the letdowns Torre experienced as a player, man-ager, and husband—when he imperceptibly evolved into a man able to try something new and uncomfortable, when his wife suggested it might be helpful. "You can't really be successful unless you've had the ability to fight your way back," Torre told me. "Instead of wish-ing something didn't happen, you need to use it to make what you do more productive."

When he joined the Yankees for the '96 season, Torre inherited a strong roster, since Steinbrenner had spent lavishly on talent, giving the Yankees the highest payroll in baseball. But every coach in sports knows that a collection of talented individuals won't necessarily form a winning team, and Torre had to figure out how to manage some of the most idiosyncratic and egotistical names in the game. The press jumped on the new manager right away, second-guessing his moves on the field and trying to stoke controversy every time there seemed to be some disagreement on the team. They were waiting for him to fail. And Steinbrenner turned out to be as much of a micromanager as everyone said, with the annoying habit of manipulating circumstances in advance so that somebody else besides him would get the blame if things went wrong. Torre knew it would be his job to insulate the players from Steinbrenner's periodic wrath and take the flack himself.

Torre, however, had learned something important about himself that gave him confidence he could handle the heat in New York. Earlier in his career, he had fled from confrontation or let others deal with it. But now that he understood why he reacted that way, he realized that his lifelong aversion to that kind of stress could be an asset that would help his team. One of Torre's top goals was to defuse the tension that so often suffused the Yankees clubhouse, as a result of a combative, scheming owner, a collection of proud players, and a double-barreled press that skillfully exploited the Yankees' weaknesses and gloried in embarrassing exposés. Torre decided that instead of getting sucked into every scrape with the media, he'd stop reading the papers and be as patient and forthcoming as he could during interviews. The players began to realize that Torre would deal with them directly and discreetly, if necessary, without airing his grievances in the press. As for Steinbrenner, Torre had a knack for humoring him and didn't get ruffled when The Boss, as he was known, called to criticize a decision he had made. Torre's confidence was no longer vulnerable to every barb or spear. Since unburdening himself about his troublesome past, he felt freer and more relaxed than he ever had before.

Showalter, Torre's predecessor, had been an intense, autocratic manager, similar in ways to Steinbrenner. He had led the '95 Yankees to the division playoffs, where they blew a two-game lead in a best-of-five series and then lost three games in a row, setting off a string of recriminations. Torre's style was totally different. He had a temper when he got emotional, but most of the time he was laid-back. He felt his role was to watch over his players and make them accountable to one another—not just to the manager—and intervene only when they needed his guidance. The '96 Yankees weren't the league powerhouse, but they played smart, scrappy ball, and, most important, they gelled as a team as the season progressed, finding ways to eke out runs when their offense was weak, with a tight defense that gave little away. They finished 92–70, the best record in their division and third best in the majors. They won comfortably in the playoffs, which put them in the World Series for the first time since 1981, against Torre's old team, the Atlanta Braves. The Braves pounded the Yankees in the first game, a 12–1 drubbing at Yankee Stadium that left the hometown fans demoralized. The Braves took the second game, too, putting the Yankees in a deep hole as they headed to Atlanta for the next three games. Steinbrenner worried incessantly that his team would end up embarrassed—a constant concern of his—and Torre himself was nervous. But the Yankees pulled off a dramatic comeback, winning the next four games, including the clincher back at Yankee Stadium, to win their first World Series in eighteen years. Torre was a hero, finally winning a World Series ring after thirty-six years in the game.

If he had never signed with the Yankees, Joe Torre would be one of those baseball names that was vaguely familiar for a while, then largely forgotten. Despite several good seasons as a player, he never made the Hall of Fame, and as a manager prior to joining the Yankees, he produced just five winning records in fifteen full seasons, and only one first-place finish. But Torre, of course, became a baseball legend. He ended up leading the Yankees to ten first-place finishes in twelve years, winning the World Series in 1996, 1998, 1999, and 2000. He was named American League Manager of the Year twice. Steinbrenner's opulent spending on players obviously helped Torre succeed, but Torre's equanimity became the glue that had been missing from the Yankees, allowing him to harness the talent, egos, and emotions that had blown apart earlier Yankees rosters. Torre had his share of frustrating run-ins with the tempestuous Steinbrenner, but he also demonstrated a singular ability to defang The Boss and keep the team on course. Torre's light touch with Steinbrenner earned him a reputation as a "lion tamer" who happened to end up richly paid. By 2007, Torre was making $7 million a year, fourteen times what he signed on for in 1996. After the Yankees, he'd manage the Los Angeles Dodgers for three years, then become one of the top executives running major league baseball.

One big factor in Torre's long-sought success was longevity. Like Lucinda Williams, Jon Luther, Thomas Keller, and many other Rebounders, he stuck with his craft long enough to overcome mid-career setbacks and capitalize on the experience that took years to build. But another key factor were the peaks and valleys of his own playing career, from the highs he hit when winning the MVP award in 1971 to the lows he endured as a part-time player in decline on a losing team. Torre knew what it felt like to be a cocky up-and-comer hiding his own fear of failure, a star, and a discouraged down-and-outer questioning his own contribution to the team. There were twenty-five talented professionals on a team, and a lot of them had to deal with less playing time or other managerial decisions that seemed unfair. "I know what it's like to play on a part-time basis," Torre said. "I knew how to sit down at somebody's locker with them. They respect the fact that I've experienced it. It made me a better manager."

Torre also felt that beneath the fear and anxiety he endured when he was younger, and the dismissive arrogance that later masked those feelings, he had a kind of empathy for the underdog that made him a good listener, another skill that helped him as a manager. "I've always had a sensitive side," he said, "which I have to trace back to the fact that I grew up with a lot of insecurities." Listening to his players, and figuring out how best to use each one of them game by game, gave Torre the kind of edge that made him a repeat World Series champ. "It's a matter of continuing to learn, continuing to find things out about people," he said. "We won four World Series, but we did it a different way each time. You've got to understand that each one of these guys has a heartbeat."

Joe Torre could have remained arrogant and self-absorbed and still ended up with an impressive playing career. There are a lot of successful people who are selfish and even unlikeable. But Torre probably would not have become a leader and a model manager if he hadn't learned how to break free of his own struggles, understand his failures, and listen to other people worth trusting. He was a Rebounder long in the making, but going the distance made the difference between a career that peaked early and then flatlined—as it would have if he had never made it to the Yankees—and a career that climaxed with an opportunity to invest everything he had learned in the pursuit of a prized goal. In sports, managers and coaches often tell their players that winning requires sustained performance over an entire game or season, rather than occasional bursts of effort or a few inspired plays. Joe Torre proved that's a pretty good career strategy as well.

CHAPTER 14

THE NINE ATTRIBUTES OF REBOUNDERS

Rebounder or not?

That's a game I began to play (with others, when I could interest them) as I learned how various people, famous or obscure, reacted to career setbacks and other hardships. Sometimes it's easy to tell, without knowing much about the person's history or background. We all know people who panic under mild pressure and seem unable to cope when something goes slightly amiss. They'd have to work awfully hard to become Rebounders—and probably complain about all that work. Other people seem to have a superhuman tolerance for stress that would wear down most people, and an uncanny ability to Rebound, no matter how abruptly or severely misfortune upends them. They're easy to categorize, too.

Most people, however, have characteristics of Rebounders and Wallowers both—the ambivalent essence of human nature. When I was researching nineteenth-century Rebounders like Thomas Edison, Milton Hershey, and Henry Heinz, I came across the maddening story of Charles Goodyear, who abandoned a family hardware business in the 1830s and spent more than a decade trying to develop a process that would make the newly discovered substance of rubber stable enough for common use in shoes, raincoats, machinery, and hundreds of other items. Though he had no scientific training, Goodyear conducted countless foul experiments with toxic chemicals in his family's kitchen, subjecting his wife and children to poverty and pawning everything in sight—even his children's books—to finance his quest. Fellow citizens of New York and Boston, where members of the Goodyear family often foraged for food or fished for it in the nearby rivers, thought Goodyear was half-mad. Some encouraged him to take better care of his family. He claimed a measure of vindication in 1844, when he earned a patent for the process of vulcanizing rubber, the starting point for a major industry. Yet after subordinating the welfare of his family to his decade-long obsession, Goodyear did a poor job of protecting his patent, spending more money on lawyers than he earned from the rights on his discovery. He also turned down partnerships and other opportunities that would have brought him and his family some wealth and comfort, because it would have forced him to share credit for his discovery and swallow some pride. Goodyear died broke, leaving his family in debt and earning little but recognition for his efforts. The Goodyear Tire and Rubber Company, founded thirty-eight years after his death, was named after him only as a posthumous honor.

Rebounder or not? To me, the answer is no. Goodyear pursued a quixotic dream without a pragmatic plan for how to execute it or benefit from it. He fixated too long on one idea and rejected new ways to think about his scheme. He lacked the awareness (or the compassion) to recognize the cost and pain that his megalomania imposed on others. But to some, Goodyear is a hero. In 1976 he was inducted into the National Inventors Hall of Fame. Look him up today, and you're likely to come across a profile that extols him as a model of persistence in the face of stupefying setbacks. His story reflects a paradox of persistence that many people face even now: Relentless determination might lead to breakthroughs, but it might also become a narrow-minded obsession that leaves you spent, broke, and alienated from the people you need. As Thomas Edison knew much better than Charles Goodyear, recognizing when it's time to change course or modify your plan is often as important as persistence itself.

We get mixed messages about resilience all the time, which makes it hard to know what kind of model to follow if we want to become more resilient ourselves. Playing Rebounder or Not with some controversial people in public life today demonstrates how tricky it can be. Take Martha Stewart, for instance. The lifestyle diva rose from working-class beginnings to form a million-dollar gourmet-catering business, which led to books, a magazine, TV shows, and the founding of her company, Martha Stewart Living Omnimedia. By the late 1990s, when her company went public, Stewart was a household name on her way to becoming a billionaire. But apparently that wasn't enough for her, and for some reason, Stewart got tangled up in an insider-trading case involving a few hundred shares of a drug company that had nothing to do with her own firm, ultimately going to prison for a short while. Stewart returned to her firm and her media ventures in 2005, saying practically nothing about her startling comedown and focusing on her business. To some, she showed dignity and fortitude by doing jail time with minimal complaint and getting back to business afterward instead of bashing her prosecutors or detractors. Yet her firm struggled from that point on, as if the shine had come off the apple, and she seemed reluctant to ever admit she did something wrong. Stewart doesn't make my list of Rebounders because the adversity she suffered was self-inflicted, and she never showed much awareness—not publicly, anyway—of her mistakes. It's a lost learning opportunity when you can't acknowledge your own flaws or talk about them.

What about Michael Vick? The football star escaped the gang-infested neighborhood where he grew up thanks to his athletic talent, playing quarterback for two years at Virginia Tech and then signing a $62 million contract with the Atlanta Falcons in 2001. He quickly helped turn a losing team into a playoff contender and became one of the most exciting and promising players in the league. But a series of personal and legal problems culminated in the discovery that Vick was operating a gruesome dog-fighting ring at his Atlanta mansion, where dogs were routinely maimed and killed. The ring earned him a 23-month prison sentence and got him banished from professional football. After Vick got out of prison in 2009, the NFL rescinded its ban and allowed him to sign with the Philadelphia Eagles, where he became a standout quarterback once again. In 2010, the Associated Press named him Comeback Player of the Year. Vick partnered with the Humane Society to help increase awareness of animal cruelty, and he made a warts-and-all documentary of his life with Black Entertainment Television, allowing cameras to film "the good, the bad, and the ugly results of my decisions," as he said. Yet some animal lovers insist that Vick should never have been allowed to return to football or earn any additional money as a professional athlete. And he, too, recovered from problems he brought on himself.

What about Bill Clinton? His otherwise successful presidency will forever be marred by his tawdry sexual encounter with a White House intern, dishonest denials about the affair, and his 1998 impeachment by the House of Representatives. Clinton complained bitterly about the hostility shown by his political opponents, as if his fall were the result of external attacks rather than his own poor decisions. Yet he artfully rehabilitated his image after leaving the White House, through foundation work, fund-raising efforts for disaster-stricken places like Haiti, and the Clinton Global Initiative, which sponsored high-powered gatherings of prominent leaders aiming to tackle some of the world's thorniest problems. By most accounts, Clinton has done genuine good deeds during his twilight career as a former president. Rebounder or not?

It's a whimsical, academic question—until you turn it on yourself.

As I was learning about Rebounders, I frequently asked myself whether I had the same qualities I saw in them. Sometimes I did, and sometimes I didn't. For a while, I thought of Rebounders in binary terms—either you were one, or you weren't. But very little in life is black and white, and I had to shake myself of the idea that people are either one thing or the other, the way Friedrich Nietzsche and Sigmund Freud thought long ago. Joe Torre didn't simply cross a threshold one day, trading in his rumpled old denial for a shiny suit of self-awareness. It happened in tiny, incremental ways, over many years. That's the way it goes, usually. Most of us learn and grow in immeasurable small steps that somehow, over time, add up to miles of travel. We go backward at times, without even knowing it. We don't always know when we're moving forward, either. Quite often, we move in zigzag patterns that aren't trackable by GPS. Sometimes we might be a Rebounder, other times, not.

This makes it hard to find Rebounders to serve as unqualified role models. Even the people I chose to profile for this book have some qualities that are desirable, but others that aren't. Reed Hastings is a bold visionary, but his boldness became overconfidence in 2011 and led to missteps that produced a sharp reversal for his company, Netflix. That left him struggling to Rebound from an unnecessary setback of his own making. As I realized how much Rebounders change, and how variegated they really are, it occurred to me that no individual possesses every required element of resilience. There's no perfect formula, and there's no such thing as the complete Rebounder. Instead, there are many qualities that can help people process adversity better and recover more quickly. So I began to identify the key attributes of the Rebounders in this book, and many others that I studied, to isolate the core qualities that allow people to overcome setbacks and learn from them. Then I compared that information with dozens of insights from the scientific literature on resilience.

When I filtered it all out, I was left with nine key attributes of Rebounders. None of the Rebounders I studied exhibited all nine attributes. Some had two or three of them. Others, five or six. But overall, these nine attributes capture the special things that differentiate Rebounders from others who are permanently defeated by setbacks or who wallow indefinitely in blame or denial. Most people will recognize a few of these qualities in themselves, along with a few others that might never fit their personalities. That's okay. What's important is adding to your ambient level of resilience little by little. All of these qualities are learnable, and some will verily force themselves upon you when necessity leaves no alternative. Rebounders like Jon Luther, Thomas Keller, and Majora Carter started out with some resilience, and developed more. Many Rebounders don't even know they're building resilience—it's just part of the natural way they react to difficulty. Anybody who has a few of these attributes, and can add a few more, will be building the vital skill set needed to get ahead over the next ten or twenty years.

All of the Rebounders I studied exhibit basic qualities that are typically associated with success, but aren't unique to Rebounders. They're relatively intelligent, ambitious, and curious. They want to accomplish things. They're lifelong learners, with enough of an open mind to realize there's a lot they don't know. And they're willing to work hard to reach their goals. But that describes a lot of people. Here are the nine additional attributes that give Rebounders an important edge.

THEY ACCEPT FAILURE

There's a catchy slogan in business, sports, and even the military: Failure is not an option. It might sound good, but for Rebounders, pioneers, visionaries, and other people who accomplish much, failure is frequently an option. That's because they attempt things that are hard to do. Most Rebounders hate to fail. But if it happens, they fail productively. They look for insights that can be gleaned from their failures, the way Thomas Edison learned things from his dead experiments that helped other inventions succeed. Some Rebounders learn to fail fast, like Reed Hastings, because they're able to quickly recognize their own mistakes. They're comfortable with the risk of failure because they've worked up to it, usually by overcoming smaller setbacks and learning how to recover. The ability to take prudent risks, the kind of risks most people need to take if they want to be successful, depends on a willingness to accept failure, if it happens. For people who don't acknowledge the possibility of failure, taking risks can be a terrifying experience, because any outcome other than success seems like a catastrophe.

THEY COMPARTMENTALIZE EMOTIONS

One of the most common attributes of Rebounders is a kind of equanimity that allows them to overcome guilt, blame, anger, and other bad feelings that often accompany setbacks. Many Rebounders are emotional people. That's where their passion and drive comes from. But when something goes wrong, they don't internalize bad feelings or become dominated by emotion, the way other people do when they feel wronged, frustrated, or disappointed. Rebounders certainly feel that kind of emotion, but compartmentalizing it allows them to apply the pragmatism that is usually the best guide through a rough patch. Jack Bogle felt furious and even had revenge fantasies when he lost a boardroom battle and got fired from the firm he had led for several years. He also had the presence of mind to recognize his anger and seek advice about how to manage it. If Bogle had spent the next several years trying to get even, it might have made him feel better, but it would have diluted his focus and energy and interfered with his efforts to establish Vanguard. It also might have generated an endless cycle of provocation and revenge that devoured his time and energy.

THEY HAVE A BIAS TOWARD ACTION

Sam Walton's phrase neatly describes the way many Rebounders react to problems: They do something. Sometimes it doesn't even matter what. "When you're in adversity and you don't quite know what it is, you just have to find a way to keep moving," Majora Carter told me, describing her own efforts to find her way over the course of a decade. Tammy Duckworth's first impulse when waking up in a hospital bed and realizing her legs were gone was to get to work, whatever that work turned out to be. Rehabilitation became her new mission, the job that had to get done, which created the inertia that helped her recover. Virtually every other Rebounder I studied felt motivated to do something when faced with a stressful situation, even if they weren't sure where it would lead. Taking purposeful action to fix a problem is one of the hallmarks of resilient people. They do it because they believe they can influence what happens next, instead of capitulating to the vagaries of fate. Responding aggressively to a challenge has the added benefit of burning up anxious energy and preventing feelings of helplessness. Wallowers, by contrast, tend to ruminate over problems without doing much about them, often finding themselves immobilized by fear or worry.

THEY CHANGE THEIR MINDS SOMETIMES

In his 2011 commencement address at Dartmouth, Conan O'Brien described how he had pursued one dream for twenty-five years—to host *The Tonight Show*. When he lost the dream, he had to develop a new vision of himself as a successful person. "Whatever you think your dream is now," he told graduating seniors, "it will probably change." The need to discard old thinking and reprogram your dreams and ambitions is so common that it's practically an adult rite of passage. Yet a lot of people cling too long to ideas that won't get them anywhere. Changing your mind often means you have to be able to recognize your own mistakes and discover the flaws in your own thinking. As venture capitalist Paul Holland pointed out when discussing Reed Hastings, recognizing your own flaws is difficult. Rebounders are able to do it because they have confidence in their ability to adjust and they're not afraid to be wrong. Tim Westergren talks about making the best decisions possible with the information you have at the time. Fresh information, including new insights into mistakes you may have made, may require new decisions. Modifying your dreams and ambitions is often the best way to attain them.

THEY PREPARE FOR THINGS TO GO WRONG

Few Rebounders expect everything to go their way just because they feel they deserve it, or because they're lucky. In fact, the word entitled isn't in the Rebounder vocabulary. Rebounders do have a powerful belief in their own ability to control the future—perhaps too much, occasionally—but that's usually because they've learned through personal experience that effort produces results. They also tend to believe, however, that if they're passive or complacent, they won't get the results they want, because plans tend to go awry without careful attention, the way weeds grow in a garden if it's not tended regularly. Jon Luther, for instance, found himself short of money and opportunities after failing to anticipate what could go wrong with a half-baked restaurant deal in Boston. From that point on, he planned for the worst, which assured that it didn't happen. I got in the habit of asking the Rebounders I interviewed whether they consider themselves to be optimists, and the answers I got were a lot more hesitant than I expected. "I'm on the fence," Thomas Keller told me. "I guess I'm cautiously optimistic." He explained that when he's in the kitchen, the one environment he can usually control, he feels a high degree of confidence that can be described as optimism. But in most other settings, there's a lot that he can't control, which makes him wary of what can go wrong. He'd prefer to be in the more comfortable environment, but he also realizes he can't hide out there. "In the kitchen, it's easy for me," he said. "Outside of the kitchen, it's a different world. But if I'm not challenging myself, then I'm not progressing either."

THEY'RE COMFORTABLE WITH DISCOMFORT

Rebounders don't live just for comfort; they also live for fulfillment. So they're willing to accept hardships and inconveniences as long as they feel they're getting closer to an important goal. Lucinda Williams could have signed a rewarding record deal years earlier if she had made the kind of music the record companies wanted her to make. Instead she continued to develop her own unique style because she felt she was getting better, even if she barely had enough money to pay the modest rent. John Ratzenberger was able to take a chance on an acting career because he was used to living with privation and relying on his own ingenuity to survive. Majora Carter never got dependent on easy living, which gave her a high tolerance for the long hours needed to fight city hall and get exemplary results as an activist. Tammy Duckworth learned to "own the suck" without letting it interfere with the job that needed to get done. Success these days is often defined as the accumulation of luxuries and privileges that eliminate life's discomforts. But Rebounders think of success a bit differently, often regarding discomfort as a small price to pay for the privilege of pursuing their ambitions.

THEY'RE WILLING TO WAIT

Everybody wants to succeed quickly, including Rebounders. But it usually takes refined skill and deep knowledge to accomplish ambitious things, and there's rarely a substitute for time when it comes to the accumulation of vital experience. It's easy to feel like a failure if you haven't made your mark by the time you're forty or even thirty, especially since popular culture bombards us with messages that make overnight success seem deceptively ordinary. Yet many people hit roadblocks and quit points that challenge their dedication to a goal, and a lot of them give up and move on to something that's easier or more convenient. What sets Rebounders apart is the determination to succeed on their own terms, no matter how long it takes. Lucinda Williams, Jon Luther, Thomas Keller, and Tim Westergren all had to wait a lot longer—and work a lot harder—than they ever expected, to reach the success they envisioned for themselves. They had to change their plans and adjust their expectations when their ideas didn't work out the first or second time. They're not unusual. Longcuts to success are far more common that shortcuts. But Rebounders don't just wait passively for a lucky break, or do the same thing over and over. They constantly learn and get better, continually improving the likelihood of success until the odds tilt in their favor.

THEY HAVE HEROES

Some Rebounders are romantics, with a surprisingly strong belief in the power of narrative and their own role in something historic. Jack Bogle is the most obvious example of a mythic Rebounder, with his frequent allusions to the naval battles of Admiral Lord Nelson and his description of the founding of Vanguard as a kind of epic quest. His characterizations might seem fanciful, even corny, but Bogle was obviously no phony fooling himself with grandiloquent daydreams. He was a highly capable visionary who found the struggles of heroic figures motivating, partly because he found them familiar. Other Rebounders may be less imaginative than Bogle, but many have mentors or role models who guide them and help them frame what they believe in. For Thomas Keller, it was the French chef and author Fernand Point. John Ratzenberger imagined himself as a modern-day Natty Bumpo, finding more adventure than he felt entitled to and subsisting on the merest basics when he had to. When James Blake felt sorry for himself, he recalled the grace and dignity of his hero, Arthur Ashe, which cured his self-pity and helped him redefine success. Tammy Duckworth emulated the inspiring peer visitors who showed up at her bedside and described how they had lived fulfilling lives as amputees. Then she became a peer visitor herself. Heroes help Rebounders set and meet higher standards than they probably would without them.

THEY HAVE MORE THAN PASSION

Most Rebounders start with passion, but they often discover that passion isn't enough. Lucinda Williams found that in addition to passion, success requires drive, which is a lot more scarce than passion. Thomas Keller called that extra quality desire, which he describes as more lasting than passion. Jon Luther had to fill in gaps in his own knowledge, at his own expense, in order to capitalize on his passion. Tim Westergren failed to fulfill his passion as a musician, but used his passion to invent a new business model that made him feel as jazzed as he felt when performing at the piano. Passion is a powerful motivator, but it also has a way of leading Rebounders into trouble, since they're willing to take risks to pursue it. But passion doesn't always get them out of trouble. That takes a higher form of resilience.

Anybody who can summon some of these attributes, even a few, when things don't go the way they want, has the tools for turning setbacks into a secret weapon. Ordinary schooling will never teach you how to learn from failure or benefit from your own mistakes. You'll probably never get on-the-job training in it. Your spouse or partner is unlikely to help you discover the secret. Most people don't even want to talk about their failures or the setbacks that genuinely hold them back. So if you recognize hardship for what it is, "own the suck," suspend instinctive judgments about why it happened and whose fault it is, keep moving, and ask what you can learn from your misfortune, you will be poised for a privileged education. Adversity is no fun, but it teaches things we can learn no other way. Instead of dreading failure, you may learn to grudgingly cherish it, because it's a unique and fleeting opportunity to learn things that a lot of other people will never be able to know.

Some people are sure that everything happens for a reason. I have my doubts, but more important, the problem with ascribing hardship to some cosmic scheme that's beyond our comprehension is that it diminishes our own responsibility to extract something valuable from something difficult. It is not inherently good when bad things happen. It's up to us to turn a bad situation to our advantage. If growth or knowledge comes from tribulation, it's only through our own effort that it happens. Rebounders don't possess a magic formula, but over time, through practice and dedication, they develop a kind of psychological muscle memory that enlarges their capacity to harness adversity. Rebounder or not? Nearly everyone has the ability to ask themselves that question, and sooner or later, answer yes.

ACKNOWLEDGMENTS

I'm lucky: I know a lot of Rebounders, who helped me figure out what this book needed to be about.

I didn't know it at the time, but I was raised by Rebounders. After my dad died in 1983, my mom, Carol "Cookie" Newman, proved that she's a gutsy and resourceful woman. She also happens to have a lot of sharp ideas and read many books, which she usually checks out of the library. As I worked on my own book, she sent ideas about people she had read about or seen on Book TV, the cable program she watches on weekends. She also read a few volumes in my stack, highlighting passages she thought might be relevant. She usually got it right. There are details in this book that are there because Grandma Cook, as she is known to her five grandkids, brought them to my attention.

My dad, Robert "Bob" Newman, died when I was a teenager. Some memories of him have faded, but many remain strong, especially the stories that our family has told over and over, turning them into oral history. Here's one of them: My dad, who grew up humbly, like many baby boomers, taught himself to play music and eventually sold his beloved saxophone to help pay his way through college. It's a good story that highlights the routine sacrifices people made easily back then, in the belief that they would lead to better things in the future. For him, it did.

Sarah Benson has been a go-to sister many times. My brother, Mike Newman, has shown up when he didn't have to and offered quiet support without ever calling attention to it. Siblings are perhaps the most underappreciated people on the planet, and I certainly don't want to create the impression that mine have redeeming qualities. I just have to admit—they've been there.

During the time I was producing this book, my daughter, Jessica, and son, Robert, grew from cute little creatures into rambunctious teenagers determined to seize every bit of independence they could grab, with brazen disregard for whatever anxiety they might cause their elders. Yet their creativity, cheerfulness, and willingness to work hard give me profound hope for the future. I feel best when I see the character they show when things don't go their way, and they suppress the urge to complain while figuring out how to make things better, on their own.

Friends. Who has enough? Many of us think we do, but boy, do they become scarce when the price of friendship goes up. So I'd like to thank those who have genuinely helped me understand how Rebounders help one another succeed. Jeanine Sieja embraced this project as if it were her own and contributed more to it through sheer example than she'll probably ever know. Thomas Jakelich has been a buoyant exemplar of resilience and an unwitting mood brightener. Ted Marzilli and Gayle Edgerton have been the kind of supporters you couldn't buy if you had the money. Ted Slafsky and Diane Prescott would probably take me in without question if I showed up destitute and forlorn, which, come to think of it, they've kind of done already. Don and Rose Shepperd offered help with research almost faster than I asked for it. Debbie Stier introduced me to some of the best people in publishing and shared one great idea after another. Kelly Leonard graciously shared her own expertise about social media and the rapidly expanding online universe—the kind of friend everybody ought to have these days. I also owe a shoutout to Chica, an eight-pound Morkie who is planet Earth's most exuberant creature.

My agent, Lisa Gallagher, got the concept for this project about three seconds after I started trying to explain it, and made numerous suggestions that helped *Rebounders* become a better book. Lisa has been a terrific advocate and a shrewd business partner, allowing me to research and write without worrying about all the rest, because I know she'll take care of it.

My editor at Ballantine, Marnie Cochran, has the best quality an author could ever hope for: making him feel as if he barely has an editor. Yet Marnie's input was momentous. She made the whole production process seem like a snap, which I know damn well it wasn't. Virtually every suggestion she made resulted in crisper writing, clearer logic, or a better experience for the reader. Standing behind Marnie were Libby McGuire and Jennifer Hershey, whose enthusiasm for this project enhanced my own and, frankly, made the whole thing happen. In fact, the entire team at Ballantine—from proofreaders to publicists and all their bosses—has been thoroughly professional, with passion for their work and a reassuring care for detail. The publishing industry, like many others, is in a state of upheaval, as eBooks, the information revolution, and many other factors transform the whole business. Ballantine remains a class act, with many staffers who are still in it for the right reason: Books give them joy.

At *U.S. News & World Report,* where I've been a longtime correspondent, I'm indebted to Kim Castro, Tim Smart, Robert Schlesinger, Christian Lowe, Chad Smolinski, Brian Kelly, and many others. My bosses and colleagues have been consistently supportive as I've juggled the demands of daily journalism with the effort required to complete this book. When I had to cut corners or beg time off, nobody complained. It's worth noting that *U.S. News* has also endured a Darwinian economic environment, and after some anxious moments emerged as a news organization that still supports serious journalism and the thoughtful exchange of ideas. That experience, along with many others over the last decade or so, has convinced me that tough times usually are not quite as bad as they might seem, for one overriding reason: Rebounders abound.

NOTES

INTRODUCTION

xi   *Parable of the Talents* The scriptural citation is Matthew 25: 14–30. To paraphrase: A wealthy man in ancient times goes on a trip, and for some reason entrusts different sums of money, or talents, to three of his servants. The first two invest the money in ways that Matthew never explains, and when the master returns, they're happy to inform him that they've doubled his money. He rewards them with the Biblical equivalent of a raise and promotion. But the third servant, afraid of the consequences should he invest the money and lose it, buries it in the ground instead, and when summoned by his master simply returns the original amount. The master blows his stack, calls the servant "evil and lazy," and orders the poor bastard cast into the "outer darkness, where there will be weeping and gnashing of teeth."

xii   *Coca-Cola president Don Keough* See, for instance, "A Bubbly Outlook from Former Coke CEO Keough," Rick Newman, *U.S. News & World Report,* January 12, 2009, available at http://money.usnews.com/money/blogs/flowchart/2009/01/12/a-bubbly -outlook-from-former-coke-ceo-keough.

xii   *Tavis Smiley* See, for instance, "How to Recover from a Career Flameout," Rick Newman, *U.S. News & World Report,* May 10, 2011, available at http://money.usnews .com/money/blogs/flowchart/2011/05/10/how-to-recover-from-a-career-flameout.

xii   *Steve Jobs commencement address* The complete text is available at http://news .stanford.edu/news/2005/june15/jobs-061505.html.

xiii   *J. K. Rowling commencement address* The complete text is available at http://harvard magazine.com/2008/06/the-fringe-benefits-failure-the-importance-imagination.

xiii   *Conan O'Brien commencement address*   This can be viewed and read at http://www
.dartmouth.edu/~commence/speeches/2011/obrien-speech.html.

xvi   *The second Iraq war*   In 2002, Pentagon advisor Ken Adelman argued in the *Washington Post* that a U.S. invasion of Iraq would be a "cakewalk." The war, which began
in 2003, ended up taking more American lives than the 9/11 terrorist attacks, costing
nearly $1 trillion, and lasting at least eight years. That's in addition to more than
150,000 Iraqi deaths, according to the World Health Organization. See "Cakewalk in
Iraq," Ken Adelman, *Washington Post,* February 13, 2002, A27.

xvi   *More apt to practice "defensive pessimism"*   A good primer on defensive pessimism
is *The Positive Power of Negative Thinking: Using Defensive Pessimism to Harness Anxiety
and Perform at Your Peak,* Julie K. Norem (Cambridge, MA: Basic Books, 2003).

xvii   *Richard Fuld and Lehman Brothers*   Sources for this capsule history of Lehman
Brothers include *The Devil's Casino: Friendship, Betrayal, and the High Stakes Games
Played Inside Lehman Brothers,* Vicky Ward (Hoboken, NJ: Wiley & Sons, 2010); *On the
Brink: Inside the Race to Stop the Collapse of the Global Financial System,* Henry M. Paulson
(New York: Business Plus, 2010); and testimony Fuld gave before the House Over-
sight and Government Reform Committee, October 6, 2008.

xviii   *Warren Buffett and the "ovarian lottery"*   See *The Snowball: Warren Buffett and the
Business of Life,* Alice Schroeder (New York: Bantam, 2009), 644.

CHAPTER 1

3   *What doesn't kill me*   In the original German: *"Was mich nicht umbringt, macht mich
stärker."* With thanks to Thomas P. Miles, adjunct assistant professor of philosophy at
Boston College.

4   *The capacity to cope with adversity*   There are various definitions of resilience in the
psychological literature. I've borrowed a definition offered by psychologist Edith Henderson Grotberg: "Resilience is the human capacity to deal with, overcome, learn
from, or even be transformed by the inevitable adversities of life." From *Resilience for
Today: Gaining Strength from Adversity,* Edith Henderson Grotberg, ed. (Westport, CT:
Praeger, 2003).

4   *Seery and his colleagues*   See "Whatever Does Not Kill Us: Cumulative Lifetime Adversity, Vulnerability, and Resilience," Mark D. Seery, E. Alison Holman, and Roxane
Cohen Silver, *Journal of Personality and Social Psychology,* 99(6), October 11, 2010,
1025–1041.

5   *Beck's innovations*   See *The Resilience Factor,* Karen Reivich and Andrew Shatté (New
York: Broadway Books), 53–58.

5   *"Positive psychology"*   Psychologists Christopher Peterson and Martin E. P. Seligman,
for instance, identify twenty-four attributes that contribute to character and virtue:
creativity, curiosity, open-mindedness, love of learning, perspective, bravery, persistence, integrity, vitality, love, kindness, social intelligence, citizenship, fairness, leadership, forgiveness and mercy, humility and modesty, prudence, self-regulation,
appreciation of beauty and excellence, gratitude, hope, humor, and spirituality. From
Character Strengths and Virtues: A Handbook and Classification, Christopher Peterson and
Martin E. P. Seligman (New York: Oxford University Press, 2004).

5   *Once called invulnerability*   *Character Strengths and Virtues,* 77.

6   *One-third of people are born with a natural resilience* Resilience for Today, 3.

6   *Maddi and his team* See *Resilience at Work: How to Succeed No Matter What Life Throws at You,* Salvatore R. Maddi and Deborah M. Khoshaba (New York: American Management Association, 2005), 16–24.

7   *Letting kids experience failure* Resilience for Today, 32.

8   *"Ordinary magic"* See "Ordinary Magic: Resilience Process in Development," Ann S. Masten, *American Psychologist,* 56, March 2001, 227–238.

8   *Starting around nine* Resilience for Today, 41–42.

9   *Parents who routinely intervene* See, for instance, *The Narcissism Epidemic: Living in the Age of Entitlement,* Jean M. Twenge and W. Keith Campbell (New York: Free Press, 2010), 78–79; *The Resilience Factor,* 22, 257; and *Mindset: The New Psychology of Success,* Carol Dweck (New York: Ballantine Books, 2007), 175–176.

9   *Super-safe playgrounds* See "Can a Playground Be Too Safe?" John Tierney, *The New York Times,* July 18, 2011, available at http://www.nytimes.com/2011/07/19/science/19tierney.html.

9   *Renowned psychologist Howard Gardner* The Resilience Factor, 18.

10 *Off-the-charts genius Chris Langan* Outliers: The Story of Success, Malcolm Gladwell (New York: Little, Brown and Company, 2008), 91–115.

10 *"Special talent"* Mindset, 11, 83.

10 *Basic resilience factors* Resilience for Today, 246–250.

CHAPTER 2

12 *Benjamin Franklin, America's first self-help guru* See *Benjamin Franklin: An American Life,* Walter Isaacson (New York: Simon & Schuster, 2004), 37–54, 95–99.

13 *George Washington lost his father* Washington: A Life, Ron Chernow (New York: Penguin Press, 2010), 10, 37, 45, 49, 50, 457, 465–67, 478–79, 552–555.

13 *Somehow those frequent struggles* The Continental Army defeated the British with considerable help from the French navy, of course. See, for instance, *American Heroes: Profiles of Men and Women Who Shaped Early America,* Edmund S. Morgan (New York: W.W. Norton, 2010), 199. My thanks also to Colonel Lance Betros of the U.S. Military Academy for help understanding General Washington's military setbacks.

13 *The Articles bound the states* Miracle at Philadelphia, Catherine Drinker Bowen (New York: Back Bay Books, 1966), 5.

14 *Bill Wilson* See *The Forgotten Man,* Amity Shlaes (New York: Harper Perennial, 2008), 231–232.

15 *"He seems to be the least perturbed"* See "Edison Starting Again," *The New York Times,* December 12, 1914, 22. With thanks to Edison biographer Paul Israel.

15 *Edison vowed* This account of the fire is drawn largely from *Edison: A Life of Invention,* Paul Israel (New York: John Wiley & Sons, 2000), 432–433. I am also indebted to Israel for considerable help presenting the salient details of Edison's life.

16 *Edison's mother, Nancy, taught him* Edison, 6–7

16 *Mrs. Edison was gentle* This account of Edison's boyhood is from *Edison,* 5–39.

16 *Edison left home for good* Courtesy of Gerald Beals, curator of the Brockton, Massachusetts Historical Society, whose brief biography of Edison is available at www.thomasedison.com/biography.html.

18 *It must have been thrilling to Edison* Edison, 41–43.

18 *Edison saw the problem right away* Beals biography.

18 *That kind of "cognitive ability"* See, for instance, *Mindset*, 11, and *The Resilience Factor*, 33, 163.

20 *William Sawyer, had made some breakthroughs* Edison, 167–208.

21 *Several months of experiments* From the Thomas Edison papers at Rutgers University, available at http://edison.rutgers.edu/transmit.htm.

21 *"I cannot stand this worrying"* Edison, 85. I've modernized spelling and punctuation, for readability.

21 *A desperate need for money* Edison, 101–104, 334, 354.

22 *Like many businesspeople* Edison, 453.

23 *He seemed to love the camaraderie* Roosevelt gave his famous speech on "the strenuous life" in Chicago in 1899, when he was governor of New York. A full text of the speech is available at http://www.theodore-roosevelt.com/images/research/speeches/trstrenlife.pdf.

23 *Edison could be susceptible* Edison, 350–362.

23 *In characteristic fashion* Edison, 403–409.

24 *Edison succumbed to hubris* Edison, 424–427.

24 *His deafness* Beals biography.

25 *He considered it an asset* Edison, 17–18.

25 *"Positive illusions"* See, for instance, *The Resilience Factor*, 55. Reivich and Shatt credit Shelley Taylor and Jonathan Brown for the seminal research on positive illusions.

CHAPTER 3

27 *Hoover had been a precocious engineer* See *The Forgotten Man: A New History of the Great Depression*, Amity Shlaes (New York: HarperCollins Publishers), 30.

27 *As a relief official* From the official White House biography of Herbert Hoover, available at http://www.whitehouse.gov/about/presidents/herberthoover.

28 *Hoover had a fatal flaw* The Forgotten Man, 102.

28 *Young boy named John Clifton Bogle* Early biographical details and the history of Wellington Management Company are from *John Bogle and the Vanguard Experiment: One Man's Quest to Transform the Mutual Fund Industry*, Robert Slater (Chicago: Irwin Professional Publishing, 1996), 9–63.

32 *"I was totally wiped out"* From an interview I conducted with John Bogle. All quotes in chapters 3 through 13 are from my interviews with the subjects, unless indicated otherwise.

32 *"Disgraceful mistake"* See *Common Sense on Mutual Funds, Fully Updated 10th Anniversary Edition*, John C. Bogle (Hoboken, NJ: John Wiley & Sons, 2009), 538.

35 *While picking out some new wall hangings* John Bogle and the Vanguard Experiment, 85.

39 *"A company that might never have existed"* From *Character Counts: The Creation and Building of the Vanguard Group*, John C. Bogle and John Bogle (New York: McGraw-Hill, 2002), 14, 130, 140, 211. For readability, I've condensed some of these quotes and eliminated the traditional ellipses.

40   *"What can go wrong?"* John Bogle and the Vanguard Experiment, 164.

41   *Pampered children* See, for example, "The Winning Edge," Peter Doskoch, *Psychology Today,* available at http://www.psychologytoday.com/articles/200510/the-winning -edge.

41   *"It is often best"* Common Sense on Mutual Funds, 560.

41   *Lessons for entrepreneurs* In *Common Sense on Mutual Funds,* Bogle lists seventeen "entrepreneurial lessons." They are: 1. Get lucky. 2. Turn disaster into triumph. 3. Get a mentor. 4. Get fired. 5. Dare to be bold! 6. Getting lucky multiple times beats getting lucky once. 7. Never get discouraged. 8. Emerson was right. Build a better mousetrap and the world will beat a path to your door. 9. Never give up. Never. Never. Never. Never. Never. [Attributed to Winston Churchill.] 10. Be a mathematical genius. (Only kidding!) 11. Never underestimate the power of the obvious. 12. Competition is easier if your competitors won't—can't—compete on costs. 13. "I'm from the government and I'm here to help you." Maybe. 14. An internally consistent strategy is one of the keys to business success. 15. Take the road less traveled by. It can make all the difference. 16. (After John Donne) "No man is an island, entire of itself." 17. Our greatest rewards come when we foster economic progress, and help to build a better world.

41   *A Yale University student* Common Sense on Mutual Funds, 535.

CHAPTER 4

47   *FedEx founder Fred Smith* See "Frederick W. Smith: No Overnight Success," Dean Foust, Businessweek.com, September 24, 2004, available at http://www.businessweek .com/magazine/content/04_38/b3900031_mz072.htm.

51   *Popeye's had started in New Orleans* See "Jon Luther: Dunkin' Chief Masters Innovation by Being a Student of the Industry," Dina Berta, *Nation's Restaurant News,* May 17, 2010, available at http://findarticles.com/p/articles/mi_m3190/is_10_44/ ai_n53730364/.

52   *When that deal went through* See "The Carlyle Group's Sweet Deal," Rick Newman, *U.S. News & World Report,* December 4, 2006, available at http://www.usnews.com/ usnews/biztech/articles/061126/4equity.b.htm.

52   *When Dunkin' went public* "Dunkin' Donuts IPO: Who's Getting Rich," Shira Ouide, *The Wall Street Journal,* July 11, 2011, available at http://blogs.wsj.com/deals/ dunkin-donuts-ipo-whos-getting-rich/.

53   *Naïve optimists* See, for example, *The Resilience Factor,* 55–56, 184–185.

CHAPTER 5

56   *"Follow your bliss"* When describing his concept of bliss in shorthand form, Campbell said it involved knowing how to "place your center," and he illustrated that by quoting a line from Upton Sinclair's novel *Babbitt:* "There's a line at the end . . . where Mr. Babbitt says, 'I never did a thing I wanted to in my life.' He's a dry stick." Campbell went on to say that "the best thing I can say is follow your bliss. If your bliss is just your fun and your excitement, you're on the wrong track. I mean, you need instruction. Know where your bliss is. And that involves coming down to a deep place

in yourself." From *The Hero's Journey: Joseph Campbell on His Life and Work*, Phil Cousineau, ed. (Novato, CA: New World Library, 2003), 216–217.

57 *The 10,000-hour rule* Outliers: *The Story of Success*, 38–51.

58 *"It wasn't this big traumatic thing"* See "Road Worthy: Lilith's Lucinda Williams Revs Up a 20-Year Career with a Moving New Album," Steve Dougherty with Beverly Keel, *People*, September 21, 1998, 113.

60 *"Frenzy of philandering"* See "Delta Nights: A Singer's Love Affair with Loss," Bill Buford, *The New Yorker*, June 5, 2000, 50–65.

62 *A "low-key, beguiling affair"* See "Lucinda Williams," Steve Pond, *Rolling Stone*, January 26, 1989, available at http://www.rollingstone.com/music/albumreviews/lucinda-williams-19890126.

63 *"Intimidated the hell out of me"* "Road Worthy," 113.

64 *Walking out on one record deal* "Delta Nights," 59.

64 *"Neurotic perfectionist"* See, for example, "Rambling Woman Blues," Karen Schoemer, *Newsweek*, July 6, 1998, 68.

65 *"Near-absolute mastery"* See "Lucinda Williams: Car Wheels on a Gravel Road," Robert Christgau, *Rolling Stone*, June 18, 1998, available at http://www.rollingstone.com/music/albumreviews/car-wheels-on-a-gravel-road-19980618.

66 *Williams never had a Top 40 hit* From Lucinda Williams's *Billboard* chart history, available at http://www.billboard.com/artist/lucinda-williams/chart-history/6024#/artist/lucinda-williams/chart-history/6024.

68 *Rebounders are able to balance* See, for instance, *Mindset*, 11, and *The Resilience Factor*, 163, 211.

CHAPTER 6

70 *On the "verge of death"* See "How Pandora Slipped Past the Junkyard," Claire Cain Miller, *The New York Times*, March 7, 2010, available at http://www.nytimes.com/2010/03/08/technology/08pandora.html.

74 *The "music genome project"* For Westergren's description of the music genome project, see http://www.pandora.com/mgp.shtml.

75 *Fifty employees but no cash* "How Pandora Slipped Past the Junkyard."

75 *Four paid employees* See "Algorithm and Blues," Linda Tischler, FastCompany.com, December 1, 2005, available at http://www.fastcompany.com/magazine/101/pandora.html.

78 *More than one million Pandora users* See "Opening Pandora's Box," Harvard Business School case study, Willy Shih, Stephen Kaufman, Melissa Blakely, and Marissa Dent, April 27, 2009.

79 *List of the one hundred most influential people* Available at http://www.time.com/time/specials/packages/completelist/0,29569,1984685,00.html.

80 *Discard static ideas* See *Mindset*, 11, 148, 230.

CHAPTER 7

82 *Blake's downfall* Some of the biographical information in this chapter is from Blake's memoir, *Breaking Back: How I Lost Everything and Won Back My Life*, James Blake with Andrew Friedman (New York: HarperCollins, 2007).

89 *Tennis legend Pete Sampras* Statistics on Sampras's career are from the Association of Tennis Professionals (ATP), available at http://www.atpworldtour.com/Tennis/Players/Sa/P/Pete-Sampras.aspx.

92 *"Cinderella Man"* See "James Blake: U.S. Open's Cinderella Man," Stephen Silverman, *People,* September 7, 2005, available at http://www.people.com/people/article/0,,1101749,00.html.

93 *Dating a model* See "Another King James? Blake Enjoying Life as Next Big American Tennis Star," Elizabeth Newman, SI.com, September 15, 2006, available at http://sportsillustrated.cnn.com/2006/writers/elizabeth_newman/09/15/queens.court/index.html.

93 *Dogged by media critics* See, for instance, this blog post on "Blake's French Flameout," posted by Jon Wertheim, SI.com, May 29, 2009, available at http://sports illustrated.cnn.com/2009/writers/jon_wertheim/05/28/french.baguettethursday/index.html#ixzz1FPfeuNr2.

94 *By the age of thirty-two* Blake's career stats come from the ATP, available at http://www.atpworldtour.com/Tennis/Players/Top-Players/James-Blake.aspx.

CHAPTER 8

101 *She learned the value of pragmatism* See "A Dreamer, Working for Beauty in the South Bronx," Amy Waldman, *The New York Times,* August 15, 2001, available at http://www.nytimes.com/2001/08/15/nyregion/public-lives-a-dreamer-working-for-beauty-in-the-south-bronx.html.

101 *Carter was jogging early one morning* Carter gave a nice account of the role her dog, Xena, played in this discovery to a website called The Bark, available at http://www.thebark.com/content/inspired-dog-majora-carter.

102 *A park was born* See "Parks Come to the Point," Linda McIntyre, *Landscape Architecture,* December 2007, available at http://www.asla.org/lamag/lam07/december/feature2.html.

105 *A reputation for getting results* See "Majora Carter: Greener Neighborhoods, Sustainable Jobs," Adam Aston, *BusinessWeek,* October 27, 2008, available at http://www.businessweek.com/innovate/content/oct2008/id20081027_254094.htm.

106 *"A relentless and charismatic urban strategist"* From the MacArthur Foundation's profile of Carter, available at http://www.macfound.org/site/c.lkLXJ8MQKrH/b.1076861/apps/nl/content2.asp?content_id={DD826DBF-DAE6-4730-A35C-8AA6FF8AF3DE}&notoc=1.

108 *"Greening the ghetto"* TED is a nonprofit devoted to connecting people in the technology, design, and entertainment fields. Carter's "TED talk" is available at http://www.ted.com/talks/lang/eng/majora_carter_s_tale_of_urban_renewal.html.

108 *A coveted public speaker* See "The Green Power Broker," Marguerite Holloway, *The New York Times,* December 14, 2008, available at http://www.nytimes.com/2008/12/14/nyregion/thecity/14majo.html?scp=1&sq he%20green%20power%20broker&st=cse.

110 *"A strong bias toward action"* *Giants of Enterprise,* Richard Tedlow (New York: Harper Paperbacks, 2003), 327.

112 *Rebounders often bounce back by channeling* Reivich and Shatté write that "The most resilient people . . . don't reflexively blame others for their mistakes in order to

preserve their self-esteem or absolve themselves of guilt. Nor do they waste their valuable reserves of resilience ruminating about events or circumstances outside their control. They channel their problem-solving resources into the factors they can control, and, through incremental change, they begin to overcome, steer through, bounce back, and reach out." From *The Resilience Factor,* 43.

CHAPTER 9

118 *Peter Oliver* See, for instance, "Peter Oliver: Pioneering Spirit of Young People's Alternative Theatre," Carole Woddis, *The Guardian,* October 24, 2007, available at http://www.guardian.co.uk/news/2007/oct/24/guardianobituaries.obituaries.

123 *The sitcom earned twenty-eight Emmy Awards* The Academy of Television Arts & Sciences, available by searching at http://www.emmys.tv/awards.

CHAPTER 10

125 *"Businessperson of the Year"* See "Reed Hastings: Leader of the Pack," Michael V. Copeland, *Fortune,* December 6, 2010, 120–130.

125 *A legendary investment* Netflix went public at $15 per share in May 2002, and its stock split 2-for-1 in 2004. In mid-2011, the stock price peaked at about $299, a 39-fold increase over its 2002 offering price, when adjusted for the split. Basic historical data on Netflix comes from the company's website, www.netflix.com/MediaCenter/Timeline. Stock prices come from Google Finance.

126 *"Slow and stodgy"* "Netflix CEO: We Fear 'Getting Long in the Tooth,'" Julianne Pepitone, CNNMoney, June 1, 2011, available at http://money.cnn.com/2011/06/01technology/d9_netflix/index.htm.

127 *More than ten million new subscribers* Netflix letter to shareholders for the second quarter of 2011, available at http://ir.netflix.com/results.cfm.

127 *Lost more than 800,000 U.S. subscribers* Netflix letter to shareholders for the third quarter of 2011, available at http://ir.netflix.com/results.cfm.

127 *The Qwikster fiasco had been a "head fake"* Hastings made these remarks at the UBS Global Media and Communications Conference in New York on December 6, 2011. A Webcast of his remarks is available at http://cc.talkpoint.com/ubsx001/120511a_im/

128 *Hastings believed in serving his country* See "Out of Africa, Onto the Web," Reed Hastings as told to Amy Zipkin, *The New York Times,* December 17, 2006, available at http://query.nytimes.com/gst/fullpage.html?res=9B0CE2D91231F934A25751C1A9609C8B63&scp=1&sq=reed%20hastings%20the%20boss&st=cse.

129 *"If you are a great people leader"* See "Lessons in Leadership—from a Failed Startup," Patricia Sellers, Fortune.com, December 9, 2008, available at http://postcards.blogs.fortune.cnn.com/2008/12/09/guest-post-lessons-in-leadership-from-a-failed-startup/.

130 *Hastings would be the CEO* I'm grateful to venture capitalist Andy Rachleff, an early investor in Reed Hastings's first company, for a plain-English explanation of how Pure Software got started.

133 *"A special talent"* *Mindset,* 11.

133 *An impressive 16 percent profit margin* Pure Software earnings statement, *Business Wire,* January 18, 1996.

133 *Pure Software went public* See "Recently Completed Offerings," *Standard & Poor's Emerging and Special Situation,* August 14, 1995.

135 *An oceanfront home in Santa Cruz* See "Fast Track to Riches," Julie Schmit, *USA Today,* December 26, 1995, 1A.

135 *Pure Atria lost $6.6 million* See "Rational to Buy Software Rival Acquisition: Deal for Pure Atria Is Valued at $520 Million," Tom Quinlan, *San Jose Mercury News,* April 8, 1997, 1C.

135 *The company lost $42 million* See "Pure Atria Posts Revenue and Operating Results for the First Quarter 1997," *PR Newswire,* April 17, 1997.

136 *"It was so different how they operated"* "Reed Hastings: Leader of the Pack."

136 *"That was the big excitement point"* See "How Netflix Got Started," interview conducted by Alyssa Abkowitz, *Fortune,* January 28, 2009, available at http://money.cnn.com/2009/01/2 //news/newsmakers/hastings_netflix.fortune/index.htm.

139 *Six years after Blockbuster first lunged* See "How Netflix (and Blockbuster) Killed Blockbuster," Rick Newman, *U.S. News & World Report,* September 23, 2010, available at http://money.usnews.com/money/blogs/flowchart/2010/09/23/how-netflix-and-blockbuster-killed-blockbuster.

139 *"We got overconfident"* UBS conference.

CHAPTER 11

141 *The namesake dish for 2007 Pixar film* Ratatouille See "A Rat with a Whisk and a Dream," Kim Severson, *The New York Times,* June 13, 2007, available at http://www.nytimes.com/2007/06/13/dining/13rata.html?pagewanted=1.

141 *A training ground for many future culinary stars* See "The Phoenix and the French Laundry," Harvey Steiman, *Wine Spectator,* April 30, 2010.

142 *"To me, that was magical"* See "A conversation with chef Thomas Keller," *The Charlie Rose Show,* March 30, 2005, viewable at http://www.charlierose.com/view/interview/983.

144 *A three-month job at Taillevent* See "How Taillevent Stays on Top," Patricia Wells, *The New York Times,* April 14, 1985, available at http://www.nytimes.com/1985/04/14/travel/how-taillevent-stays-on-top.html.

144 *Keller threw him out* See "On the Road to Acclaim, a Chef Learns Lessons in Humility," Marian Burros, *The New York Times,* October 16, 1996, available at http://www.nytimes.com/1996/10/16/garden/on-the-road-to-acclaim-a-chef-learns-lessons-in-humility.html.

152 *"Having the Dream Is Hard"* See "The Gift: Having the Dream Is Hard. Living It Is Harder," Elaine Sciolino, *The New York Times,* September 19, 1993, available at http://www.nytimes.com/1993/09/19/weekinreview/the-gift-having-the-dream-is-hard-living-it-is-harder.html.

154 *Best Chef in America* See "In Napa Valley, a Restaurant Scales the Peak," Ruth Reichl, *The New York Times,* October 29, 1997, F1.

154 *French Laundry earned the top three-star rating* See "Bay Area Stars Fail to Make

Michelin Cut," Carol Ness, *San Francisco Chronicle,* October 3, 2006, available at http://www.sfgate.com/cgi-bin/article.cgi?f=/c/a/2006/10/03/MNGSULH7QL1 .DTL.

CHAPTER 12

157 *Iraq had become far bloodier than Mogadishu* These casualty counts come from the independent research organization Global Security, available at http://www.global security.org/military/ops/iraq_casualties.htm.

164 *The Soldier's Creed* The Soldier's Creed can be found readily on the Web, such as here, http://www.gotrain.org/~emgeer/army-creed.html.

CHAPTER 13

173 *Clueless Joe* See "We Wuz Clueless on Torre: Joe Proves the Skeptics Were Off Base," Ian O'Connor, *New York Daily News,* October 27, 1996, 68.

173 *Manager of the Year* Major League Baseball issues two Manager of the Year awards, one for the National League and one for the American League. Torre won for the American League in 1996, sharing the honor, in an unusual arrangement, with Johnny Oates of the Texas Rangers. Baseball-Reference.com is one source of this information, available at http://www.baseball-reference.com/awards/manage.shtml.

173 *A business-list bestseller* See, for instance, the *Businessweek* bestseller list for December 6, 1999, available at http://www.businessweek.com/1999/99_49/b3658097.htm. *Joe Torre's Ground Rules for Winners* ranked fourteenth.

174 *The ugly family secret* Many of the biographical details in this chapter are taken from Torre's 1997 memoir, *Chasing the Dream: My Lifelong Journey to the World Series,* Joe Torre with Tom Verducci (New York: Bantam, 1998).

176 *He steadily improved, batting over .300* Statistics on Joe Torre's career as a player and manager, and on other teams and players mentioned in this chapter, come from www.baseball-reference.com.

184 *"I was able to connect the dots"* Since attending that seminar in 1995, Torre has spoken publicly many times about his experience with domestic violence. One example is a brief speech he gave at the White House on October 27, 2010, which can be viewed at http://lifesuccessseminars.com/jtorre.html.

187 *Finally winning a World Series ring* Some details of Torre's career from 1996 onward come from *The Yankee Years,* Joe Torre and Tom Verducci (New York: Anchor Books, 2009).

CHAPTER 14

190 *Story of Charles Goodyear* Biographical information on Goodyear comes from *They Made America: From the Steam Engine to the Search Engine, Two Centuries of Innovators,* Harold Evans (New York: Little, Brown, and Company, 2004), 107–123; a biography of Goodyear published by the Goodyear Tire and Rubber Company, available at http:// www.goodyear.com/corporate/history/history_story.html, which is reprinted from

Reader's Digest, January 1958; and a history of the Goodyear Tire and Rubber Company, available at http://www.goodyear.com/corporate/history/.

192 *Take Martha Stewart, for instance* Biographical details come from Biography.com, available at http://www.biography.com/articles/Martha-Stewart-9542234?part=0. The stock price of Martha Stewart Living Omnimedia mostly declined after Martha Stewart ended her prison term in 2005. The stock peaked at about $36 in early 2005. Over the next six years it drifted down to a range of $3 to $6.

192 *What about Michael Vick* Biographical details come from Biography.com, available at http://www.biography.com/articles/Michael-Vick-241100?part=1.

193 *Documentary of his life with Black Entertainment Television* From Vick's official profile published by the Philadelphia Eagles, available at http://legacy.philadelphia eagles.com/eagles_files/html/vick_1.html.

193 *Animal lovers insist* The advocacy group People for the Ethical Treatment of Animals has remained a vocal Vick critic, which is evident by searching for Vick's name at the PETA website, www.peta.org.

197 *Tend to ruminate over problems* See, for instance, *The Resilience Factor,* 24–26.

197 *"Whatever you think your dream is now"* Conan O'Brien's commencement address.

INDEX

ABOUT THE AUTHOR

RICK NEWMAN is chief business correspondent for *U.S. News & World Report* and a frequent TV and radio commentator. Before moving to New York in 2001, Rick spent twelve years in Washington, where he covered the Pentagon and earned the Gerald R. Ford Prize for Distinguished Reporting on National Defense. He's also the co-author of *Firefight: Inside the Battle to Save the Pentagon on 9/11* (2008) and *Bury Us Upside Down: The Misty Pilots and the Secret Battle for the Ho Chi Minh Trail* (2006). Rick has two kids and lives in suburban New York. Follow him on Twitter: @rickjnewman.

ABOUT THE TYPE

This book was set in Garamond, a typeface designed by the French printer Jean Jannon. It is styled after Garamond's original models. The face is dignified, and is light but without fragile lines. The italic is modeled after a font of Granjon, which was probably out in the middle of the sixteenth century.